# A HISTORY OF THE WORLD'S GREAT RELIGIONS

Ward McAfee
California State College
San Bernardino

UNIVERSITY
PRESS OF
AMERICA

LANHAM • NEW YORK • LONDON

Copyright © 1983 by

University Press of America,™ Inc.

4720 Boston Way
Lanham, MD 20706

3 Henrietta Street
London WC2E 8LU England

Printed in the United States of America

ISBN (Perfect): 0-8191-3395-7
ISBN   (Cloth): 0-8191-3394-9

Library of Congress Catalog Card Number: 83-12435

To God belong the East and the West,
Whichever way you turn
The Face of God is there.

                    --Qur'an, 2:109

# Table of Contents

# Preface

As I was finishing this book, I had a conversation with a New World archeologist about my project on world religions. "Will your book have anything to say about native American religions?" he inquired. In the moments of silence that followed, I wondered whether my quest had been irretrievably stained by limits I had set in the beginning. All of "my religions" had been born in Asia--Judaism in the land of Canaan (later known as Palestine), Hinduism and Buddhism in India, Christianity also in Palestine, and Islam on the Arabian peninsula. Other faiths, briefly covered in my work, were also distinctly Eastern Hemisphere in origin--Zoroastrianism from Iran, Jainism from India, and Taoism and Confucianism from China.

Trained as an American historian, I had earlier written books on California railroads and the origins of the Mexican War. After a decade of teaching and researching solely on American subjects, I felt an itch to discover the wider world beyond America's shores, and world religions became my new passion. I proudly scorned my "Americanist" colleagues. I was like the young man leaving his innocent home in the country for the more complex life in town. I was off to discover the world.

"I've only covered those religions that have had an impact on world history," I heard myself answering the archeologist. For all of its majestic sweep, my reply somehow sounded unsatisfactory to me. Yet, upon later reflection, I concluded that it was generally a valid statement. Possibly, if Europe had been less ravaging in its colonization of the New World, religious thought from the Western Hemisphere might have influenced the modern world more than has been the case. Certainly, some Pre-Columbian practices and beliefs can be found in Christian forms in modern Latin America, but they are not covered in this volume, any more than are Anglo-American variants of Christianity, such as Christian Science and Mormonism. In writing this book, my concern focused on the main themes of each of the world's principal, living religious traditions. Consequently, the story has been restricted from venturing off onto numerous religious cul-de-sacs.

The following chapters fall far short of being encyclopedic. Important personages and developments are omitted, if their inclusion would serve to distract attention from what this author considers the major trends within each living tradition. In the opinion of some, my narrative might give too much play to minor themes. Some may conclude that it dwells too much on the impact of Reconstructionism in modern Judaism, or the significance of the Hare Krisha phenomenon in modern Hinduism, or Zen in Buddhism, or Dietrich Bonhoeffer in Christianity, or the Ayatollah Khomeini in Islam. These emphases obviously represent my own understanding of what is important and essential. They hardly represent an objective last word, if such a thing is indeed possible.

In the pages that follow, the terms "East" and "West" recur with some frequency. My use of "West" relates to European cultural aspects which are clearly dominant in the Western Hemisphere of the modern world. Likewise, "East" is not used to mean the Eastern Hemisphere in its broadest context. Rather it means those influences which are otherwise known as Oriental or Asiatic, as distinguished from Occidental or European. Of course, several of the religions covered in this work straddle East and West, as defined above. All of the West's great religions, with their origins among Semitic peoples, have been touched by Oriental tendencies. At the same time, they have been shaped to a great extent by people of European culture. This is especially true of Judaism and Christianity. Islam is a special case, truly integrating Eastern and Western tendencies, albeit upon a base of Western religious tradition.

My hope in writing this work is that its readers will come away with a greater understanding of many of the living critical religious issues of human history. What motivates Jews from throughout the world to support the survival of Israel with such passion? What in Hinduism makes it attractive to Western intellectuals and the children of the street, the dropouts of American middle-class culture? Why, for the first time since the last days of Rome, are Westerners finding Oriental religious thought, today typified by the Spartan-yet-lunacy-prone expression known as Zen, so appealing? What is the nature of the spiritual malaise that seems to characterize our erstwhile Christian culture? What is the outlook of Islam? Why is it the world's fastest growing religion? Why is it so adamantly opposed to the state of Israel? These are but a few of the questions addressed in the following pages.

Not that long ago, a majority of Americans would have regarded an exploration into religions other than Christianity as irrelevant, if not dangerous. "'I am the way, the truth, and the life,'" Jesus states in John 14:6. "'No man cometh unto the Father, but by me.'" This verse has served as a bulwark for those seeking to limit their study to Christianity alone. Nonetheless, several leading, modern Christian teachers have rejected a narrow, doctrinaire interpretation of this passage. One of these, Paul Tillich, has written: "Faith is not an acceptance of doctrines, not even Christian doctrines, but the acceptance of the power itself out of which we come and into which we go, whatever the doctrines may be through which we accept it."[1] This more liberating, existential view awakens curiosity concerning how God-empowered persons of non-Christian traditions have explained their own particular viewpoints.

As my own background is Christian, I have found that my exploration into other faiths has enriched my understanding of Jesus's message. Jesus was a mystic who taught liberation through a consuming love of God and humankind. He urged individual ego to surrender its will to that of God. This same message is to be found in the teachings of other world religions—for example, Hinduism, Buddhism and Islam, the latter especially in its Sufi expression. Jesus also preached an ethic of social justice: "'I was hungry and you gave me meat; thirsty, and you gave me drink; a stranger, and you took me in.'" (Matthew 26:35) This message is also vibrant in Judaism and Islam. Truly, for a believer schooled in any of these traditions, inspiration may be found in the others. Hopefully, this book will serve to promote such insights and broad ecumenical toleration and human unity.

My exploration has convinced me that each of the world's major religions is deserving of respect. Occasionally, books of this nature subtly seek to prove the superiority of one tradition over others. That is not done here. It is the view of this author that each of the major religions point to God, sometimes in similar, sometimes in distinctly unique, ways. Accordingly, each religion is described in these pages from a perspective that is devotional while also striving for objectivity. Warts are not ignored, but neither are they magnified so as to disfigure the essential beauty of each portrait.

The narrative describes the significant differences among the world's great religions. The tendency of Jews to think in terms of a communal destiny as opposed to the individual Hindu soul's journey through numerous reincarnations is described. Christianity's preference for divine mystery is compared to Buddhism's almost objective, step-by-step program. And, of course, Islamic jihad (or holy war) stands in stark contrast to Buddhist ahimsa (or non-violence). Nonetheless, a common theme running throughout all of these traditions is also apparent. Each of them teaches that evil easily masquerades as a savior, that there is meaning above self-indulgence, and that human suffering can ultimately be transcended.

Our world is beset with problems of human want, which can alternately be described as resulting from "overpopulation" or maldistribution of the world's wealth. Our planet is burdened by a crisis of the spirit that is fed by anxiety-producing (hopefully war-deterring) weapons of mass destruction. Speaking to the pessimism of our age, each of the world's major faiths has provided an account of how the world will end: In Judaism the end time will be marked by the Messiah; in Hinduism, Kalkin; in Buddhism, Maitreya; in Christianity, the return of Christ; in Islam, the Mahdi or Hidden Imam. These stories tell man that he is not the end-all--that his history is not a story of endless achievement but rather is relative to divine purposes. The tenor of our times naturally leads to curiosity about what people in the past have seen as the meaning of existence and the purpose of the human condition. This book has been written to address that curiosity. It claims to be no more than a brief introduction to a complex subject. While it is designed to inform the reader, hopefully it will also inspire further investigation.

Many have assisted me in the preparation of this work. Lyn Young and the staff of the library of California State College, San Bernardino, were most helpful in locating scholarly resources relating to the project. Mary Schmidt and the secretarial staff of the School of Social and Behavioral Sciences of the same institution not only provided secretarial services but also encouraged me in my search. I am most grateful to Marilynn Chovick who proofread the entire manuscript. My students at CSC, San Bernardino, are thanked for their questions and comments concerning the manuscript as it developed. Bill Harwell, the pastor of my family's church, also helped shape my thinking, and Ben and Miriam Kovitz and Ray and Mary McCombs encouraged the ecumenicism underlying this work. Finally, my wife Lois was instrumental not only in her support, but also in providing cherished religious insights.

Wrightwood, California<br>
June 1983

NOTES

1. Paul Tillich, A History of Christian Thought (New York, 1968), p. 247.

Chapter One:   Judaism

## The Rise of the Hebrew People

It is commonplace that humankind is divided into
two great cultural traditions. The Orient,
representing one, looks inward toward the essential
nature of man for answers to ultimate questions. In
comparison, the Western tradition finds clues to the
divine in social and political events. For the West,
God demonstrates His intent for mankind in such events,
and, therefore, the world of human action is valued.
Contrasted to the Asiatic, who tends to view the
worldly drama as peripheral, the Occidental has been
closely identified with an activist's approach to life.
The root causes for the Oriental tendency to be passive
in the world will be explored later. In this chapter,
the origins of Western man's preference will be
examined.

In the ancient West, a cyclical view of existence
was commonly held. People thought not in terms of
linear historical progression, but rather of endless
repetition. Human events were not regarded as unique,
never to reoccur. Rather, the accepted perception that
nothing was new under the sun seemed irrefutable. The
Book of Ecclesiastes would later record this ancient
opinion, which had been encouraged by the seasonal
patterns of nature. Then a new interpretation
appeared. It was nurtured by a nomadic people, not yet
bound by the cyclical routines of agriculture. Having
experienced a series of what they considered miraculous
occurrences, this people proposed that events are
directed by a personality external to mankind and that
this supernatural power had a special plan for them.
Ultimately, this divine outline came to be called
history, a faith that human affairs had been
inaugurated and directed by an omnipotent God who would
eventually bring an end to His creation. This new
mental referencing system focused attention on what
Oriental philosophers would regard as illusion that
distracts the mind from its true being. In valuing
history, the Hebrew people would relate easily to the
material world as the stage of their God's unfolding
plan.[1] Here was a wedge of difference between East and
West.

Fully developed, the Hebrew mind would be founded
on a conception of a god apart from this world but

1

intimately involved with its affairs.  On occasion, Hebrews would experience the direct presence of God, as mystics would always know Him.  Increasingly, however, these encounters would be replaced by an indirect knowledge of divine will gained by historical analysis. As other peoples would read tea leaves or look for meaning in the chance patterns of trivial phenomena, Jews would look to history to guide them.  This faith would be slow in growing.  Provided a major catalyst by their liberation from Egyptian bondage, it would root itself in the convictions of this stubborn nation. Then all that had come before, all of their folk myths of the ages, would be reinterpreted in its perspective. And all that would come afterward would be understood on an historical dimension.

When this people would come to record their historical relationship with God, they would see it originating with Abraham.  He had moved his clan from Ur, an ancient city along the Euphrates River, to Canaan, which is today Israel, in about 1900 B.C. Chosen by God to establish a new people, Abraham nonetheless had cause to doubt his ultimate success. Apparently unable to carry on his line through his barren wife Sarah, the patriarch gained a temporarily acceptable heir by mating with Hagar, Sarah's maid. Through divine intervention, Sarah herself was later allowed to bear a son, who would be proclaimed the legitimate carrier of the Hebrew destiny.  Named Isaac, this son was born in his mother's old age.  Here was the first miracle of God furthering the growth of the Hebrew nation.

Isaac would in time sire two sons, one of whom named Jacob would father the progenitors of the twelve tribes of Israel.  Joseph, one of Jacob's twelve sons, was betrayed by his elder brothers and sold into Egyptian slavery.  Here again, God was seen directing the progress of His chosen people.  Rising from slavery to become the Pharaoh's second in command, Joseph later used his new position to save his family from famine in Canaan.  He subsequently told his brothers that they should not feel remorse for their earlier treachery against him, for God had directed their actions so that the Hebrew people might later be saved.  The faith that God directs history and through it reveals Himself was evident.

Multiplying for centuries among the abundant grazing lands of Egypt, the people of Israel were enslaved by a Pharoah who knew not Joseph.  Their subsequent liberation by Moses clearly indicated to them God's revelation in history. This experience, occurring about 1270 B.C., convinced the Hebrew people of their special relationship to God, who promised His favor to those of them who would keep His commandments. God's commandments to the Hebrews partly concerned ethical behavior among men. The concept of a covenant between a god and his people, oriented toward human beings living ethical lives here on earth, was in stark contrast to the Egyptian religion which centered on an afterlife acquired not through ethical behavior but rather by tricking the gods. Magic could hide the evil deeds of the Egyptian believer. This was not possible in Judaism, whose God was known not only for His omnipotence but also His omniscience. Unlike their Egyptian oppressors, with their thoughts on life after death, the early Hebrews' attention was solely on their unfolding relationship with God in this world.

Possibly the Hebrews were encouraged by their experiences in bondage to believe concepts diametrically opposed to those of the hated Egyptians. Early Judaism developed strong feelings against idolatry, by contrast a distinguishing characteristic of Egyptian religion. The Hebrew God was the only god His followers were instructed to worship, in comparison to the polytheism of Egypt. Disdained by Egyptians as filthy stock breeders, the Hebrew people were conditioned to accept beliefs that would discredit their enemy's orientation to life. This interpretation is strongly suggested by the numerous points of difference between the religions of these two ancient peoples, who once lived side by side in a master/slave relationship.$^3$

Having escaped from Egypt and travelling in the wilderness with their eyes on Canaan, the Hebrew people felt the temptation of more permissive gods. As their backsliding demonstrated, they did not yet believe theirs to be the only god of the universe. Indeed, even Moses's first commandment had merely stated that Hebrews were to have no other gods before their God. At that stage of its development, Judaism had a strong tendency toward monotheism, but was not monotheism itself. That would come later.$^4$ For the time being, Hebrews would marvel at the power of their jealous God and their special relationship to Him. Exodus, Chapter 19, verses 4-6, would describe their covenant in poetic language:

You have seen what I did to the

3

Egyptians, and how I bore you on
eagles' wings and brought you to
myself. Now therefore, if you will
obey my voice and keep my covenant,
you shall be my own possession
among all peoples; for all the earth
is mine, and you shall be to me a
kingdom of priests and a holy nation.

God did not involve only part of their lives, but
rather their whole lives. They were wholly dedicated
to Him and therefore a holy nation. The emphasis is
not intended as a clever play on words. A dictionary
will show that the word "holy" derives from the word
"whole." An understanding of the Hebrew people's
status as a holy nation can be gained only by realizing
that as a people they were totally dedicated to their
God. They demonstrated this commitment in the events
of this world. In their unfolding history, they
interacted with their God.

As mentioned earlier, other peoples at that time
thought of life not as history, the development of
unique occurrences, but rather as endless repetition.
In the cyclical view encouraged by observing nature's
recurring seasons, that which was similar in
corresponding events was emphasized in mental
processing. The never-to-be repeated character of an
occurrence was discarded as trivial, unimportant, and
meaningless. Sameness and permanence were valued by
this widespread style of mind. By contrast, the Hebrew
conception emphasized the novel aspects of events.
Judaism was a religion devoted to change. Unlike
neighboring peoples, the Hebrews saw meaning in the
unrepeatable aspects of life, for God's hand was in
altered circumstances.

The Hebrew concept of time, moving in linear
progression, was novel and unique. God was the ruler
of a world moving toward a divine goal. His chosen
people would play a key role in the unfolding of that
goal. Implicit in this belief was a corollary faith
that God cares about the struggles of this world. The
ancient Hebrews recorded this in their folklore--the
stories of Adam's fall, of Noah and the flood, and of
the Tower of Babel. As God involved Himself in human
events, the world had meaning and value. It was not to
be rejected as in Hinduism, Buddhism, and in some
variants of Christianity. In Judaism, God gave man
dominion over an earth created and cherished by
Himself. It was no accident that Jews later played

4

important roles in the development of modern science. Curiosity and interest in the physical universe is the mark of every scientist. Judaism encouraged this attitude.[5]

The duty of God's chosen people was to be involved in worldly concerns. While notable men among them would occasionally retreat from society, their absences characteristically would be brief. As a holy nation, they were required to do His will in human struggles. Their duty was to bring about what ought to be. In contrast, their neighbors' nature religions accepted the world as it was. In doing God's will, the Hebrews sought to make the world better, for they were an active agent in His historical plan. The fertile seed of the idea of progress was ancient Judaism's most precious gift to succeeding generations. While their neighbors confidently expected life's regeneration each Spring, the ancient Hebrews looked years into the future for the fulfillment of their hopes. They thought in terms of destiny and of an end to suffering. Justice was their goal, and ultimately the scope of their ethical concern would come to include all mankind.

Other nations' gods at that time tended to be amoral and indifferent to man. Not so with the Hebrew God. He wanted men to be good, yet He gave to man the power of ethical choice.[6] Dramatized in the Hebrew story of Adam and Eve, ethical choice suggested that man is free. Doubts remained on this point, for was not God the omnipotent and omniscient director of history? As such, could He really allow men to be free? This problem would later plague Christian and Islamic theologians as well. In any case, none of the Western religions, including Judaism, would doubt that God is the ruler of mankind. Consequently, human decision contrary to God's will would be punished by Him.

The Hebrew God was invisible and in many ways unknowable. His commandments were made known by Moses. But, as Moses himself was informed, to see God was to die. Because of His essential mystery, representations of God in the form of idols constituted human presumptuousness and blasphemy. As an invisible God, the Hebrew deity had no limited jurisdiction, but could see the entire desert and the hills beyond, as befitting a god of a nomadic, shepharding people. This was in contrast to the agriculturalists of that region whose gods lived in definite places, had spatially

5

limited domains, and were represented by stationary idols. The temptation to locate their God would be strong among the ancient Hebrews. First Mt. Horeb and later the Temple in Jerusalem would be claimed as the home of the Lord. But ultimately, the vision of Psalm 139, verses 7-10, would dominate Jewish thinking:

> Whither shall I go from thy spirit?
> Or whither shall I flee from thy
> presence? If I ascend up into
> heaven, thou art there: if I make
> my bed in Sheol, behold, thou art
> there. If I take the wings of the
> morning, and dwell in the uttermost
> parts of the sea; even there shall
> thy hand lead me, and thy right
> hand shall hold me.

While invisible, the Hebrew God was not an abstract impersonal force. He could be angry or filled with rejoicing. As a deity who cared about the events of humankind, He had personality. Man was created in His image and likeness. Therefore, in many ways, the Hebrew God was like men. Consequently, man had worth and dignity. As His highest earthly creation, man was loved by God as a child by a father. However, the full concept of God as a loving father was slow in developing. As a divine personality, His characteristics were at first representative of man's darker nature. God at times required the extermination of whole clans--men, women and children. And when His requirements were only partially met, as in King Saul's failure to destroy completely the people of Amalek, He coldly planted the seeds of the royal slacker's destruction. In any case, God from the outset took a keen interest in the affairs of His chosen nation. Gradually, this interest came to be interpreted as love. Early He had shown His intimate concern for the Hebrew people by delivering them from Egypt into Canaan. He molded history so that His chosen people returned to their rightful home. He would continue to reveal Himself through worldly events. This simple belief would make Hebrew religious scholars keenly interested in the political and economic developments of men and nations. Ultimately, this interest would shape the values of many far beyond the boundaries of the Hebrew people.

## The Establishment of Hebrew Politics

When Moses died after having led his nation to the

outskirts of Canaan, his recorded successor, Joshua, developed a strategy for entering the promised land. Warned by scouts of the power of the Canaanites, Joshua focused on capturing the weakest outlying settlements, leaving the stronger ones alone. His attack on Jericho fit into this pattern. Contrary to myth, the walls of Jericho were dilapidated at the time of the battle, which resulted in the annihilation of all the inhabitants. New Hebrew settlements arose. At a safe distance from the stronger Canaanite centers in the fertile plains and valleys, these new communities were located in the hills and mountains. Similar to what Jews would do in the same area over 3000 years later, new areas were made habitable by stout pioneering efforts, while peace was kept with the lowland Canaanites by the payment of Hebrew tribute.[8]

Moses had led Israel out of Egypt in about 1270 B.C. Forty years later, his followers entered Canaan. Roughly 100 years after that, the prophetess, Deborah, persuaded the Hebrew tribes to challenge the lowland Canaanites, and the payment of tribute ceased. Then, the arrival of a Greek tribe, known as the Philistines, ushered in a new chapter in Hebrew history. Dominating the Canaanites with superior iron weapons, the Philistines invaded the Hebrew hill country, threatening the very existence of Israel. Unification was needed to resist this new powerful enemy. In the middle of the 11th century B.C., the twelve tribes of Israel agreed that Saul of the tribe of Benjamin should centralize their government in a monarchy, now required by this new external threat. For a time, King Saul kept the Philistines at bay. Eventually, he was trapped and killed by his own hand, his body taken as a trophy by the Philistines. Why had this failure occurred? The Hebrew answer was characteristic. Saul had failed to follow God's will and consequently had been destroyed by historical events.

Saul's successor was David, formerly the doomed king's armor bearer. The name "David" was a military title, given him later in life. His original name is unknown, and the details of his youth are encrusted by myth, the prime example being the story of Goliath. Scholars hold that one of David's lieutenants slew a Philistine giant and that the heroic deed was later ascribed to David's youth in order to enhance his legend. In any case, David became the champion of the southern tribes, a grouping known as Judah after the largest of these tribes. From this base, David defeated the Philistines and liberated the northern

7

tribes. David's first problem in victory was to reunite the southern and northern tribes. He selected Jerusalem, which was located near the boundary of these two tribal groupings, with this purpose in mind. With the promised land won, and their first covenant with God apparently fulfilled, Hebrew pundits began talking of a second covenant involving David and what was fast becoming the holy city of Jerusalem. Recorded in Psalm 89: 3-4, and Psalm 132: 11-14, the second covenant described Judaism's new royal family as blessed by God "for all generations." As for Jerusalem, it was chosen by God as His eternal home. From that point forward, this former Canaanite community would be the holy city for the Hebrew people. Subsequent events would make it revered by Christians and Muslims as well. Also, the divine selection of the house of David would later become part of Christian theology, as Jesus of Nazareth reportedly would be of Davidic descent.

David wished to enhance Jerusalem's reputation by building a temple, a house for God, in that city during his lifetime. But this was not to be. Hebrew tradition then held that the tabernacle, a portable sanctuary used during the 40 years in the wilderness, was Israel's only house of God. David did not press the issue. Instead, he moved the Ark of the Covenant, the sacred talisman containing the stone tablets of the Ten Commandments, to Jerusalem in order to give his capital added authority.

David, it truly appeared, was divinely blessed. He had started as a runt of a shepherd boy and had become the first successful king of the children of Israel. The king had every reason to be proud of his many accomplishments. But as Proverbs 16: 18 would later note, pride precedes destruction. David was not to be an exception. Viewing the wife of one of his soldiers at her bath, David wanted her for his own. He was king, and ordered the soldier concerned to the most dangerous area of the frontier, where his death quickly followed. David's subsequent marriage to Bathsheba, the murdered soldier's wife, did not go unnoticed. Nathan, the prophet, chastised a contrite David and pointed out that even a king is not above God's commandments. As for punishment, Nathan prophecied that evil would befall the house of David because of the transgression. A cloud now threatened the glory of the second covenant.

The remainder of David's life was beset with tragedy. Amnon, his eldest son, was slain by another son, Absalom. Temporarily banished and out of favor, Absalom raised a revolt with the aid of the northern tribes, who had never really regarded the king as one of their own. The revolt was quashed, and Absalom was killed against his father's orders. David's spirit was crushed by these events. His anguish cries through the ages: "O my son Absalom, my son, my son Absalom! would God I had died for thee, O Absalom, my son, my son!" (II Samuel 18: 33)

In David's old age, Bathsheba persuaded him to abdicate in favor of their son Solomon, who ascended the throne in 973 B.C. at the age of 13. The young king pushed ahead with a project that had been close to his father's heart--the construction of the Temple, the permanent house of God in Jerusalem. Skeptical voices were raised in Israel: "'Will God indeed dwell on earth? Behold, heaven and the highest heaven cannot contain thee; how much less this house which I have built!'" (I Kings 8:27) Remembered for his wisdom, Solomon showed little of this attribute in conscripting labor from the northern tribes to build the controversial Temple. Possibly, the rebellious northern tribes might have been reconciled to the project through a policy of honey. Instead, they got vinegar, made doubly odious by the fact that the southern tribes also were not forced to build the Temple.

Predictably, the alienated northern tribes reasserted their dissatisfaction upon Solomon's death. Naming themselves Israel, they thereupon broke with the house of David, unthinkingly weakening their new state as a consequence. Judah, the southern remnant of the once powerful Davidic kingdom, continued to be ruled by the great man's descendants. It thereby enjoyed the authority of the second covenant. The monarchy in Israel seemed somewhat illegitimate by comparison and suffered relative instability as a result. In addition, Israel's secession made the divided Hebrews prey to their neighbors. The next 300 years depicted the decline of this once powerful people.

This unhappy period was the heyday of the Hebrew prophets, who had few doubts concerning the cause of the trouble. Elijah castigated Israel's King Ahab and Queen Jezebel for bearing false witness against Naboth and expropriating his estate for their royal gardens. The resulting legal murder of Naboth was not their only sin. Queen Jezebel further defiled the northern kingdom by her worship of Baal, the Canaanite fertility god.  Consequently, both Ahab and Jezebel ended their lives at the hands of others.  Here was God's punishment, written in events as a warning to a sinful people.  But the message was temporarily disregarded. King Jeroboam II of Israel later set a tone of pleasure loving and dissipation for his kingdom, ignoring the growing gap between rich and poor.  The prophet Amos reminded Israel of the meaning of Moses' covenant:  The Hebrew community must live up to God's laws of social justice or forfeit the benefits of a chosen people. Israel's destruction was predicted if this selfish pattern of behavior continued.

Within a generation after Amos, Israel was no more.  God's instrument of destruction was Assyria, one of the most ruthless imperialist powers in all of human history.  Seizing Israel in 733 B.C., Assyria deported her upper and middle classes to distant lands. Assyria's technique of obliterating a nation's identity was to scatter its leadership and replace their number with displaced peoples from other conquered countries. The Assyrians moved 27,000 Hebrews out of Israel and a corresponding number of foreigners into the vanquished kingdom.  Over hundreds of years, this forced mixing created a new people, who became known as Samaritans. They were partially Hebrew and accepted only the scriptures of Genesis, Exodus, Leviticus, Numbers, and Deuteronomy, collectively known as the Pentateuch.  The undefiled southern tribes hated them as a bastardized sect.  Thus, the 10 northern tribes were lost to history.  Thereafter, Judaism would develop from the southern tribes of Judah.

Seers in Judah had an easy explanation for these events.  The northern tribes had broken God's covenant with the house of David and had suffered predictable results.  Yet they could not afford to be too smug, for Assyria's hot breath now threatened the southern kingdom as well.  In 701 B.C., the Assyrian host besieged Jerusalem.  The prophet Isaiah foretold the enemy's destruction, a most unlikely event surprisingly fulfilled by a plague that swept the enemy camp.  This seeming miracle enhanced Jerusalem's prestige as a holy city and firmly established the credentials of Isaiah. With the northern tribes gone, Jerusalem no longer had detractors within Judaism. The city was now confidently proclaimed as the center of the earth, and the Temple of Solomon as the center of Jerusalem.  And in the center of the Temple rested the holy Ark of the Covenant.[10]

Thereafter, peace was bought by paying tribute to Assyria. For the next 100 years, Judah enjoyed relative prosperity under a succession of kings, the most important of whom was Manasseh. This infamous monarch systematically violated the first commandment by worshipping Baal in the Temple. He also encouraged belief in the Assyrian astral cult (astrology), which contradicted Judaism's historical orientation. The major assumption of astrology is that one's fate is written in the stars. By contrast, religious Hebrews saw their fortunes resulting from the degree to which their community upheld its unique covenant with God. Hebrews conceded that astrology might determine the fate of others, but as for themselves it was irrelevant. Manasseh ignored this fundamental precept even though his Assyrian masters did not require his religious subservience. Accordingly, when Judah was eventually overwhelmed by powerful enemies, it was seen as a result of Manasseh's idolatry.

Babylon became Judah's new threat in 612 B.C., when that power unexpectedly crushed Assyria. For awhile, Judah paid tribute to Babylon, but then suddenly refused. The prophet Jeremiah harshly predicted that Babylon would serve as God's instrument, punishing Judah for Manasseh's idolatry. Manasseh's successors had rejected Baal and returned to the God of Moses. Nevertheless, Jeremiah proclaimed the coming doom, sealing his name for all time with pessimistic foreboding. Unfortunately for Judah, his prophecy proved accurate, at least to the degree that Babylon destroyed Judah and carried away its creative elites into captivity in 588 B.C. The Temple of Solomon was reduced to rubble, and the Ark of the Covenant was never seen again. Only Judah's most impoverished peasants were left behind to scratch out a living as they had done before.

Was the proud history of the Hebrew people at an end, mocking the promise of high destiny that had been implicit in the several covenants with their God? Would the exiles of Judah become lost forever, as had the deportees of Israel? The first covenant was apparently broken. God had not protected His chosen people as He had done when the Assyrians had earlier threatened to destroy Judah. The second covenant was also violated. Jerusalem lay in ruins, and the descendants of David were in chains. We moderns could hardly have disdained the ancient Hebrews if they had thereupon concluded that their faith was misplaced. Those beaten people would not have seemed weak to us

11

had they quit their notion of being unique and divinely chosen and had silently merged with other Mediterranean cultural traditions.

The exiles of Judah held to their ancient faith. They accepted their trials as God's punishment and discipline for their transgressions. They closely examined their behavior to eliminate habits contrary to their God's commandments and looked forward to a time when His favor would again be restored. Despite the taunts of their Babylonian conquerors, they continued to regard themselves as God's chosen people and foresaw a restoration of the house of David. In Judaism's darkest hour up to that time, the new idea of the coming Davidic Messiah soothed their agony. The ability of the Hebrew spirit to endure and grow, a characteristic which would be seen again and again, now heroically asserted itself.

## Judaism's Response to Babylonian Captivity

Jewish scripture describes the Baal cult of the ancient Canaanites as the enemy of Judaism. Yet, during their Babylonian captivity, it is quite possible that Baalish symbolic thinking gave the defeated Jews the needed hope to survive as a people. History is replete with ironies of this kind. Baalism traditionally had emphasized that life is never crushed out completely. As a nature religion, it taught that new life always emerges after death, that spring always follows winter, and that night is always darkest just before the dawn. Certainly, the Hebrew captives were experiencing their darkest hour up to that time. Yet Baalish analogies from nature encouraged optimism. In the depressing night of Babylonian captivity, Jewish theologians suggested that a brighter day lay ahead, that God would soon conclude His story for mankind, and that the righteous remnant of the Jewish people would win ultimate victory.

Up until Babylonian captivity, Judaism had no developed conception of life after death. The scriptures did tell of Sheol, a Hebrew nether world where the dead lived temporary, shadowy existences. This focus would change with the experience of national destruction and mass deportation to an alien land. Increasingly, Jews would not expect God's rewards in this world. Instead, Judaism would look to an end to history, when the best elements within the faith would enjoy immortality with their God. Before the fall of Judah, Hebrew believers had been solely concerned with

12

affairs of this world, but as worldly conditions no longer encouraged hope, Jews now looked beyond human history.

True to its origins, Judaism could not easily conceive of eternal life as disembodied existence. Instead, in Judaism's developing concept of a life beyond, the dead would physically rise from their graves. Those living in immortality would have the physical bodies they had known on earth. Similarly, the Jewish afterlife would not be in some cloud-bound heaven. Instead, it would be on a reconstituted earth. In short, their new conception of life after death would be harmonious with the rather earth-bound orientation of pre-Babylonian Judaism.[12]

Had Jewish life been truly oppressed in Babylon, it is unlikely that any new theological elaborations would have developed or that even the original faith would have survived. In point of fact, the uprooted Hebrews did quite well in Babylon as merchants. This was the first Jewish venture into this line of work. Heretofore, herding and agriculture had been their economic mainstays. Interestingly, Hebrews had previously regarded traders as parasites. Hosea 12: 7 indicates this earlier attitude; "He is a merchant; the balances of deceit are in his hand: he loveth to oppress." In Judah, the despised Canaanites had been the shopkeepers. Now the alien Jews in Babylon came to succeed in these trades. Divorced from the land and knowledgeable in several languages, the Jewish people would increasingly find the best available economic opportunities in buying and selling merchandise. Over the ages, these facts of life would encourage the unfortunate stereotype of the greedy, grasping Jewish merchant.

Commercial intercourse has encouraged the disappearance of many distinct ethnic groups throughout history. Babylon's Jews successfully resisted this tendency. Far from their homeland, the Jews managed to retain their separate identity largely through strict Sabbath observance, which had been rather lax before Babylonian captivity. In Babylon, a community rule came into existence that no work be performed from Friday's sundown to sundown on Saturday. The commandment was ancient, but now it was enforced. The Hebrew deportees interpreted the destruction of Judah as God's punishment for straying from His law. They were determined to reverse the trend of divine disfavor, and so the Sabbath was now strictly observed.

13

This helped segregate the Jewish community in Babylon, as strict Sabbath observance was highly visible and disruptive of any regular relationships with outsiders. Accordingly, community identity was maintained in a foreign land.[13]

Then, after 50 years of Jewish exile, Cyrus the Great of Persia conquered Babylon. Friendly to the Jewish captives who cheered him as a liberator, Cyrus encouraged a caravan of 42,000 Jews to return to Judah and make it a Persian province. In addition, reconstruction of the Temple in Jerusalem was begun under Persian patronage. This dramatic turn of events spoke to the Jewish people. Truly, their God was most great. Indeed, even before this event, the Jewish captives had concluded that theirs was the only God. Under the mocking dominance of the Babylonians, the Jews had made the case for the strict monotheism which would thereafter characterize their faith. This development indirectly had been encouraged by Babylonian pundits who had claimed that Judah's demise proved the superiority of Babylon's gods. The Jewish captives had answered this by categorically denying the existence of those gods. They had proclaimed that their God, the God of Israel, was also the God of all humanity, including Babylon. Therefore, Jewish captivity in Babylon had not been a result of the superior power of rival gods, but rather the judgment of the omnipotent God of the universe. Persian liberation reinforced this belief.[14]

Increasingly, YHWH came to be used as the name of God. An ancient belief in Biblical lands was that to know the name of a god was to have power over him. The ancient designation YHWH, by its mysterious and unpronouncable nature, suggested the omnipotence of God, and so it was increasingly used in place of past names such as El-Shaddai. YHWH can be made pronounceable with the addition of vowels at appropriate places. However, the word Yahweh is a modern invention. The returning Babylonian captives did not refer to God by this name in oral conversation, for to do so would have shown disrespect. In written accounts, He was referred to as YHWH.[15]

The view that YHWH was the God of all peoples, which had been long speculated upon, had a reforming influence upon the "chosen people concept." The language of Exodus 19: 4-6, which had described the Hebrews as a "kingdom of priests and a holy nation" now took on richer meaning. The chosen people would be

14

ministers to the world. This new role was dramatized in the book of Jonah, which emphasized the duty of the chosen people to spread God's message to all nations. Proselytizing efforts were mounted. For the next millennium, the chosen people would not be a closed club but rather an expanding community of believers. This new attitude cut both ways. It not only widened the possibility for non-Hebrews becoming Jews but also indirectly encouraged the absorption of foreign ideas into Judaism. Zoroastrian beliefs would impregnate Judaism through this entering wedge.[16]

Zoroastrianism was the religion of Judaism's Persian benefactors. Its founder was Zarathustra (Zoroaster), who is thought to have been born in Media in about 660 B.C. Similar to Judaism, Zoroastrianism was an ethical religion, placing a premium on moral behavior. It also had a well-developed eschatology (a term which means a theology concerning the end of time), which was very attractive to the Jews of that day. When people die, Zoroastrian belief held, they go to heaven or hell depending on how they lived their lives on earth. There they reside in disembodied spirits until the end of days (the end of history), when the bodies of the dead will be resurrected and reunited with their souls. At that time, final judgment will occur and the truly evil people will be destroyed forever. The good will live on in an earthly paradise. Zoroaster preached the existences of both a good god and an evil god. These two forces struggle through time until the end of history when the good god will emerge victorious. Just before the end of days, the struggle between good and evil will become intense and the righteous will temporarily suffer.

Judaism did not absorb all of Zoroastrian eschatology. The idea of two gods, while neatly identifying the source of evil in the world, ran too afoul of Jewish monotheism to be accepted. The farthest that Judaism would go in this direction was in accepting the existence of Satan, whose powers were in no way equivalent to God's. Some Zoroastrian concepts were successfully grafted onto Judaism. The ideas of an end to history, the general physical resurrection at the end of days, the final judgment of good and evil persons, the destruction of evil souls and the establishment of the Kingdom of God on a reconstituted earth were all adopted by Judaism over the next several centuries. Christianity would also later espouse these concepts, except for the notion that truly evil persons would be destroyed after the final judgment. Christian theology would have these unfortunates live on in hell.[17]

Judaism wove an additional idea into this eschatology. The Messiah, a term meaning God's anointed one, would inaugurate the Kingdom of God at the end of days. He would be a descendant of King David. That was clear. His attributes and style were disputed. Some held that he would be like David, a warrior king. Others would think of him as a suffering servant who would atone for the sins of mankind. All agreed that once the Kingdom of God had been instituted, the righteous inhabitants of His kingdom would have the divine law written in their hearts and would be incapable of sin. In that day, the children of Israel would win ultimate victory and preside over the nations of the earth.[18]

It would be inaccurate to claim that Judaism was solely inspired by Zoroastrianism in developing its eschatology about the coming Kingdom of God. Independent influences within Judaism had been suggesting these themes before and during the Babylonian captivity. For example, the early chapters of Isaiah, composed before the fall of Judah, record the ideas of both the coming Kingdom of God and the Davidic Messiah. The idea of the general resurrection at the end of days was offered as early as the Book of Ezekiel, named after the chief prophet who lived at the time of the Babylonian captivity. The political turmoil swirling in the area, resulting in the destruction of Assyria and then Judah itself, and the subsequent fall of Babylon, all seemed to suggest a climax to history. It is even possible that some of Zoroaster's theology was inspired by Jewish sources. In any case, Judaism was ripe for the eschatology articulated in Zoroastrianism, and the seedling ideas held in common with the Persian faith came to flower in Judaism as well.[19]

Yet not all in Judaism would accept these ideas. Even up to the time of Jesus of Nazareth, powerful elements within Judaism would reject the notions of a coming Messiah, the end of days, the inauguration of the Kingdom of God, and the general resurrection of the dead. The Book of Ecclesiastes, thought to have been written in about the third century B.C., indirectly expressed this skepticism and ironically demonstrated the human need for the new eschatology. The ancient Hebrews had conceived the concept of linear history, but the author of Ecclesiastes described the passage of

16

time more as a tale of mindless repetition and upheaval than a story with a divine purpose. To him, all appeared to be vanity. In such a world without purpose, what reason could be given for human exertion in any cause? The experiences of the Jewish people in Babylonian captivity had suggested the new eschatology. Their need for it was indirectly articulated by the quiet despair of Ecclesiastes. The next several centuries would witness both the expansion of their need and their resulting faith that the end of this world was coming fast.

## Judaism's Era of the Second Temple

Persian rule over Judah lasted roughly 200 years, until Alexander the Great of Macedonia swept through the area on his way to India in about 330 B.C. Consequently, the Seleucids governed the province for nearly two centuries. This dynasty, founded by one of Alexander's generals (Seleucus Nicator), tested the mettle of the Jews. The Greek way of life proved a great temptation for aristocratic Jews, as their Greek overlords represented a civilization unsurpassed in the ancient world. Also, Jewish youth were lured by Greek glorification of both athletics and the human body. Naked athletic performances, common among the Hellenistic population, greatly offended faithful Jews. The story of Adam and Eve reflected Judaism's traditional bias against nudity, as sin had first been revealed by that couple's awareness of the naked condition. Also, Noah's son, Ham, had been cursed because he had gazed upon his sleeping father's nakedness. Greek attitudes were quite the opposite, as they regarded the unclad human form as a divine temple. Whereas Jews were shocked by Greek norms, the growing Hellenistic population was offended by Jewish circumcision, which to the latter represented a surgical desecration. The Greek cultural influx threatened Jewish loyalty to the one outward symbol that indelibly bound them as a nation.

In 168 B.C., King Antiochus, the Seleucid ruler of the Jews, commanded that a statue of Zeus, looking very much like Antiochus himself, be placed in the Temple of Jerusalem. Antiochus then added the title Epiphanes, or "god made manifest," to his name. In addition, he commanded that the Jewish people forsake YHWH and worship Zeus, and he outlawed circumcision on pain of death. What were the Jewish people to do? The answer rose spontaneously from the hearts of courageous folk facing impossible odds: Revolt! Their leader was

17

called "the hammer," or Maccabaeus, and his followers became known to history as the Maccabees. At times it appeared that their struggle must fail, but national independence was eventually won in 142 B.C. The outcome appears truly miraculous, even through the fog of millennia. A new Jewish state, resulting from the first systematic anti-Jewish religious persecution, existed after four and a half centuries of foreign domination.[20]

Interestingly, both the belief in the end of days concept and that concerning individual immortality had been encouraged during the Maccabean war. As Jewish warriors fell in battle, faith that they would find their reward in paradise deepened. The Book of Daniel, believed to have been written in the early years of the conflict, prophesied that the end of history would come in "70 weeks" of years (490 years) after the return of the Jews from Babylonian captivity. This dated the predicted end at roughly a century after the Maccabean revolt, helping explain the high expectations of the coming Kingdom of God in the days of Jesus of Nazareth. With the conquest of the Maccabean kingdom by the Roman general, Pompeii, in 63 B.C., the prophecy of Daniel seemed to be coming true. In 37 B.C., Herod, who was tied to the Maccabean line by marriage, was appointed by Rome to govern the province of Judea. While nominally a Jew, King Herod was hated by Jews as a tyrant, an epithet he richly deserved. Herod ruled by assassination and terror. He virtually wiped out his entire family, because he feared the imagined plots that consumed his tortured mind. Herod's acts and methods contributed to the growing popular belief that the end of history was fast approaching.[21]

A group of Jews, known as Zealots, believed a human assist was necessary to inaugurate the divine climax of time. As the end was to be characterized by a life and death struggle between the forces of good and evil, they called for good Jews to fulfill their eschatological duty by participating in the contest. In their belief, armed conflict was a divinely appointed necessity. The Messiah, they predicted, would be a warrior, as David had been. This precept was probably shared by most Jews. The Zealots held that there could be no compromise with Roman rule, as Roman emperor-worship represented rank idolatry, and the first commandment of the Jews stressed that YHWH alone deserved worship. Roman tradition and Jewish religious principles could not be reconciled. The Zealots called for war against Rome on the Maccabean mode.[22]

18

The Essenes, another Jewish group, prepared for the expected end in other ways. Whereas the Zealots sought to inaugurate the Kingdom of God, the Essenes concentrated on purifying themselves in preparation for the last judgment. It has often been speculated that this sect did much to influence the founders of Christianity. A case can be made for this, as the Essenes advocated a rigorous anti-materialism that went far beyond traditional Judaism. For example, they viewed commercial activity as violating the commandment against stealing and interpreted the commandment against killing as prohibiting war. They viewed women and sexual relations as corrupt influences and therefore encouraged the very un-Jewish condition of celibacy. They lived in communes based on the principle of simple subsistence and believed that righteous Jews should be completely unselfish, meek and humble. They were more characteristically Jewish in holding that suffering confers power, and they practiced spiritual healing supposedly made possible by their ascetic, purifying way of life. Some speculate that John the Baptist was once an Essene monk, as he practiced their belief in the value of frequent baptisms as a purifying exercise.

Nevertheless, the self-segregated Essene communes were in stark contrast to the behavior of Christianity's founder. The Essene's objective of self-purification, a goal which would be injured by contact with the defiled world beyond their settlements, made them more reluctant than even the Pharisees to have contact with sinners. Also, the Essenes were more legalistic regarding strict Sabbath observance than were the Pharisees, whom Jesus chastised for their rules and regulations. Another significant difference separated Jesus from the Essenes, as the latter did not believe in the resurrection of the body at the end of days. Different in this respect from most Jews as well, the Essenes believed in a disembodied afterlife in heaven or hell.

Some have speculated that the Essenes may have been influenced by religious thinking from the Indian subcontinent. It is known that King Ashoka, who ruled India in the third century B.C., sent missionaries as far west as the Mediterranean. This conjecture has certain merit as many Essene beliefs traditionally have been part of the Indian mind. For example, Indians typically associate meekness and holiness and have believed that pure persons contaminate themselves by

association with lesser humans.  Also, an Indian holy
man characteristically abstains from sex, and when
informed of the resurrection idea, traditionally
religious Indians find it without validity as did the
Essenes.  On the other hand, the Essenes did not
believe in reincarnation, a core concept in any Indian
belief system.  Nevertheless, the suspicion of some
Indian influence upon Essene doctrine remains.[23]

The Zealots and the Essenes are both easily
contrasted with the Sadducees, a group representing the
worldly, politically minded Jewish leaders of that day.
The Sadducees rejected all eschatological concepts.
Talk of an end to history and the coming Messiah
undermined respect for worldly authority, which the
Sadducees held dear.  In addition, it threatened
trouble with Rome.  As scions of the Jewish
aristocracy, the Sadducees were dominant in not only
the economy of Jerusalem but also in the religious
ceremonies, which were central in ancient Judaism.  In
that age, Jews from throughout the diaspora would come
to Jerusalem to sacrifice small animals in the Temple.
The Sadducees controlled this primitive rite from the
ancient Hebrew past.  Accordingly, they held that only
the priestly performers of the Temple sacrifices lived
up to the full letter of the written Jewish law.
Self-satisfied and content with existing conditions,
the Sadducees lived in fear of the changing currents
within Judaism.[24]

With changing times and circumstances, questions
of legal interpretation within Judaism naturally arose.
With the progress of civilization, Judaism increasingly
acquired additional ethical concerns, requiring a
further development of religious law.  The combined
result was the accumulation of an oral legal tradition
during the era of the second Temple.  This oral law was
made elaborate by the seemingly endless scholarly
discussions and debates on legal fine points encouraged
by the Pharisees, yet another of the Jewish groups of
the period.  Whereas the Temple was identified with the
Sadducees, the synagogue, a simple building where pious
Jews could discuss the law, was the center of Pharisaic
activity.  In place of ornate ritual and animal
sacrifice, the Pharisees put scholarship and
intellectual acuity, traits which would eventually
become associated with the Jewish temperament.  Ancient
Hebrews had listened for prophets, but the Pharisees
distrusted the spontaneous and mystical qualities
associated with living prophets.  Instead, their
attention focused on God's words delivered to the

ancient prophets and the meaning of these prophecies in day-to-day Jewish life. The Pharisees were Judaism's puritans, seeking to train the Jewish masses to live by the tenets of the evolving and increasingly rigorous Jewish law. In contrasting their purposes with those of the Sadducees, the Pharisees were especially fond of God's words in Jeremiah 7:21:

> In the day that I brought them out of the land of Egypt, I did not speak to your fathers or command them concerning burnt offerings and sacrifices.
> But this command I gave them, "Obey my voice, and I will be your God, and you shall be my people; and walk in all the way[s] that I command you that it may be well with you."

The Temple could not continue much longer as the fountainhead of Jewish religious experience, as proselytizing was swelling the Jewish population in lands far from Judea. Accordingly, the synagogue had distinct advantages as a rival institution. The synagogue had no priests. As a house of God, it could be erected wherever the faithful gathered to worship. It was not restricted to the limiting confines of David's holy city of Jerusalem, nor even Judea. All faithful Jews were theoretically on an equal footing in the synagogue. Any attender could read from the scriptures and discuss their meaning with the congregation. Jesus of Nazareth did this himself on occasion, but the practical masters of the synagogues were the Pharisees due to their great learning. After the destruction of the second Temple, the synagogues became the primary places of Jewish worship, and schools arose to ordain rabbis to lead the synagogues. But in Jesus's day, the term rabbi (or teacher) was applied to anyone learned in the scriptures, including Jesus himself.

The gospel attacks on the Pharisees are well-known. For the last two thousand years, Christians have associated the word "Pharisee" with mindless legalism. But in fairness to the Pharisees, their attitude was "possibilistic" rather than one of adherence to unachievable norms. In comparison to the prophetic, charismatic style of Jesus, the Pharisees were legalists indeed. But in contrast to the Sadducees, the Pharisees stressed that the law should be practicable. For example, the Pharisees rightly charged that by centering Judaism in Jerusalem's

21

Temple, the Sadducees made their version of the law impractical for Jews who lived outside of Judea. The Essenes, too, were impractical by Pharisaic standards in ruling, for example, that babies could not be delivered on the Sabbath. The goal of the Pharisees was a legal system that practicably could be followed by all Jews. They came into conflict with the Christians as, unlike the Essenes and Sadducees, Pharisees did missionary work among the common people, the same audience appealed to by Jesus and his disciples.[25]

In contrast with the Essenes, who observed the Sabbath with a most somber attitude, the Pharisees welcomed the holy day with joy, calling attention to the wonder of God and His creation. In addition, unlike either the Essenes or the Sadducees, they believed in the resurrection at the end of days. The Pharisees basically agreed with the Zealot conception of the Messiah and the struggle between good and evil at the end of time. But, unlike the Zealots, they generally preferred passive resistance to active confrontation. Here was a soft spot in the Pharisaic world view which the Zealots ultimately exploited. As the Pharisees admitted that a contest between good and evil would mark the last days, they could not refuse to participate in the Zealot uprising once it came in 66 A.D. (or C.E., "Common era," as Jews designate the Christian era). The Essenes, for all of their supposed allegiance to the pacifistic ideal, also had to join the conflict against evil when the fighting started. Interestingly, these would-be pacifists proved to be heroic warriors and ultimately perished to the last man. The Sadducees, too, were ruined by the war, which resulted in the destruction of the Temple in 70 A.D. With no Temple, the Sadducees' reason for being quickly eroded, and the sect faded from history. Judaism's future destiny would rest with the Pharisees.

The earlier success of the Maccabees against impossible odds encouraged this tragic resort to arms, as did the belief that God would inaugurate His Kingdom in the midst of the struggle. Correspondingly, when defeat came it was all the more devastating, for it suggested that God was punishing his chosen people for some wrongdoing. Such thinking can justify passive acceptance of inhuman treatment at the hands of a conqueror, for, as in the times of Babylonian captivity, the conqueror can be perceived as a punishing agent of God. However, this is not always the case, as the example of the defenders of the

22

fortress Masada demonstrated. Faced with an impending Roman seizure of the fortress, Masada's Jewish garrison, together with wives and children, put each other to the sword rather than satisfy the expectations of their conquerors. While Ecclesiastes had earlier proclaimed that it was better to be a living dog than a dead lion, Masada's defenders chose the latter alternative. Their example lives on to inspire Jews even today.

At the time of the Maccabean revolt, the population was relatively dispersed and roads were poor--two conditions which aided the rebels in waging guerrilla warfare. By the time of the Great War with the Romans, greater population density and new, excellent Roman roads helped deny the rebellious Jews similar advantages. Many Jews were killed and carried off into slavery as a result of their defeat, but enough remained to renew the struggle 62 years later in the Bar-Kokhba Revolt, which lasted from 132 to 135 A.D. Deriving his name (which means "son of a star") from messianic prophecy, Bar-Kokhba's effort also resulted in destruction and defeat. This time, the Romans worked to eliminate the source of Jewish resistance in Palestine--the Jews themselves. Most of the survivors were sent into foreign slavery or otherwise removed from the area, yet a substantial remnant remained. Later, in the fourth century, when Christianity became the official religion of the empire, the remaining Jews in Palestine underwent special persecution. Consequently, more and more Jews fled their homeland. For the next 16 centuries, Jews could always be found in Palestine but increasingly representing no more than a small minority of their promised land's population.[26]

The era of the second Temple was over, and the long age of the Jewish diaspora had begun. Actually, the Jewish diaspora dated back to the Babylonian captivity, for a large number of Jews remained in Babylon even after the reconstruction of the Temple. But as long as there was a Temple in Jerusalem, the diaspora had been on the outskirts of Jewish history. After the Great War and the Bar-Kokhba Revolt, the dispersed Jews would increasingly represent the best in Judaism, and their story would be the essence of Jewish history until modern times.

The Talmudic Millennium

When the Jews had returned from Babylonian

23

captivity, they came home with the new certainty that the God of Israel was the God of all peoples. This realization had spurred them into proselytizing efforts, fulfilling their ancient charge to be a priest people unto all the world. Journeying throughout the periphery of the Mediterranean, Jewish missionaries found eager converts. The high ethical principles of Judaism, together with its emphasis on stable family life and social justice, were good drawing cards for the expanding faith. Jewish proselytizing activities naturally increased with the growing expectations that the end of history was drawing near. Those righteous Gentiles capable of becoming Jews deserved the opportunity to accept God's commandments and eventually share in the coming Kingdom of God. With flocks of Gentiles joining Jewish communities, belief in the approaching end became all the more firm. God indeed appeared to be preparing the world for universal acceptance of his divine sovereignty, an expected sign of the end of days.

Ironically, with the destruction of the Temple in 70 A.D., Jewish proselytizing increased even more. One might suspect that the Roman victory would have led Jews to retreat immediately into a shell of secure tradition. This was not the case. With the Temple gone and the national moorings of the Jewish faith weakened, the Pharisees were further encouraged to spread their version of Judaism, which was more suited to the necessities of a universal faith. The Christian gospels begrudgingly noted their proselytizing successes, which had been facilitated by the Jewish resistance against Rome. In those days, Judaism was synonymous with heroism. Who else had so boldly challenged Roman authority with so few material resources? Downtrodden elements throughout the empire eagerly investigated the Jewish way of life as an alternative to the hated, exploitative Roman order. In the generation immediately preceding the Temple's destruction, roughly 4.5 million Jews lived outside Palestine, with only one million in Judea. During the next several centuries, this ratio grew larger still.[27]

Eventually Judaism retreated from this attempt at expansion. Several reasons explained the turnabout. For one, in sharp contrast to the rival Christian sect, the Jews themselves made it relatively difficult for newcomers to join their community. Christianity offered the promise of instantaneous spiritual rebirth. The rapid conversion of Saul of Tarsus, a persecuting Pharisee, into St. Paul, the foremost Christian missionary, was a guiding model to newcomers to that faith. By contrast, Judaism required that a family of converts must uphold the Jewish law for three generations before being fully welcomed into the congregation. As a result, Jewish converts of that time were designated Noachides ("God Fearers"). These God Fearers were permitted to attend the synagogue but were not completely integrated into the Jewish community. The requirement of circumcision was also a hindrance to adult male Gentiles who were attracted by Judaism.

In about 200 A.D., Rome outlawed Jewish proselytizing, an edict that was largely effective. Christianity suffered similar persecution, but its missionary successes continued apace, largely due to the conversion of Jewish God Fearers to Christianity where they could enjoy immediate entree. Viewing the Christian church as a bastard offspring, Jewish leaders could see that it was among Judaism's most recent converts that Christianity scored its easiest successes. Indeed, Christianity was in many ways a parasite that fed upon Jewish proselytizing successes. Predictably, distrust of the God Fearers grew within the Jewish community, further encouraging their flight to Christianity, and Jews increasingly came to regard religious expansion among the Gentiles as a bankrupt policy.[28]

Meanwhile, the legalistic approach to religion, always present in Judaism was growing apace, further discouraging outsiders from seeking entrance. The Pharisees' emphasis on the universal aspects of Judaism had encouraged them to spread the faith beyond the confines of Judea. But as masters of the growing oral law, the Pharisees early exhibited exclusive tendencies that would eventually strangle their proselytizing mission. For example, as Judaism's lawmakers they gave emphasis to Deuteronomy 7: 3-4, which commanded that Jews not intermarry with Gentiles. Under their leadership, this legal prohibition was enforced, in spite of the fact that Ruth, an ancestor of King David himself, had been a Gentile. With the enforcement of the prohibition against intermarriage and the dying out of proselytizing, the chosen people increasingly became a closed entity. Of course, despite the legalists' best efforts, some mixed marriages continued to occur. The rule devised for these situations was that if the mother was Jewish, the children would be similarly regarded. To this day, the most legalistic elements in Judaism continue to be disinterested in converting

25

Gentiles. On the other hand, Reform Jews, who have retained only those laws with ethical content, are most eager to renew proselytizing efforts, in order to make up losses suffered in the Nazi Holocaust.

With the rise of Christianity, Judaism retreated within itself, giving a greater aura of exclusivity to the chosen people concept. With this restricted vision, the belief slowly arose that a Jew could never lose his elect status. This was unique among the world's great religions. Other faiths placed sole emphasis on belief and practice. Medieval Judaism promoted a different theory. "A bad Jew," R. Judah Halevi proclaimed, "bears within himself the latent or slumbering qualities of election and singularity, which pass from him to his good son or grandson." With active proselytizing defunct, Judaism could not afford to lose members through attrition caused by individual flaws of character and lack of religious dedication. Hence the implication that Jewishness was carried racially through the generations was given religious sanction. On rare occasion, whole groups of Gentiles would adopt Judaism for reasons of state. Maimonides, the most famous Jewish sage of the Middle Ages, would welcome these newcomers to the Jewish family. But new additions were not actively sought as a matter of course. Accordingly, the believing offspring of apostate Jews were eagerly welcomed back into the now restricted ranks of Judaism.[29]

In most of life, the cause of sad developments have happier results as well. The slow death of proselytizing was the negative face of Judaism's growing legalism. By contrast, the finest product of medieval Judaism was the Talmud, which was the oral law reduced to written form. The Talmud, which means "learning" or "teaching," consists of two parts. First is the Mishnah, which was the oral law of the Pharisees compiled and categorized. This was found to be insufficient by itself, for changing conditions required further elaboration and interpretation. This was given in the second aspect of the Talmud, called the Gemara.

The Talmud was the work of scholarly rabbis, most of whom are anonymous to history. After the destruction of the Temple, the rabbis of Palestine took the lead in drafting a text. But with increasing persecution of Palestine's Jews, which accompanied the rise of Christianity to political power, the center of Talmudic development shifted to Babylon, which was

safely outside the reaches of the Roman empire. Two
Talmuds were produced, but the Babylonian model was
ultimately far superior to the Palestinian version.
For most situations, the Babylonian Talmud was the
Talmud. Its bulk alone is impressive, consisting of 22
volumes and 2,500,000 words.

The work was finished after a millennium of
scholarly discourse and discovery. Nonetheless, the
development of Judaism's legal tradition has not yet
ended. Changing conditions continue to call for legal
reinterpretation. For example, modern Jews debate
whether turning on electric lights during the Sabbath
constitutes lighting a fire on the seventh day, which
is prohibited in Exodus 35: 3. Talmudic scholars,
unable to foresee the invention of the electric light,
obviously did not cover this contingency, and so legal[30]
discourse within Judaism continues even yet.

During the thousand year process of compiling the
Talmud, a style of argumentative, scholarly discourse
came to characterize Judaism. It is no accident that
the faculties of modern colleges and universities have
a higher percentage of Jews than is found in the
general population. Talmudic Judaism delighted in
argument, as does modern academia. The Talmud reflects
this by containing not only the rulings of the position
that eventually won out on any given question but the
opposing viewpoints as well. Talmudic Judaism placed a
high value on rationalism and persuasive discourse, for
these were the human tools through which divine law was
realized. The attitude of the Talmudic rabbis was
similar to that of modern scientists seeking to uncover
the secrets of the universe. They trusted in the
powers of human logic to translate God's legal
blueprint, given to man in the Pentateuch, to the
changing conditions of their day. An anecdote from
those times amply illustrates the scholarly,
intellectual, curious style of mind that was developed
in the Talmudic debates. The story tells of a disciple
who hid under his rabbi's bed to learn how his teacher
behaved with his wife at night. When discovered, the
student justified his unusual behavior by recalling
that the Jewish law applied to all aspects of life,
including his master's sexual practices. Curiosity and
intellectual ability became highly valued within
Judaism. Consequently, a new aristocracy of learning
was formed as many a poor man with a scholarly bent was
elevated to the pinnacle of public acclaim within the
Jewish community.[31]

Some examples of Talmudic law must be given to provide the reader with a better understanding of the subject. Everyone is familiar with the commandment against stealing. Curious and inventive, the Talmudic scholars examined various kinds of thievery to determine which deserve the greater punishments. For example, is a robber with a mask worse than one who steals without disguise? The Talmudic answer was that robbery with a mask is the more serious crime, for in this case the robber demonstrates that he respects men more than God. Clearly, God knows a thief's identity, whether or not he wears a mask. Therefore, the mask's only purpose is to shield the robber's identity from the eyes of men. The robber undiscovered by use of clever disguise thereby retains the respect of others, and demonstrates his values accordingly. By this reasoning, greater punishments were reserved in the Talmud for those thefts involving deception or disguise. Similarly, the rabbis debated what was equitable in making restitution to the victims of robberies. If a thief stole a block of wood and was later caught with the wood unchanged, the answer was simple: the wood should be returned to its original owner. However, what if the thief made a beautiful carving from the wood before his arrest? Should the original owner of the wood be allowed to claim the carving? The Talmudic answer was no, as the carving was the product of the thief's creative labor. In such cases, the discovered thief would be required only to pay the owner the value of the original block of wood.

The scholars also debated the meaning of the requirement to do no labor on the Sabbath. Did it necessitate that a man remain in bed on the seventh day? They concluded that it did not. Labor was defined as essentially creative activity. God had spent the first six days of history in acts of creation, and on the seventh day He had abstained from creating. Man was obliged to do likewise. On another matter, Leviticus 19:9 commanded that the farmer not harvest the corners of his field but leave this remnant for the poor. But what if the farmer wished instead to leave a portion in the center of his field for the poor; would not that suffice? Did the law apply only to grain or to leguminous plants, olive trees, date orchards and pomegranates as well? If a farmer left a corner of his field unharvested for the poor, and the poor stayed away, was he required to let the produce rot? These were the kinds of questions that consumed generations of the best minds in Judaism.

The commandment of Exodus 23: 19("Thou shalt not boil a kid in his mother's milk") was interpreted to mean that cheese (a milk product) and meat could not be eaten together. The prohibition of Exodus 16: 29 ("Let no man go out of his place on the seventh day") encouraged interesting and long discussions, for how should "his place" be defined? His house? His neighborhood? His village? Setting an appropriate "Sabbath boundary" is still a necessity for Orthodox Jews.[32]

With all of this energy spent on defining and refining the divine law, the question necessarily arose of God's relationship to it. Could God abrogate the Talmudic law, even part of it, with a miracle? If so, the work of the scholars would have a finite quality, which could undermine their labors. The entire culture of Talmudic Judaism tilted in the opposite direction. It valued rationalism over dogmatic credulity, logical discovery over miracles, and verbal acuity over mysticism. Accordingly, the Talmudic rabbis portrayed God as bound to the law. One explanation of this condition used the analogy of a father's love for his daughter. Though he gave her in marriage to another man, he could never forsake her. So it was with God and His law. Lest this analogy not communicate the message to some, the Talmud included a quite specific account of the immutability of the law and God's powerlessness to change it. Once upon a time, the Talmud relates, a group of Talmudic scholars were arguing a fine point of the law. All the scholars but one agreed, a condition which would normally have closed debate. However, in this case, the dissenter appealed to God who answered with a heavenly voice that the minority position was correct. At that, a spokesman for the majority shot back, "The law is not in heaven." His defiance meant that after God gave His law to man at Mt. Sinai, it was beyond divine control. The story continued. The prophet Elijah then appeared before the scholars and told them that God's response to this incident was one of joyous resignation. According to Elijah, "God laughed with joy saying: 'My children have conquered me, my children have conquered me.'" When one considers the stature of man in defining Jewish law, it is interesting to note that the name Israel, given to the father of the Hebrew people, means "he who struggles with God and wins."

The concept that the law was beyond God's control heightened the authority of the Talmud. Psalms 62: 11 states: "Once God has spoken; twice have I heard."

29

The reference to God speaking signified the initial revelation of His law. As the application of His law in changing circumstances required human interpretation, it was heard again. In short, the findings of the Talmud had divine authority as much as if God Himself had made them. The attitude of the Talmudic scholar was similar to that of the scientist, who regards himself as discovering truths not of his own making. Accordingly, the truths discovered by the debating rabbis were not human laws but rather God's laws, a blueprint for eternity.[33]

Jews mocked the notion of a preexistent Christ, charging that Christianity was not truly monotheistic. Now the Talmudic claim that even God could not alter the law invited an Islamic view that Judaism also was not monotheistic, that the Law was the second god of Judaism. These attacks and criticisms are part of the polemics common to competing religions. Islam would weaken its self-proclaimed title as the world's purest form of monotheism with the claim that the Qur'an, the holy book of the Muslims, had been preexistent with God in heaven. The temptation of the world's great religions to elevate aspects of their faiths beyond the realm of criticism would prove too great to resist. Consequently, each would compromise somewhat its claim to pure monotheism.[34]

By protecting the Jewish law from even divine tampering, the Talmudic scholars were in fact restricting the growth of Jewish mysticism. Mysticism, while never dominant in Judaism, had its roots deep in the Jewish past, as the Essene sect amply demonstrated. Yet mysticism and a religion based on law are natural enemies. Modern Jewish Hasidism is a rare exception to this rule of thumb. The unique blend of mysticism and legalism common to the Hasids will be described as this narrative approaches the modern era. More typically, mystics are characterized by antinomian, or anti-legalistic, tendencies. For example, St. Paul, transformed from a law-abiding Pharisee into a Christian mystic, proclaimed that the coming of Christ abrogated much of the law of his forefathers. Sufi mystics within Islam would proudly refuse to obey some of the Muslims' most fundamental religious laws. The significance of Hindu law, or dharma, would fade in the minds of Vedantist mystics, and Zen masters would burn Buddhist scriptures exhibiting their contempt for all structure and form. The Talmudic ruling that the Jewish law was to be solely the product of a rational debate among experts served to curb the development of similar tendencies within Judaism. Masters of the kabbalah, the name given in the 11th century to the secret practices of Jewish mystics, could not effectively appeal beyond the law to God Himself. As a result, although Jewish mysticism flourished in 13th century Spain, where Zohar, the Book of Splendor was compiled, and later in Safed (Palestine) during the 15th and 16th centuries, kabbalism is today practically non-existent within Judaism. A small group of kabbalists still meet in secret in Jerusalem, but that is all. One authority has concluded: "Jewish mysticism has become a museum piece, an interesting if grotesque offshoot from the normative Jewish tree." The Talmudic rabbis, by building a fence around the law, helped insure this result.[35]

Almost by definition, a religion based on legal observance emphasizes good works, which is tantamount to observance of the law. Talmudic homilies emphasizing this point are picturesque. For example, a man who performs good works is as a tree with a well-developed root system, whereas a person whose wisdom is more than his works is as a tree with many branches but shallow roots. The latter will inevitably fall victim to the first strong wind. The Talmudic rabbis taught that good deeds are a shield against misfortune. The Book of Job had raised the eternal question of theodicy: Why does misfortune befall good men? The authors of the Talmud responded in several ways. Some held that righteous Jews, undermined by cruel events, would receive their reward in the Kingdom of God at the end of days. Others reemphasized a communitarian theodicy which antedated the eschatology grafted onto Judaism after the Babylonian captivity. Deuteronomy 29: 10 had proclaimed the community of Israel. Accordingly, God did not evaluate individuals but rather the whole community. "You are all responsible for one another," the rabbis had commanded. "If there be only one righteous man among you, you all will profit from his merits....But if one of you sins, the whole generation will suffer." This theodicy had explained the destruction of Israel, the Babylonian captivity, and defeat in the wars with Rome. It explains why ancient Jews stoned sinners and why modern Jews feel a cultural obligation to help the downtrodden members of society.[36]

Judaism would endure as a law-bound religion with a strong sense of community. Persecution would destroy other peoples, but not the Jews. By accident or divine decree, this unique people would survive into the 20th

31

century despite the conscious efforts of demonical elements to end their 4,000 year history. Arnold Toynbee would call them "a living fossil."[37] What gave them the resources to survive? Secular historians would emphasize two related factors--their distinctive Talmudic law which set them apart and gave them identity, and their sense of community. Religious Jews knew yet another explanation.

## The Persecution of the Jews

The last thousand years of Jewish history have been marked by persecution in nominally Christian lands. Attacks on Jews, fed by negative stereotypes, rumors, outright lies, and Gentile anger over the Jewish will to survive as a people, ultimately led to the Nazi Holocaust. Judaism withstood this test but bearing terrible scars not easily erased from memory. The people lived on, some with their faith shaken, believing that their God had led them along treacherous paths. Yet many continued to regard the Jewish destiny as "chosen," albeit not as enviable as once hoped. Some Jews, disillusioned by the terrible events of the 20th century, discarded their traditional God altogether. Many of these retained a fierce clan loyalty, generated both by their forebears' religion and the persecution of unrelenting enemies. Both they and believing Jews subsequently resurrected the state of Israel as a fortress in which both the faith and the ethnic group could receive ultimate succor.

The story of modern Judaism's defensive state of mind began in Europe's Middle Ages, if not before. At that time, two principal themes were exploited to justify anti-Jewish persecution. One was the charge that the Jews had killed Christ. Referring to Jesus of Nazareth as "the mortal, corrupt one" and the "son of lewdness," Jews did not help abate Christian hatred on these grounds. Nevertheless, the ridiculous extremes to which gullible Gentiles pushed this theme remains a blot on the intelligence of medieval Christianity. Too many Christians of that time believed in what would later come to be called the "blood libel." This rumor held that after killing the perfect Jesus, Jews continued to lust for innocent blood, a craving which led them to kidnap Christian boys and girls for ritual sacrifice. Consequently, every missing Christian child served to excuse acts of torment and violence against Jews. After the Church ruled upon the doctrine of transubstantiation in 1215 A.D., another foolish but terrible charge was leveled against Jews as the killers of Christ. As bread and wine used in the Eucharist were now regarded as the actual body and blood of Christ, Jews were accused of stealing these elements for supposed rites of torture in their synagogues. This was the "desecration of the host libel," which could effectively be used to whip up anti-Semitic frenzy at those times when no Christian children were missing without account.

The other main theme under which anti-Jewish hatred multiplied was the stereotype of the greedy, grasping Jewish merchant. It will be recalled that Jews first entered middlemen, trading occupations during the Babylonian captivity. Later, with the rise of Islam in the seventh century, Jewish merchants exploited their unique trading contacts across the hostile chasm separating Muslim lands from Christendom. Jews further gravitated toward trading centers as they were effectively barred from agriculture, due to the close interrelationships between feudal loyalties, land holdings and the Church. The growing elaborateness of Jewish dietary laws also encouraged concentrations of Jewish population as kosher experts could only be found in the cities. That urban manufacturing was not open to Jews because of the anti-Semitism of the guilds simply reinforced the Jewish tendency toward commercial life, which was also encouraged by the medieval church's prohibition against usury. European economic expansion created a need for money lenders, who in the closed society of the Middle Ages could not be Christians. The money-lending Jew, often reaping more than 30 percent on his investment, fast became a hated symbol in an increasingly unsettled and anxious society.

The record of persecution suffered by Christendom's Jews creates an ugly catalog of events. For example, in 1096 A.D., Crusaders on their way to fight Muslims in the holy land sharpened their skills by wiping out Jewish communities along the way. In the 12th century, France expelled her Jews. In the following century, Jews were driven from England, and a Europe suffering under the bubonic plague persecuted Jews for "poisoning the wells." Fifteenth century Spain witnessed forced Jewish conversions to Christianity. These unfortunates were labeled "Marranos" (swine) for their continuing resolve to practice Judaism in secret. Spain's anti-Semitism came to a rapid boil at the end of the century with the expulsion of that country's prosperous Jewish community and the efforts of the Spanish Inquisition to force

33

religious confessions from the hated Marranos. Martin Luther, at first viewed by Jews as a positive new force within northern European Christianity, eventually called for the destruction of European Judaism. At the outset of the Protestant Reformation, it seemed as if Protestants and Jews were not that far apart. Both debunked Catholic idolatry, valued written scripture and Hebrew as the language of God, and rejected celibacy while upholding chastity. Indeed, Luther's subsequent hatred of Jews was fed by his disappointment that they refused to convert to Protestantism. For their part, Roman Catholics joined Lutherans in burning every copy of the Talmud within easy reach. In 1516, the year before Luther began his rebellion against the Church, Venice's authorities confined its Jews to a small, crowded section known as the "ghetto" (foundry), and a new mechanism was thus devised to contain and suppress Judaism. In the coming years, both Catholics and Protestants would continue to persecute Jews in their respective efforts to capture the banner of leadership within Christianity.[38]

The Messiah would come at a time when the righteous would be sorely tested, or so ancient Jewish eschatology had told. Accordingly, a claimant to the Messianic title arose in the mid-17th century to capture the tired hopes of world Jewry. Named Shabbatai Zevi, this pretender ultimately converted to Islam after receiving threats on his life from a Muslim ruler. Christianity had flourished on the crucifixion of its Messiah. Seventeenth century Judaism was shaken to its roots by Zevi's betrayal. Thereafter, the traditional Messianic belief would suffer a decline within Judaism. This was not due solely to the deep disappointment felt after the apostasy of Shabbatai Zevi, for the rationalistic tendencies of Talmudic Judaism had continued to develop apace. The Messianic idea, with its emphasis on divine miracles, had survived in Judaism because of its ancient pedigree, not because it harmonized with the rationalistic thrust of the Talmud. As the 18th century approached, all of Western culture tilted toward rationalism, which was glorified in that century's chief intellectual flowering known as the Enlightenment. Given its rationalistic tendencies, Judaism adjusted to the secular intellectual trends of modern life, but not without an internal struggle.[39]

Born in the disillusionment of Shabbatai Zevi's failure, the Hasidic movement reasserted Judaism's mystical aspects in an effort to save the ancient faith

34

from sterile rationalism. The main emphasis of Hasidism, which arose in the 18th century, was and is that "the Jewish condition must be lived rather than studied." An Hasidic tale elucidates this point. It tells of a rabbi in Cracow who was told in a dream to go to a distant city where he would find a treasure. Upon his arrival there, he told his dream to a stranger, who in turn related a dream he had had. The stranger's dream pictured a treasure buried in the home of a rabbi from Cracow. Armed with this new revelation, the rabbi returned home and found the treasure. The message was clear: religious truth is as close as your own heart. Hasidism, which centered in Poland and Russia, sought to capture in every passing moment the joy and celebration that should accompany the Messiah's arrival. The message of the Hasids (meaning "the pious ones") was that one need not be a scholar to discover God and that men could experience God before the Messiah's time. The Hasids hallowed all of life, exhibiting another deep-rooted tendency in Judaism, that being to live all of life as a sacrament. They were legalists in that they adhered to the Talmudic law, but they were more. For them, the law was more than ritual; it was a divine way of life. They were mystics in their almost pantheistic celebration of every detail of their existence as a translation of God's love, but they were more, for they refused the otherworldly, secretive elitism of the kabbalah.

The movement gravitated around various "rebbes" or Hasidic masters, to whom their followers showed a loyalty similar to that due to the Messiah himself. Yet, the rebbes did not pretend to be the Messiah, in whose eventual coming the Hasids continued to believe. The Hasidic message was that life should be celebrated, that joy need not wait for the coming of the Messiah. Dancing and ecstatic song would characterize the Hasids, most of whom would later be consumed in the Nazi Holocaust. But even in the dungeons of that experience, some Hasids, with their distinctive side curls, beards, and black hats, would celebrate life. Their German persecutors would not easily forget the sight and sound of these Jews dancing and singing in death-camp-bound cattle cars.[40]

Meanwhile, in western Europe, rationalistic Judaism evolved into what came to be called the Reform movement. Arising in 19th century Germany, the Reform movement rejected those aspects of Judaism which separated Jews from the Gentile community. Viewing

35

ancient Jewish laws as self-segregating mechanisms, Reform Jews advocated that only those laws with ethical content be retained. The distinctive dietary laws were rejected, while Moses' Decalogue remained in vogue. By watering down the traditional law, Reform Jews revealed strong assimilationist tendencies, which western European countries reinforced by removing various legal restrictions which had long kept Jews in a pariah status. Through legal emancipation, which occurred in the 1860's and 1870's, the Gentile communities seemingly showed that they too were willing to extend a friendly hand.

Not all Jews viewed these events with sanguine feelings or a willingness to integrate with the majority, Gentile culture. Those Jews who reacted to these modernizing tendencies by strictly adhering to the inconvenient but revealed laws of the Torah were labeled Orthodox. The Conservative movement, still another branch of modern Judaism, evolved out of the Reform group. Splitting from the latter in 1845, the Conservatives criticized the Reform movement for overemphasizing philosophical abstractions while abandoning Jewish tradition. In a sense, Conservatism represented a half-way position between Orthodoxy and Reform Judaism. While more observant of Jewish tradition than the Reform group, Conservatives disallowed the age-old segregation of women in a separate gallery in the synagogue, permitted congregation members to ride to synagogue on the Sabbath, and proclaimed that the Torah was not the literal word of God.

Reconstructionism grew out of the more secular-oriented elements of the American Conservative movement. Its leader was Mordecai Kaplan, who began to develop his Reconstructionist views early in the 20th century. God, in Kaplan's eyes, was reduced from a divine person to a process which helped bring about Jewish salvation, which in turn was defined as the individual reaching his highest potential through the Jewish way of life. Kaplan assumed that Jewish culture could survive as a secularized blend of humanism and Jewish folkways. Drawing upon the American philosophy of pragmatism, Kaplan sought to refashion Judaism by stressing function over form and process over intellectual or spiritual content. In denying a supernatural God, Reconstructionism was questioned by more traditional Jews who wondered out loud whether Kaplan's variant deserved to be considered religion at all.[41]

The sectarianizing of modern Judaism occurred in response to the challenges posed by an increasingly technological, rational, worldly, Western environment. Some Jews viewed these trends as inviting a new era of hope and progress, while others were not as optimistic. Traditional European politics had oppressed Jews. Accordingly, some 19th-century optimists interpreted the rise of secular Marxism as aiding the cause of Jewish liberation and assimilation. Socialist programs harmonized nicely with Judaism's traditional emphasis on social justice. Correspondingly, many Jews joined socialist movements. The growth of nationalism in 19th century Europe was also seen by many Jews as a positive force. With national feelings on the rise, the European Christian community became increasingly divided and consequently less oriented toward a unified Christian consciousness. Reform Jews speculated that nationalism might spell the end to Judaism's long history of persecution, and German Jews proclaimed their common nationality with German Christians. The advance of science and technology in the 19th century was also viewed as a positive force by many Jews. Had not irrationality fed the anti-Semitic upheavals of the past? Science would civilize the Gentiles and nurture their growing tendencies toward equitable treatment and reasonableness.

In the midst of this mounting western European Jewish optimism appeared an interesting but disturbing book by Leon Pinsker, entitled Auto-Emancipation. Appearing in 1882, its thesis claimed that anti-Semitism would not be checked effectively until a Jewish state again appeared on the world scene. It foretold that until that time Gentiles would regard Jews as unnatural. Until the resurrection of a Jewish state, Jews would be a nation without a homeland, a soul without a body, a ghost people, abnormal and hated. Pinsker argued that legal emancipation in western Europe had come from Gentile paternalism, but if anti-Semitism were ever to be put on the course of ultimate extinction, action would have to come from the Jews themselves. They would have to undergo great sacrifices to recreate a homeland to end their ghost-like status; it would have to occur through self or "auto" emancipation.

Zionists (or those Jews agreeing with Pinsker about the necessity of founding a Jewish homeland) saw danger signs in the same elements viewed more optimistically by other Jews. For example, Zionists noted that Christian socialists had an ugly tendency to identify the capitalist enemy with Jewish bankers. Some socialists had argued that this was an effective strategy to win the working class to Marxist perspectives. But if anti-Semitism was the "socialism of fools," and if a large segment of mankind was foolish, did the rise of socialism auger well for Jews? Similarly, the Dreyfus affair in France caused Jews to question the benefits of nationalism. Dreyfus, a Jewish French army officer, was accused falsely of selling state secrets to the Germans. The episode dominated the headlines of the 1890's, and most Frenchmen believed Dreyfus guilty. As the Dreyfus case demonstrated, rising nationalism could easily breed a fear of "fifth column" Jews. As such, could nationalism effectively diminish anti-Semitism, as the assimilationists had hoped? Scientism also cut both ways. If the hard sciences of physics and chemistry encouraged rationality, the pseudo-science of racial differences offered anti-Semites a forum of hate under the guise of science. By the end of the century, it was widely accepted that science demonstrated the biological superiority of Aryans over Semitic peoples. Several generations later, the triad of socialism, nationalism, and scientism would merge to form Nazism, whose inhuman acts would lead the surviving assimilationists to see the wisdom of Leon Pinsker's argument.[42]

The Ottoman Empire, which controlled Palestine until 1918, officially had discouraged the immigration of Jews to their ancient homeland. Nevertheless, they came. In 1840, only 10,000 Jews could be found in the region; by 1881, 24,000 Jews lived there, and by the outbreak of World War I, 85,000 Jews lived in Palestine. During that war, Great Britain's Foreign Secretary issued a statement that was designed to win the support of American Jews for the Allied war effort while weakening the resolve of German Jews to continue the struggle. Later to be known as the Balfour Declaration, this pronouncement promised that Germany's defeat would result in the Turkish loss of Palestine, which would be transformed into the long-awaited Jewish homeland. With the Allied victory, Palestine became a British protectorate, but Balfour's statement was not honored for strategic reasons. After the war, the British were most reluctant to anger Muslims with a pro-Jewish policy, for Arab patriots could all too easily sabotage the Suez Canal, the British Empire's lifeline to India. With Hindu nationalists rioting for independence in India, the British were wary of any action that might encourage the subcontinent's substantial Muslim population to add to the turmoil. Consequently, Britain outlawed Jewish immigration to Palestine. Nevertheless, it came. By 1933, the year that Hitler came to power, 250,000 Jews were in Palestine. After six years of Nazi persecution, a half million Jews were in Zion.

At the end of World War II in 1945, an exhausted England, now tired of imperialism, chose to surrender its Indian colony and Palestine as well. Palestine would belong to the force that could back up its claim with arms. The Jews met the challenge. Six million Jews had recently died in the Nazi Holocaust, but from the horror of their deaths came the catalyst to found the state of Israel. As the ancient prophet Ezekiel had foretold, the dry bones of murdered Jews now became a creative force. On the other side stood resurgent Arab expectations. Arabs had traditionally never regarded Palestine as a separate nation, for the very concept of a separate Palestine was a product of Jewish history. The Ottoman Turks had lumped the entire Mediterranean coastline from Egypt to the Taurus mountains into a single administrative unit called Syria. Therefore, the struggle was not initially between two rival nationalisms, but rather between Jewish nationalism (Zionism) and Pan-Arab resolve to retrieve all lost Islamic territories. In Arab eyes, the state of Israel represented a continuation of European colonialism. While many of Israel's Jews were Sephardim (or Jews native to the region), the leadership of the new nation were immigrants from Europe (or Ashkenazim). Hence to Arabs, the Jews were no different than the Christian crusaders of a millennium before. They were foreign invaders, representing a disintegrating European imperialism. Eventually, Sephardim would raise charges of discriminatory treatment by the dominant, better-educated Ashkenazim, lending credence to the Arab view. Nevertheless, Jewish superiority was evident on the battlefield, first creating the state of Israel in 1948, and subsequently defending its existence against unforgiving Arab neighbors.[43]

Israelis now claim that during the war for Jewish independence, Arab military strategists called for a mass exodus of Arabs from Palestine to motivate all nearby Arab states to join the struggle. Fleeing refugees heightened Arab anger, and Egypt, Jordan, Syria, and Iraq joined in war against the Zionists. But this combined force failed to drive the Jews from

39

the promised land. In 1949, with the negotiation of a cease fire, Israel refused to allow Arab refugees to return to their homes, as they would undermine the majority status of Jews in the new nation. These refugees ironically would assume the name "Palestinians," a designation that earlier had been identified with Zionism. Many of them were denied citizenship by neighboring Arab states who feared that the world would accept a new Jewish version of European imperialism without the heartrending spectacle of miserable camps of dispossessed people. In turn, Israeli anthropologists and sociologists would argue that before the flight of these Palestinian refugees, many of them had been recent arrivals from Egypt, drawn to the area by economic opportunities created by industrious Jews. Having constantly to justify their existence in the region, Israelis now claimed that many of the so-called Palestinians were little more than displaced Arabs, used by their Islamic brethren for purposes of pan-Arab chauvinism.[44]

At the creation of the state of Israel, the Soviet Union was its strongest foreign supporter, but this situation rapidly changed. Initially, the USSR had strongly backed Zionist goals in an effort to embarrass the British in their retreat from the area. By contrast, the United States at first gave Israel only lukewarm recognition in spite of the influential American Jewish lobby within the ruling Democratic Party. The change in Soviet attitude came when the new state of Israel captured the imagination of Jewry behind the Iron Curtain. Thereafter, Stalin referred to pro-Israel Soviet Jews as "cosmopolitans" and backed the Arab cause of destroying the Zionist state. Meanwhile, American policy worked for the survival of Israel without alienating petroleum-rich Arab countries.[45] In 1979, American purposes would win a tactical victory with the signing of an Egyptian-Israeli peace, breaking the heretofore solid Arab phalanx against Israel. Nevertheless, the issue would continue to loom as a future source of turmoil and an ever-present temptation to detonate an atomic world-holocaust. Most Arab peoples continue to demonstrate a resolve to destroy the state of Israel. Similarly, steeled by memories of long and terrible persecution, the Jews of Israel show every willingness to fight to the death to retain their hard-won, small refuge against a hostile world. Such is the modern legacy of the thousand years of suffering recorded in these few pages.

NOTES

1. Mircea Eliade, Cosmos and History, The Myth of the Eternal Return (New York, 1954), pp. 3-5, 27-29, 34-36, 42-43, 86-88, 96-97.

2. Werner Keller, The Bible as History, A Confirmation of the Book of Books (New York, 1956), pp. 52-67.

3. James Henry Breasted, Development of Religion and Thought in Ancient Egypt (New York, 1959), pp. 308-309; William A. Irwin, The Old Testament: Keystone of Human Culture (New York, 1952), p. 28; Max Weber, Ancient Judaism (New York, 1952), p. 262; George Foot Moore, History of Religions (2 vols.; New York, 1947), II, 157-163, 168, 177.

4. Irwin, The Old Testament, pp. 27-42; James Michener, The Source (Greenwich, Conn., 1965), p.178.

5. Moore, History of Religions, II, 30.

6. Irwin, The Old Testament, p. 105; Weber, Ancient Judaism, p. 203.

7. Weber, Ancient Judaism, pp. 224-225.

8. H.H. Ben-Sasson, ed., A History of the Jewish People (Cambridge, Mass., 1976), pp. 52-53; Keller, The Bible as History, pp. 153-162.

9. Keller, The Bible as History, pp. 175-213; Weber, Ancient Judaism, pp. 113-114; Ben-Sasson, ed., History of the Jewish People, pp. 97-111.

10. Maimonides, the greatest of medieval Jewish sages, claimed that the site of Jerusalem's Temple was the spot on which Adam had been created, where Abraham had offered Isaac in sacrifice, and where Noah had settled after leaving the ark. See Salo Wittmayer Baron, A Social and Religious History of the Jews (17 vols.; New York, 1952-1980), VI, 228. For the age of the prophets, see Michael Avi-Yonah and Emil G. Kraeling, Our Living Bible (New York, 1962), pp. 229-230; Ben Sasson, ed., History of the Jewish People, pp. 129-130, 145-158; Weber, Ancient Judaism, p. 322.

11. Keller, The Bible as History, pp. 267-293.

12. Weber, *Ancient Judaism*, p. 156; Irwin, *The Old Testament*, pp. 167-171; Keller, *The Bible as History*, p. 275.

13. Weber, *Ancient Judaism*, p. 354.

14. *Ibid.*, p. 182; Irwin, *The Old Testament*, p. 29; Huston Smith, *The Religions of Man* (New York, 1958), p. 248.

15. Adin Steinsaltz, *The Essential Talmud* (London, 1976), pp. 213-215; Weber, *Ancient Judaism*, pp. 221-222; Michener, *The Source*, p. 380; Edmund Wilson, *Israel and the Dead Sea Scrolls* (Toronto, 1954:1978), p. 257.

16. Ben-Sasson, ed., *History of the Jewish People*, p. 277.

17. George William Carter, *Zoroastrianism and Judaism* (Boston, 1918), pp. 77-79, 105-106; Moore, *History of Religions*, I, 360-365, 375, 386, 394, 398, 404-405; Albert Schweitzer, *The Kingdom of God and Primitive Christianity* (New York, 1967), pp. 33-41.

18. Ben-Sasson, ed., *History of the Jewish People*, p. 181; Arthur Hertzberg, ed., *Judaism* (New York, 1962), p. 216.

19. Baron, *Social and Religious History*, I, 96; Carter, *Zoroastrianism and Judaism*, pp. 105-106.

20. Keller, *The Bible as History*, pp. 322-335; Michener, *The Source*, p. 380.

21. Baron, *Social and Religious History*, II, 38; Michael Grant, *Jesus, An Historian's Review of the Gospels* (New York, 1977), p. 96; Hugh J. Schonfield, *The Passover Plot, New Light on the History of Jesus* (New York, 1965), pp. 22-23; Keller, *The Bible as History*, pp. 358-360; Ben-Sasson, ed., *History of the Jewish People*, pp. 285-286; Robert M. Grant, *Augustus to Constantine, The Thrust of the Christian Movement into the Roman World* (New York, 1970), p. 26.

22. Ben-Sasson, ed., *History of the Jewish People*, pp. 254-256, 274.

23. *Ibid.*, pp. 272-274; George A. Barton, *The Religion of Ancient Israel* (New York, 1928), p. 27; Christian D. Ginsburg, *The Essenes, Their History and*

42

Doctrines (London, 1864:1956), pp. 13-14, 24-25; Weber, Ancient Judaism, pp. 406-408; Paul Johnson, A History of Christianity (New York, 1976), pp. 18-19, A.L. Basham; The Wonder that Was India (New York, 1954), pp. 484-485; Rudolf Augstein, Jesus, Son of Man (New York, 1977), pp. 121-124.

24. Irwin Edman, The Mind of Paul (New York, 1935), pp. 54-55; Grant, Jesus, p. 177; Weber, Ancient Judaism, pp. 387-388; Steinsaltz, The Essential Talmud, p. 21.

25. Solomon Grayzel, A History of the Jews, From the Babylonian Exile to the Present (New York, 1968), pp. 120-122; Weber, Ancient Judaism, pp. 284, 382, 385-387, 391; Hertzberg, ed., Judaism, p. 233; Johnson, History of Christianity, p. 18.

26. William Whiston (trans.), The Works of Flavius Josephus, The Learned and Authentic Jewish Historian and Celebrated Warrior (Philadelphia, n.d.,), pp. 847-855; Keller, The Bible as History, pp. 398, 408; Michener, The Source, p. 1039; F.E. Peters, The Harvest of Hellenism (New York, 1970), p. 533; Ben-Sasson, ed., History of the Jewish People, pp. 296, 303, 314; Baron, Social and Religious History, II, 50-51, 91, 112-113; Steinsaltz, The Essential Talmud, p. 29; Wilson, Israel and the Dead Sea Scrolls, p. 321.

27. Baron, Social and Religious History, I, 180; Ben-Sasson, ed., History of the Jewish People, pp. 288, 364; Weber, Ancient Judaism, pp. 419-420; Grayzel, History of Jews, pp. 140-141.

28. Baron, Social and Religious History, II, 164; Johnson, History of Christianity, p. 12; Weber, Ancient Judaism, p. 423; Grayzel, History of Jews, p. 150.

29. Weber, Ancient Judaism, p. 417; Ben-Sasson, ed., History of the Jewish People, pp. 536-538.

30. Ernest R. Trattner, Understanding the Talmud (New York, 1955), pp. 9, 25, 40, 140-141; Steinsaltz, The Essential Talmud, p. 53; Ben-Sasson, ed., History of the Jewish People, pp. 367, 373.

31. Baron, Social and Religious History, II, 235; Steinsaltz, The Essential Talmud, pp. 5, 9, 57, 96, 259, 269, 272; Weber, Ancient Judaism, p. 154.

32. Barton, Religion of Ancient Israel, pp.

155-156; Steinsaltz, The Essential Talmud, pp. 109-110, 113, 115, 155-156, 185-187; Hertzberg, ed., Judaism, pp. 100-101.

33. Trattner, Understanding the Talmud, pp. 90, 154-155; Steinsaltz, The Essential Talmud, pp. 217-218; Erich Fromm, You Shall Be As Gods, A Radical Interpretation of the Old Testament and Its Tradition (New York, 1966), pp. 28, 46-47; Wilson, Israel and the Dead Sea Scrolls, p.28.

34. Smith, Religions of Man, p. 205; Alfred Guillaume, Islam (New York, 1954), pp. 130-131; F.E. Peters, Allah's Commonwealth (New York, 1973), p. 53; Abu Bakr Siraj Ed-Din, The Book of Certainty (New York, 1974), p. 13n.

35. Perle Epstein, Kabbalah, The Way of the Jewish Mystic (New York, 1978), p. 158; Newsweek, May 26, 1980, p. 94.

36. Trattner, Understanding the Talmud, p. 169; Leo Auerback (ed. and trans.), The Babylon Talmud in Selection (New York, 1944), p. 38; Baron, Social and Religious History, II, p. 200; Hertzberg, ed., Judaism, p. 201; Weber, Ancient Judaism, p. 263.

37. Ben-Sasson ed., History of the Jewish People, pp. 728, 732.

38. Ibid., pp. 388, 397, 401, 409-417, 463, 470-472, 481-485, 558-559, 629, 639, 646-647, 653, 875; Trattner, Understanding the Talmud, pp. 198-201; Michener, The Source, pp. 655-656, 764-765, 798; Weber, Ancient Judaism, pp. 253-255; Steinsaltz, The Essential Talmud, pp. 71, 74-80, 189; Friedrich Heer, The Medieval World, Europe 1100-1350 (New York, 1961), pp. 87-88, 310; Grayzel, History of Jews, pp. 309-310, 314-315, 341-352, 358-365, 374.

39. Ben-Sasson, ed., History of the Jewish People, pp. 617-618, 701-707; Grayzel, History of Jews, pp. 443-453.

40. Elie Wiesel, Souls on Fire, Portraits and Legends of Hasidic Masters (New York, 1972), pp. 38, 92; Martin Buber, The Origin and Meaning of Hasidism (New York, 1960), p. 172; New York Times, Feb. 4, 1979, Sec. 1, 44:5-6; Grayzel, History of Jews, pp. 453-461.

41. Ben-Sasson, ed., History of the Jewish People,

pp. 834, 837, 847, 870; Jacob Neusner, ed., _Understanding American Judaism, Toward a Description of a Modern Religion_ (2 vols., New York, 1975), II, 199-242; Isidore Epstein, _Judaism, A History Presentation_ (London, 1959), p. 298.

42. Ben-Sasson, ed., _History of the Jewish People_, pp. 872-873, 895; Grayzel, _History of Jews_, pp. 550-557, 568, 575-576.

43. Ben-Sasson, ed., _History of the Jewish People_, 876, 892-895, 916, 919, 921, 940, 945, 947, 990-991, 1010; Steinsaltz, _The Essential Talmud_, p. 66; Michener, _The Source_, pp. 472-474; Raphael Patai, _The Arab Mind_ (New York, 1976), pp. 13-14, 41.

44. Arthur Kahn and Thomas F. Murray, "The Palestinians, a Political Masquerade" (Pamphlet distributed by Americans for a Safe Israel; New York, 1977), pp. 12, 14-15, 27; Ben-Sasson, ed., _History of the Jewish People_, pp. 1055-1056, 1058, 1062, 1078; Gil Carl Alroy, _Behind the Middle East Conflict: The Real Impasse Between Arab and Jew_ (New York, 1975), pp. 141-158; Grayzel, _History of Jews_, pp. 686-687.

45. Ben-Sasson, ed., _History of the Jewish People_, pp. 1069-1070; Grayzel, _History of Jews_, p. 695.

## Ancient Vedic Religion

Western religion, influenced by Judaism, generally values the affairs of this world. ⌐By contrast, eastern philosophy and religion cherishes the goal of detachment from the world. Hinduism, as one form of this latter orientation, teaches that the individual suffers innumerable reincarnations until self can be dissolved and spiritual liberation realized⌐ Hindu philosophers teach that ignorance sustains worldly creation. ⌐Consequently, Hindus seek knowledge to transcend phenomenal existence. Hindus worship many gods, albeit never losing sight of the unity underlying that which is truly real. The ultimate understanding that Hindus seek is that freedom comes not from worldly achievement but rather in the extinguishing of all ego-filled desires. While sharing with western faiths the impulse to curb selfish cravings, Hinduism has developed this common theme with its own unique touch, as shall be shown in this chapter.⌐

Hinduism derived from ancient Vedic religion, practiced in India over a thousand years before Christ. This primitive religion was brought to India by a people who called themselves Aryas. The Aryas, or Aryans as we identify them, came from somewhere northeast of present-day Iran and Afghanistan. Scholars speculate that the Aryans originated far from large bodies of water, as they had no words for ocean or sea in their earliest known language. From this region, they migrated northward into Europe. Their presence as far west as Ireland is suggested by the linguistic relationship between the Gaelic name for the island, Eire, and the word Aryas. Aryans also moved into what is today Iran, whose name similarly reveals its ancient heritage. They came to India in waves lasting from 2000 to 1000 B.C.

Their religion was ultimately recorded in the Vedas, which literally translated means "knowledge." This knowledge, in the form of somewhat cryptic poetry, was orally transmitted through the generations, as there was no known writing in India before the 4th century B.C. The Rig-Veda, the oldest of these works, was created some time between 1500 and 900 B.C., making it the oldest extant composition associated with a living world religion. By contrast, the oldest section of the Hebrew Genesis is believed to date back to the

9th century B.C.  Vedic priests recited their richas, or praises to their gods, thereby accounting for the word rig in the scripture's title.  The religious practices of the ancient Aryans are revealed in its pages.

The Aryans were a light-skinned people, whereas the native inhabitants of India were dark and flat-nosed, two physical characteristics negatively commented upon by the foreign invaders.  The blending of the two races was discouraged by the caste system, which was maintained by the Aryan conquerors in part for that segregating purpose.  The history of these events is in many ways lost and has been painfully reconstructed only through archeological efforts.  The Aryans and their Indian descendants did not value historical consciousness, and for this reason any intentionally recorded history is lacking.  One frustrated historian has written of the Indians:  "A more unhistorical people would be difficult to find."[2] By contrast, the ancient Hebrews saw God revealing his intentions to man through historical events.  For that reason, they placed a great importance on recording and interpreting history.  The books of the Torah were devoted to telling the history of the Jewish people and their evolving relationship with God.  This was not the orientation of the Aryans.  While Judaism had a series of founding fathers--Abraham, Moses, and David--Vedic religion had none, at least none that was recorded. Ultimately Vedic religion developed both the concept of reincarnation and a cosmology that described creation as an on-going, never-ending process.  In this world view, any one life, or any history of all the known world, was only a tale of relative insignificance. Hindu attention would focus beyond history to that which would be called moksha, or liberation from phenomenal existence.

To witness the development of Hinduism, we need to start at the known beginning and examine the religious practices and beliefs of the early Vedas.  The Aryans worshipped many gods, the principal one being Indra, a god of war somewhat like the Germanic Thor or the the Greek Zeus.  By nature, Indra was an amoral male figure, fond of indulging in sexual and alcoholic escapades. His worshippers would sacrifice to him for victory in war or rain for plentiful crops.  Indra's role as the destroyer of Vritra, the god of drought, created the former's status as a rain god.  Indra is portrayed in Vedic imagery armed with thunderbolts to hurl at his enemies.  His devotees petitioned his services by means of the Soma sacrifice, involving consumption of an alcoholic beverage, which this god seemingly enjoyed more than any other of his divine cohorts. Indra is pictured staggering around the sacrificial fire after consuming great quantities of the inebriating Soma.

The Rig-Veda describes Soma as an invigorating drink that enabled both men and gods to achieve great deeds, such as the conquest of Vritra. The means by which Indra would receive this drink, and the roasted horse flesh that would accompany it, was Agni, the god of fire. Agni had many faces, not the least of which was the sacrificial fire, the divine mouth by which gods such as Indra received the offerings of humans. Accompanied by a pillar of smoke, Agni served as a messenger between men and the gods. In his role as the fire of the hearth, he was also the divine witness to human events and thereby much closer to mankind than were other Vedic deities. Coming from a colder climate than is common to the Indian subcontinent, the Aryans valued fire. They feared it as well, for Agni could easily become a destroyer of human possessions and raw materials.

Rudra, the god of the storm, suggests a feature of ancient Vedic religion that has possibly had an influence upon modern-day Hinduism. Rudra, which means "the howler," was a god of destruction, which we have just seen was an aspect of Agni. As a destroyer, Rudra was also a hurler of thunderbolts, a role associated with Indra. The example of Rudra demonstrates that there was a marked overlapping of traits among the ancient Vedic gods, suggesting a possible germ of monotheism within a polytheistic framework. Some western observers have criticized ancient Vedic religion for its contradictory, repetitive nature in which "the personalities of the gods [were] only slightly developed and [lacked] a distinct individuality of character."[3] But behind this apparent flaw was both a tendency that possibly contributed to the Hindu characteristic to see all divine forces in ultimate unity and a dim recognition that divine forces cannot be tightly compartmentalized among clear and distinct personal gods. While modern Hindus pay homage to many distinct gods, they generally claim that they are merely aspects of the one, true God. The vague boundaries separating ancient Vedic deities perhaps encouraged the development of this later mentality.

Varuna was a Vedic rain god, a role which we have

seen was identified with Indra. More importantly, he was also the guardian of the Rita, literally translated as "the course of things," or the cosmic order. Varuna governed the alteration of day and night, the sequence of the seasons, and the patterns associated with changes in the weather. He was associated closely with his brother Mitra, who alternatively was portrayed as the sun, light generally, or the power that rules the sun. Here again was a duplication with the function of another Vedic god, Vishnu, the sun god who would later evolve into one of the two principal deities of Hinduism. An Indo-Aryan connection with ancient Iran can be seen in Mitra's similarity to Mithra, the Persian god of light. While the Rita supposedly was under Varuna and Mitra's jurisdiction, Indo-Aryans gradually came to believe that the cosmic order was also controlled by the sacrificial rites of the Brahmins, the Vedic priests. Originally, the sacrifice was intended to persuade the gods to respond favorably to desired outcomes: success in war, long life, and male progeny. With time's passage, an additional notion came to be accepted--that the Rita would not be fully operational unless the Brahmin priests performed their sacrifices. In short, the cosmic order itself became dependent upon the correct enactment of the sacrifice. This conception greatly enhanced the importance of the priestly class, as the world supposedly would fall into chaos without its ministrations.[4]

The sacrificial rites involved both blood sacrifice, normally an offering of horses to the gods, and the sacrifice (and drinking) of Soma. Melted butter was also poured on the flame, as Agni responded most dramatically to this offering. Blood sacrifice, certainly prominent in Vedic rites, would carry on into Hinduism, which would generally disdain the killing of sentient beings. To this day, goats are sacrificed in the great temple of Kali in Calcutta, and human sacrifice was practiced among some Hindus as late as the 19th century. The participants in the ancient Vedic blood sacrifice saw themselves as sharing the sustenance of roasted horse flesh with the gods and acquiring divine powers accordingly. The more liberal the offering, the more acquisition of divine power would occur. A Vedic believer could make simple sacrifices over the home fires, but the more regal ceremonies presided over by the Brahmins had far greater potential for success. Of course, only wealthy patrons and Brahmin priests could partake in these more important sacrificial events.[5]

The Brahmins tightly maintained their monopoly on the production of Soma juice, the recipe of which has long been lost to history. Scholars believe that the juice was extracted from a climbing-vine plant which grew wild. Its juice was mixed with milk and butter or honey, producing a stimulant capable of inspiring this response as recorded in the Rig-Veda:

> One half of me is greater than both
> worlds: Have I been drinking Soma?
> My greatness reaches beyond the
> heavens and  this great earth:
> Have I been drinking Soma?
> Shall I carry this earth hither
> and thither?
> Have I been drinking Soma?
> Shall I shatter this earth here or
> there?
> Have I been drinking Soma?
> One half of me is in the heavens and
> I  have stretched the other down deep:
> Have I been drinking Soma?
> I am most great; I reach up to the
> clouds:  Have I been drinking Soma?[6]

The search for liberation from human limitations, as represented in the above Vedic poetry, would become the principal goal of all eastern religion. However, Hindus would later normally abstain from alcoholic aids in seeking this end. As for the ancient Indo-Aryans, they believed the Soma beverage divine, as the god Soma allowed his essence to be sacrificed for the good of men and gods. The drink was portrayed as bringing men and gods together in mysterious communion. Here was a hint of mysticism from the Rig-Veda which would eventually be fully developed in the more advanced religion of Hinduism. The priests believed that without the sacrificial sharing of Soma with the gods, the latter would die. Thanks to the ancient Brahmins, these deities stayed very much alive. "We have drunk the Soma; we have become immortal," said the Rig-Veda; "we have entered into the light; we have known the gods." This feeling became known as Brahman, a name similar to the that of the priest class.[7]

Ancient Vedic religion was primarily oriented to success in worldly endeavors, as we have seen. Nevertheless, unlike ancient Judaism, another religion focusing on this world, the faith of Aryans included a reasonably developed conception of an afterlife. Vedic religion gave only the barest attention to the pit or

51

abyss, where evil doers were sent upon death. Far greater emphasis was given to the kingdom of Yama and his twin sister Yami, who had been the first people to die. Their realm was a paradise blessed with a plentiful amount of Soma. Consuming corpses in flame, Agni transported souls to Yama's kingdom. The practice of cremation would continue into Hinduism along with a sacrificial offering of food and drink to dead ancestors. The latter still occurs despite its apparent incompatibility with the concept of reincarnation, which plays a dominant role in Hinduism. This is reflective of the accumulative character of Hinduism, which discards not even those elements which logically should be rejected.

Indian religion has consistently manifested a love of ritualistic and theological elaboration, a trait that has made Hinduism the most complicated and intricate of mankind's major faiths. In the days of the ancient Indo-Aryans, this manifested itself in the growing formalism of the sacrifices, so that all spontaneity was finally eliminated. One mispronounced word from a Vedic priest cancelled his desired result. The sound of the phrases used in the rites ultimately became far more important than their meaning. Inspired men outside the Brahmin class witnessing the gradual demise of Vedic religion in mindless ritual began to search for a deeper meaning in their spiritual tradition. The Kshatriyas, comprising the soldier-governor class, took the lead in reforming, expanding and developing Vedic philosophy. Their efforts would lead to the development of Hinduism, as well as of Buddhism and Jainism, the latter now only a minor Indian religion. They expanded the meaning of sacrifice into self-denial. First interpreted by them as a means by which to coerce the gods, self-sacrifice was eventually seen as a path to the divine. Gradually, the exhilaration induced by alcoholic Soma was replaced by ecstasy accompanying self-denial.[8]

The Kshatriya reformers taught that Brahman, the divine force experienced during the Vedic sacrifice, is available to all of us. The individual's knowledge of this experience was called Atman. They taught that Atman/Brahman, while given two names, is in fact the unified, ultimate reality. To realize this truth became the highest goal of Hindu religion. Sorrow and even death could be transcended by the person wholly comprehending this discovery. Whereas ancient Jews had thought of God as a being separate from themselves, the Kshatriya reformers of the Vedas looked at their many gods and themselves as emanations from an indivisible, divine force. Ultimate reality was not dualistic, not divided into a heavenly God and a material world created by Him. Ultimate reality was simply and magnificently Atman/Brahman. Atman/Brahman is devoid of attributes, for to define it would be to limit that which is beyond human categories. Nevertheless, these innovating philosophers described Atman/Brahman as ultimate peace and tranquility. In their hands, the original goals of Vedic religion--worldly happiness and material abundance--developed into something more sublime. Tranquility beyond the world of ego attachments became a new objective.

This transcendentalist philosophy appeared in compositions known as the Upanishads, dating from 800 to 500 B.C. "Upa ni shad," meaning "to sit near," apparently referred to students clustered around their teacher to receive this new knowledge. The Upanishads are commonly regarded as the culmination of Vedic wisdom and the transition from ancient Vedic religion to Hinduism. The religion of the Upanishads teaches the goal of self-realization through intense, inward-looking meditation. By contrast, the western religions of Judaism, Christianity and Islam generally place a higher value on deeds and emotions that are extensions of personality. The West has long sought to change the world. The East, first under the guiding light of the Upanishads and later the Buddha's teaching, has sought to transcend it.

What was this inward saving knowledge taught by the Upanishads? These holy scriptures described it in these words: "When all desires which cling to the heart fall away, then mortal becomes immortal, and in this life finds Brahman. When all the earthly ties of the heart are sundered, then mortal becomes immortal. This is the end of all instruction." In other words, anything engendering attachment to this world is suspect. Strong emotion of any kind--even love of one's own children--is dangerous. Aldous Huxley, a 20th-Century Westerner attracted to Upanishadic philosophy, put it well: "The more there is of self, the less there is of God. Our pride, our anxiety, our lusts for power and pleasure are God-eclipsing things."[9] The same thoughts abound in the recorded sayings of Jesus of Nazareth, whose teachings on this score have often been subordinated to creed and dogma within the Christian church.

A variety of visual and auditory techniques have

been employed by Hindus seeking to achieve detachment through control of the mind. Specially constructed visual images, called yantras and mandalas, symbolize the complexities and energies of life, and help center thought on principles beyond ego. Mantras use auditory senses to the same end. Westerners are not totally ignorant of such devices. The star of David and the cross are good examples of yantras, while a Roman Catholic's "Hail Mary's" represent a Christian mantra. Those who use such methods of worship attest that they are frequently more efficacious than thought-prayers which distract the mind with verbal concepts. The visual and verbal tools of meditation briefly described here allow the worshipper to journey beyond the limitations of thought and speech.[10]

Ancient Vedic religion, which began with primitive blood sacrifice, gradually evolved toward a vision of both God as the only reality and God's nature as tranquility. In contrast with Western religions, which stress remolding the world to suit God's justice, highly refined Hinduism teaches passive contemplation of divine things. Consequently, Hinduism, unlike Judaism, devalues the study of history. While foreigners have called this religion Hinduism, in reference to the faith of those living beyond the Sindhu (or Indus) River, Indians themselves call their belief the sanatana dharma, or the eternal, unchanging order.[11] To the Hindu, religious truth is constant and unchanging and can be found by meditation rather than by interpretation of external, historical events. The Upanishads show the way: All reality is Brahman; all that is the individual is Atman; Atman is Brahman.

Samsara

When the Aryans came to India, they subjugated the native Dravidian population and called them dasas, or slaves. They allowed only fellow Aryans to participate in Soma sacrifices, as they regarded the dasas as only slightly better than animals. Gradually, they developed an explanation for this inequitable social situation: A person is born into a desirable or oppressed status depending on how he lived his past lives. Similarly, the manner in which he lives his current life will influence the condition of his future existence. Aryan theologians called this ongoing process of birth-death-and-rebirth samsara, which translated means the flow of change in all things. A spinning wheel located in the center of India's national flag symbolizes this concept of unending flux,

54

which is at the heart of Hindu religion.

Westerners generally consider the idea of reincarnation positively as a form of personal immortality. By contrast, Indians typically see samsara as a prison, for human existence is filled with pain and suffering. Prosperity in this world is not Hinduism's ultimate goal, which is rather moksha, or liberation from samsara. Such liberation can come only after many thousands of lifetimes, which provide an individual soul with innumerable opportunities to refine itself for eventual union with its divine source. This world is not unimportant to Hindus. To be reborn a human, at best a Hindu and a Brahmin, is more desirable than to return as a dog or an insect. In turn, a dog is further along the path of spiritual evolution than an insect, and a human outside Hindu religion is further advanced than a dog. And, the Aryan holy men declared, the Brahmin is more advanced than any other being in samsara.[12]

The Aryans brought the germ idea of inequality with them, but on Indian soil it blossomed into the complex social stratification known as the caste system. The connection between this establishment and the concept of samsara is clear and direct. For example, if one fails to follow his caste duty, his spiritual progress is interrupted. Thereby, a bad Brahmin can become a non-Hindu or worse in a future life. Advancement toward moksha is by no means inevitable. Every action in life is important, for it contributes to one's future status.

Hindu attention focuses on dharma, or unchanging caste duty. Dharma literally means "maintenance," in the sense of maintaining one's harmony with the nature of things. Dharma is fulfilled or denied by each individual alone. He who conforms to caste norms is rewarded in future lives. Interestingly, while both Hinduism and Judaism stress the role of religious communal law, Hinduism ultimately leads its devotees' attention away from community concerns. Traditional Judaism's concept of salvation binds the individual to his worldly community even after death, when hope is deferred until the resurrection of Israel at the end of days. By contrast, the Hindu at death leaves his community behind, his group identity at rebirth being dependent solely upon his own actions and thus subject to change. Consequently Hinduism's fundamental message is not one of community service but rather of spiritual individualism.

In Hindu society, each caste has its own unique dharma. The dharma of a king is different from the dharma of a merchant, which in turn is different from the dharma of a warrior, which may be contrasted to the dharma of a farmer. Prostitutes have a different dharma than thieves. In fact, no one within Hindu society is without a dharma. Hinduism developed a general dharma or universal ethic that commanded everyone to injure no living beings, to tell the truth, not to steal, to live purely, and to control one's passions. But this general dharma is superseded when it conflicts with the dharma of a particular caste.[13] For example, the dharma of a warrior is to kill. How then can he injure no living being? The dharma of a thief is to steal. How then can he not steal?

The caste system occasionally gave religious sanction to persistently anti-social conduct. Criminal castes have been known in the past. The English word "thug" derives from the name of a Hindu caste of assassins who strangled and robbed wayfarers in honor of their goddess. Their dharma, until suppressed by their Victorian British overlords, was to kill the weak, just as a tiger feeds upon deer. Westerners raised in the tradition of the Ten Commandments, which is in effect a universal dharma, find it difficult to understand a system of religious law that could allow criminal behavior. In contrast to the universality of ethical norms in the West, orthodox Hinduism effectively compartmentalized Indian society into separate units, each with its own unique set of rules. Consequently, the European concept of natural law would be alien to the Hindu mind. The American Declaration of Independence talks of self-evident truths, that all men are created equal and are endowed with the same set of inalienable rights. By contrast, Hindus think in terms of divergent sets of duties and the self-evident truth that all men are not equal.[14]

The Hindu conception of sin is also fractionated, as a Hindu's sins differ according to his caste. Accordingly, the Western conception of the universal sinfulness of man has not characterized Hinduism, and Hindus typically are struck by what they consider the Western obsession with the sinful nature of mankind. On the other hand, Western travelers to India quickly identify a Hindu preoccupation with maintaining ritual purity. Traditional Hindus live in fear of the glance of an impure person upon their food or the touch of one who is classified as a pariah. Water from the holy

56

river Ganges, cow dung and cow urine are commonly used as purifying agents for those who have been so defiled.[15]

With the development of this compartmentalized system of social duties, the sanctioned role of women was delineated. At the time of the Rig-Veda, women had enjoyed a rough equality with men and had partaken in the ancient sacrifices. Their social status was to change for the worse. As Aryan males married the women of conquered, indigenous peoples, the status of females generally became tainted by that of the lowly dasas. Consequently, a unique dharma came to be associated with women. Ironically, it was most oppressive for high caste women as the higher castes most conscientiously aspired to uphold Brahmanic expectations. While the spiritual degradation of Hindu women has been dated as beginning at about the time of Christ, we can see its tendency much earlier. Even as early as the Rig-Veda, when women supposedly enjoyed a relatively high status, we can see shadows of what was to come. In that ancient scripture, Indra offers these comments: "'The mind of woman brooks no discipline. Her intellect hath little weight....The hearts of women are those of hyenas.'"[16]

As Upanishadic philosophy caught hold, with its ideal of moksha and detachment from the world, other seeds were sown for the degradation of women. In the male mind, women are associated with sexual passion, which is perhaps the strongest of all worldly attachments. Hence, any world view advocating that men break with earthly desires was bound to be accompanied by a misogynist polemic. There is an Indian proverb which states that a woman's lust for eating is twice as great as a man's, her cunning, four times as great, and her sex urge, eight times as great. Accordingly, women were to be distrusted by a seeker of moksha.

Beginning with the 5th and 6th centuries of our era, some Hindus would use women in sexual yoga. This version of Hinduism would be called tantrism of the left hand. Most Hindus rejected tantric practices, fearing the enslaving potential of human sexuality. Indeed, sexual self-control is one of Hinduism's highest ideals. Some Hindu ascetics have been known to test their powers by lying with beautiful, naked women and abstaining from sexual intercourse. Mahatma Gandhi himself is reported to have done this in his old age in the belief that it maximized his spiritual powers.[17] Hindus may be right that sexual self-restraint enhances

57

one's spiritual growth.  However, one thing is clear. This belief helped contribute to the decline of women in Indian society.

Some of the more interesting general rules developed for Hindu women were: 1) A woman must do nothing independently, even in her own house.  In childhood, she must be subject to her father and in youth, to her husband; when her husband is dead, to her sons.  Hindu teachings claim that women are dependent creatures by nature.  Accordingly, their dharma is to fulfill their natural constitution and not rebel.  2) A woman may marry a man of higher caste than herself without penalty, but if she marries into a lower caste, her children will be of lower status than even her husband.  Endogamy, or marriage within one's own caste, is the most common Hindu practice.  3) A girl should be married before her first menstruation.  A father who allows his daughter to remain unmarried beyond this time incurs guilt equivalent to one abortion for every menstrual period in which she remains single.  As women are naturally libidinous, they should marry young, for unless bound by marriage and watched constantly, a woman will consort with every stranger, even hunchbacks and dwarfs, and will engage in lesbian practices.  4) A female should marry a man three times her age.  An ideal match traditionally was between a 24 year old man and an 8 year old girl.  As great shame accompanied an unmarried, fully-grown woman, some fathers married their older daughters in absentia to opportunistic Brahmins who were party to this paper arrangement for a fee.  5) A widow should not remarry, even if her husband died when she was but a child.  A practical consideration contributed to this rule:  If a widow remarried, her family would have to pay a second dowry; further, her new husband would acquire the goods she inherited for her family from her first husband.[18] Ideally, in centuries past, a widow would practice sati, or self-immolation on her husband's funeral pyre.

Sati came into vogue among the higher castes between 650 and 1200 A.D.  In Rig-Vedic times, Aryan widows were known to marry again, but with the growth of Hinduism widows faced a most dreary existence. Consequently, sati for widows was often a welcome escape.  In the Hindu world, women were expected to predecease their husbands.  In the first place, to be born merely a female was taken as a sign of relatively low spiritual status.  Additionally, if a woman achieved widowhood, Hinduism taught that sins from her previous incarnations accounted for it.  A widow could eliminate both her own and her husband's past sins by practicing sati. Being burned alive was weighed against the guarantee of a blissful reincarnation for both herself and her deceased husband. Commencing about 1000 A.D., Islamic invasions of the Indian subcontinent threatened to end the practice of sati, but the Muslim attempts to suppress it were unsuccessful. Interestingly enough, Muslims did succeed in persuading Hindu males to accept the Islamic practice of veiling and secluding women. Not until 1829, did the British, who were then fast becoming the new overlords of India, systematically start to prohibit widow burning in areas under their control. Nevertheless, to this day, good Hindus revere as holy places sites where sati is known to have occurred.[19]

Traditional Hinduism still excludes women from full participation in religious life. Women attempting to acquire spiritual powers are labeled yoginis, a term which is linguistically similar to yogi. However, the word yogini has a negative connotation which is in stark contrast to the reverence associated with the title yogi. Yogini is defined as witch or female demon.[20] Hindus defending their religion's treatment of women will note the inclusion of many female deities in the Hindu pantheon. Indeed, young Hindu males are taught reverence toward these devas, and such respect and admiration is often transferred in a male Hindu's behavior toward a woman of high status. Certainly, if Hindu society regarded women as does Islam, Indira Gandhi would never have become prime minister of her country.

As we have seen, one's caste and sex helps indicate the current level of a Hindu's spiritual progress. One's birth sign does also. Astrology came to India from the Middle East at about the time of Christ. Before that, Indian fortune tellers relied on interpreting dreams, omens and the facial features of their subjects. These methods became secondary with the arrival of astrology. We have seen that Judaism, with its strong emphasis on human free will, rejected astrology because of the latter's apparent identification with fatalism. By contrast, Hinduism welcomed the ancient Babylonian art. While also accommodating free will in its theology, Hinduism cried out for explanations of the mysteries of samsara. For example, how can an individual tell where he currently is located in his own evolutionary development toward spiritual perfection? One's sex and caste are seen as several indicators. Astrology is also a help. In

59

addition, the stars provide clues how an individual's life might yet evolve. Each of the signs of the zodiac indicate potential virtues and faults, auspicious possibilities and events to be avoided. Just as caste and sex create certain rules or dharmas, a person's astrological endowment does also. To this day, traditional Hindus obey their astrological dharmas. For example, they consult their astrologers before initiating important acts, such as those involving travel or plans of marriage.[21]

In describing the concepts of samsara and dharma and how they relate to male/female relationships, caste, and zodiacal signs, another concept may be introduced that closely relates to all of the above. This is the idea of karma. Karma is defined as the moral law of cause and effect. It can be expressed in the biblical maxim, "As you sow, so shall you reap." Or, as a Hindu saying puts it, "Even as a calf finds his mother among a thousand cows, an act formerly done is sure to find the perpetrator."[22] In short, if we are born into a sex, a caste, and under a particular sun sign, we earned this status by our choices in past lives. Similarly, our behavior now will determine the situation of our future incarnations. Interestingly, in contrast to Judaism, Hinduism united astrology and free will into an internally consistent world view. This was accomplished only through the concept that the human soul experiences many lifetimes on earth.

In the Western view, a person has only one lifetime to effect his destiny for eternity. Therefore, Westerners see this life as all-important, as it is the only opportunity we have to make our mark. By contrast, Hinduism teaches that while our actions in any one lifetime are important, they are not irreversible. For the Hindu, the Western necessity to experience all of life in a 70 year time span is lacking. For the West, life is valuable and should be savored. The Hindu conception is different. As we have thousands, perhaps even tens or hundreds of thousands of incarnations, life in samsara is basically distasteful. Samsara's joys are ephemeral and surrounded by pain. Hinduism's ultimate goal is to be rid of life's suffering. Accordingly, the West describes Hinduism as "life denying."

Scholars don't know how or when the conception of samsara came into existence. It is lost in the ancient past. We do know that the dharma concept was brought to India by the Aryans. Scholars have concluded that the karma idea was born on Indian soil soon after the Aryan conquest.[23] Karma could explain why some were rich and well-born and why others suffered as slaves. In short, Vedic teaching said that if one fulfilled his dharma he would earn good karma, which would result in a better incarnation in the next round of samsara. In brief, this is how the ideas of dharma, karma and samsara are interrelated within Hinduism.

Karma

As we have seen, karma is the Hindu doctrine of cause and effect. Every action in life in which a participant is emotionally involved produces karma. Westerners talk of someone's chickens coming home to roost. They also have a saying that those who live by the sword, die by the sword. These thoughts are close to the concept of karma, with the difference that the idea of karma is intimately linked to a belief in reincarnation. In Hinduism, actions of a past life can come home to roost in this life.

It is thought that the karma idea originated in the ancient Vedic belief that the Brahmins' sacrificial acts determined the workings of the natural order. From this evolved the notion that every act in life, not just those involved in the Soma sacrifice, produces a karmic effect. Expressed in everyday terms, each of our thoughts and actions makes an impression upon the mind. This impression might be imperceptible at first, but if the thought or action occurs again and again a habit is formed. These tendencies define ourselves as distinct personalities.[24] In Hindu terminology, they are our karmas.

Westerners often define karma as fatalism, plain and simple. This is a misconception. Karma is used to explain why a person is born rich or poor, strong or weak, whole or crippled, male or female. Nonetheless, Hinduism emphasizes that this supposed fate was earned. The karma idea stresses that our past thoughts and actions alone determined our present condition. Correspondingly, our future situation depends upon our choices now. The person who obeys his dharma will generate new karma that will bear good fruit in the future. This is hardly fatalism.

Nevertheless, there are good reasons why the karma doctrine is easily associated with fatalism. Very few Hindus believe that human free will can work immediate transformations. Some Hindus engage in ascetic practices to starve passionate cravings within them. But most Hindus do not view past karma as something that can be willed out of existence. This majority view argues that internal urges should not be suppressed, for if such an attempt is made these desires will merely surface in future lifetimes. There is an old Indian saying that a cobra swept out of sight under a bed troubles the rest of the man who sleeps there. This same idea is expressed somewhat differently in Hermann Hesse's well-known novel <u>Siddartha</u>. In Hesse's story, the hero (Siddartha) starts as a religious Brahmin lad, who decides to live as an ascetic in the forest. There, he feels lust welling up within him. He moves back to town, lives with a courtesan and spends his time seeking pleasure. After living through these urges, he returns to the forest without possessions. Hesse stresses that this diversion in town was a necessary part of Siddartha's evolution toward a higher plane. "Everyone follows his nature," an ancient Hindu holy book notes; "what can repression accomplish?"[25]

Hinduism acknowledges pleasure-seeking as a legitimate end of life, albeit a base one. To fulfill one's dharma is life's highest purpose, followed by earning wealth through honest means. The lowest acceptable end of life is kama, or engaging in pleasure of all kinds. Many Westerners have made their first and only contact with Hinduism through the <u>Kamasutra,</u> a manual on the art of sensual lovemaking written at about the time of Christ. Also demonstrating the acceptability of kama in Hindu life, erotic art, which leaves little to the imagination, covers the exteriors of many Hindu temples. Unlike Christianity, Hinduism has not placed human sensuality beyond the pale. In Hinduism, sexual urges are seen as forces that have to be mastered, not suppressed. Hindu eroticism acknowledged the tremendous temptations of life without making kama an ideal. Accordingly, erotic art was put on the outside of the temple, not in the central, most sacred, rooms.

Hinduism acknowledged that an enemy ignored is far more dangerous than one directly challenged in open confrontation. Accordingly, contemplation of pornographic sculpture decorating temple walls is advocated as a first step toward a life of spiritual meditation. With these thoughts mastered, the devotee can progress to the next plateau in his ascent to realization of Brahman. Jesus of Nazareth warned of the dangers of merely mastering one's overt behavior, while allowing sexual desire to rage uncontrolled in one's heart. Hindus have agreed and have been more conscientious than Christians in developing this idea. Accordingly, Hinduism has found that the real culprit is human desire, rather than its manifestations.[26]

As Hinduism taught that karma must be lived through, it certainly flirted with being fatalistic. Yet it stopped short of being so. Hindus have a saying that the mudfish lives in mud, is surrounded by mud, but it does not become mud. In the same way, the individual living in a world of lust, playing out his past karma, can choose to disengage from it by developing mental detachment.[27] In gradually achieving mental liberation or detachment from sense objects, a person slowly consumes or destroys past karma without creating new karma and is enabled to move to a higher plane. In this way, the karma philosophy ultimately advocates the power of human choice. That which appears on the surface as fatalism is really a philosophy of total individual responsibility.

Hinduism's emphasis on individual responsibility can be seen most clearly in its explanation of why extraordinary tragedies befall some and not others. Questions of this nature are common to all religions. In Judaism, the Book of Job wrestles with this issue. In that scripture, Job, a good man, is visited with one personal misfortune after another. As Judaism taught that goodness would be rewarded, Job challenged God for an explanation of his suffering. The clearest answer that he received was not to question the ways of the Lord. In short, the Book of Job answers the human inquiry into the existence of suffering with divine mystery. Westerners typically have not been satisfied with this answer. Acknowledging this frustration, one author has noted: "Either God can prevent evil and He will not; or He wishes to prevent it and He cannot."[28] In contrast to the Book of Job, Hinduism's karma doctrine provides a clear explanation of human suffering. A Hindu comment on the Jewish text might be: If Job suffered, even though he had been good in this life, it was because of evil habits he had acquired in past lives.

Theodicy is a theological explanation of human suffering. The most clear and thorough theodicy on record is Hinduism's karma concept. See a crippled beggar in the street? A Westerner would typically think, "What tough luck, there but for fortune go I." The Hindu sees the beggar's twisted body and thinks,

63

"As he sowed, he reaped." Pity or empathy in such situations would be inappropriate emotions. The crippled beggar deserves his condition. In fact, he earned it through his past thoughts and actions. Perhaps he crippled others in a previous life. So would the Hindu think.

Indian prime minister Indira Gandhi once commented that Hinduism's stress on individual responsibility was both her country's primary strength and fundamental weakness. It had given the people an inner strength but had also put a veil between the individual and others in society. She lamented that social welfare programs could not succeed in India unless this basic Hindu attitude of mind would change. In short, the karma doctrine interferes with the Western idea of social welfare. The karma idea teaches that one can earn good karma by giving to the poor, but this can be done only on an individual charities basis. Therefore, gift giving to the individual beggar has always been prevalent, while the social welfare idea, even though it has been central to the ideology of the Indian socialist state, has never been truly effective in the land of Hinduism. One primary reason for this failure should be clear. The West has generally assumed that if the government improves the environment of the ignorant and disadvantaged, social improvement will result. In brief, the West has assumed that society can uplift the individual. The karma doctrine rejects this.

According to the karma concept, only the individual can uplift the individual. The path of any individual's progress is long and treacherous, filled with endless suffering over thousands of lifetimes. The individual's evolution from bad to good karma culminates finally in liberation from the chains of karma altogether, at least for the few that achieve moksha in any cosmic cycle. In the Hindu view, no individual is responsible for another, but is totally responsible for himself. This orientation should not be confused with the Social Darwinism commonly associated with American conservatives. Hinduism does not preach a doctrine of untrammeled individualism. Quite the opposite is the case. Dharma (social duty) and self-renunciation are principal themes of traditional Hindu thought. The individualism of the karma idea is weighted with social duties. By contrast, the Western brand of individualism stresses inalienable rights free from societal restriction.[29]

Hindus are most sensitive to the Western perspective that the karma doctrine is merely an aristocratic rationale to oppress the poor. Accordingly, they typically turn the mirror of social criticism back upon the West. Are not the poor of the West, they ask, exploited by a culture that identifies happiness with the acquisition of material possessions? Furthermore, Hindus contend, are not the poor of the West, who are taught from birth that they are mere products of their social environment, and consequently incapable of resisting the evils around them, reduced from human beings to animals? Hindus comment that Western societies neglect the soul. Western humanism, they argue, makes material well-being a necessary prerequisite for living, and this value system results in spiritual suffocation. Hindus note that even Western religion is corrupted in the process. Typically oriented toward service to mankind, religious Westerners too easily fall prey to the mistaken idea that God needs them. This notion, Hindus argue, heightens the egoism of the Western believer and blocks his spiritual enlightenment.[30]

Rather than emphasizing the need for the larger community's material improvement, Hinduism looks to the individual's liberation from human cravings. The Hindu seeks to exhaust his past karma, for it is karma that ties his soul to samsara, or the endless cycle of rebirths. Moksha, or liberation from samsara, is Hinduism's ultimate goal. Good karma is better than bad karma, but no karma is the Hindu ideal. To the Hindu, good and evil are concepts that belong in samsara. Detachment from such concepts is seen as the means toward final liberation. Even after achieving a state of mental detachment in every action performed, the individual lives on until all past karma is exhausted. Then the cycle of samsara is broken, and the individual soul making this ultimate achievement finds rest in the divine Presence.

Very few Hindus make a serious attempt to achieve moksha, believing it to be within reach only to the few at the end of samsara's long trail of spiritual evolution. More common is to work for an improved status in future births and fear the consequences of bad karma. Hindus are taught that if one's emotions are thoroughly mired in lust, he might return from death as a tree, a condition devoid of consciousness deserved by a proven inability to control human passions. Some Hindus claim that once a soul reaches the human plane it cannot revert to animal, insect, or

65

vegetable forms of life. This is only a minority voice. Most Hindus acknowledge the great risks of the human condition. Human actions, unlike those of animals, are tainted with malice. Hence the chances of earning bad karma in the human condition are great.[31]

The karma doctrine is ever on the minds of practicing Hindus. It defines not only their relationship to divine truth but to their material environment as well. And there is the irony, for Hinduism's concern with karma dwells to some extent on considerations of individual advancement in social and economic status. For example, a Hindu is commonly motivated to fulfill his caste dharma in hopes of achieving a more comfortable incarnation in his next life. Good karma has its worldly rewards. The Hindu critique of Western materialism has a certain validity. At the same time, it must be acknowledged that karma consciousness is oriented to a degree with similar preoccupations, which make true detachment from worldly concerns difficult to achieve.

## Rules of the Hindu Social Order

It is estimated that today's India has about 3,000 castes, some numbering only a few hundred persons, with others running into the millions. Each caste has its own unique set of dharmas which bind the lives of its members. For example, caste dharma limits the acceptability of various occupations, foods, marriage partners and social customs. These dharmas are not set by general norms of fair play. Rather, they are the result of traditions lost to history.

Hindu holy books give this explanation for the hierarchical caste system: In the beginning, God created the Brahmins, the highest caste, from his mouth; the kshatriyas, made up of warriors, kings and governmental officials, came from his arms; the Vaishyas, farmers and tradesmen, sprung next from his thighs; and finally the Shudras, or menial laborers, came from the Lord's feet. Such is the mythological explanation of the four major caste categories known as varnas. Literally translated, the word varna means color, as each caste category is associated with a particular color. White is the color of the Brahmins; red of the Kshatriyas; yellow of the Vaishyas; and black of the Shudras. Scholars have debated the origins of these color designations, some claiming that they derived from the racial prejudices of the Aryan conquerors. Others have seen them as more symbolic in meaning. Nevertheless, all concede that Aryan racial preferences had some role to play in the origins of the caste system. Indeed, to this day Hindus value a light skin color, as is most apparent in the arrangement of Indian marriage contracts.[32]

Early Vedic scriptures refer to only the first three caste categories. It appears that the Aryans came to India with a three-layered class structure and that the Shudras later derived from the dark-skinned, conquered, native inhabitants of the country. Today, one can find fair Shudras and black Brahmins, but in Vedic times racial distinctiveness appears to have been maintained. Pratanjali, the great grammarian, wrote as late as 150 B.C. that "'the physical characteristics of a Brahmin were fair skin and tawny hair,'" in contrast to the black skin of the Shudra.[33] Intermarriage across caste lines, pairing higher caste men with lower caste women, contributed to the fractionating of the four simple caste categories into the thousands of castes that are in India today. Other factors were as important in contributing to the proliferation of castes. For example, intercontinental migration paths terminated in India, leaving peoples of different races, cultures and levels of civilization living in close proximity. The compartmentalization of society known as the caste system allowed these diverse groups to maintain a degree of cultural distance, despite crowded population conditions.[34]

The name given to caste in India is jati, which means a group into which one is born. The word caste itself came from the Portuguese, who upon observing the social rules of various jati, used their word casta, meaning race or family, to describe the groups they saw. The jatis are associated together through the varna system. A jati in south India may have only a local existence, without roots in other regions of the subcontinent. Nevertheless, its claim to a particular varna status will tie it to jatis elsewhere.

Scholars have discovered that the relationship of jatis to the more general varna system is not unchanging in nature. Jatis have been known to switch their varna claims in hopes of achieving higher status. The process of successfully maintaining such a claim has been termed "Sanskritization." To maintain the claim successfully, the whole caste has to live by the highest standards of the ancient Brahmanic codes recorded in Sanskrit. In the earliest stages of this process, neighboring castes belittle the pretentions of the aspiring jati. But after two or three generations, the myth can become firmly established, moving a jati from, say, the Shudra to the Kshatriya classification, a vast improvement in social status. Catastrophes have encouraged Sanskritization in the past. For example, an entire caste fleeing its native region in wartime or famine was provided with a unique opportunity to upgrade its social status. Resettling far from those familiar with its traditional varna, a jati could commence the process of Sanskritization with greater than normal expectations of success.

Lower castes look to Sanskritization as a means toward upward social mobility. By contrast, higher castes are attracted to Westernizing influences which weaken the traditional social order. A Brahmin, receiving the benefits of Western education, moves to the city and is increasingly liberated from the strictures of caste dharma. In turn, the low caste villager picks up the social rules of traditional Hinduism discarded by the city dweller in hopes of improving the reputation of his jati.[35]

High status within the traditional Hindu social order is not without its price. The higher the caste, the greater the social obligations of its members. For example, a low caste Hindu is more or less free to eat a variety of foods, including meat. Vegetarianism is an obligation associated with the higher castes. The food of a low caste Hindu may be prepared by almost anyone, although some low caste jatis are not lax on this issue. That of a high caste member invariably can be cooked only by those of equal or yet higher rank. The glance of a low caste person upon the food of one of high rank can make the latter's meal and cooking utensils ritually unclean, resulting in their destruction, among other inconvenient purification rites. Perhaps it is not surprising that persons bearing the burdens of these traditions often find Westernization attractive.

A century ago, when Hindus first began to travel to England to receive Western education, the caste burdens of making such a move were enormous. Difficult purification methods, including drinking a mixture of cow dung and urine, were prescribed for returning scholars. Contact with the West produced more serious problems for traditional Hindus as well. When, in the 19th century, the importation of cheap British textiles undermined the traditional weaving trades of West Bengal, starvation ensued for millions in that region.

68

The jati dharma of Bengali weavers required that they stay at their occupation even after it had been made economically irrelevant. Eventually, these castes took up new, nontraditional lines of work, but not until 30 percent of their members had perished. This example illustrates in tragic terms the weight of social duty upon the Hindu conscience.[36]

Even today, those Indians little touched by Western ways feel bound to maintain the traditional social order. Untouchable latrine cleaners have been known to forego attractive economic opportunities in order to maintain their unsavory dharma, and hope for a better reincarnation has not been their sole motivation. A person who breaks jati dharma risks rejection by family and peers. Such rejection carries not only social and psychological costs. It also means discarding the only meaningful hope for care and maintenance in one's old age. Traditionally, the caste has served as a mutual assurance society in India, filling the role that welfare systems provide in Western countries.[37]

In traditional Hindu society, innovation is evil and caste rules are more significant than individual personality. Many Westerners, especially Americans, are raised with the idea that innovation is the highest value. The fruits of this belief can be seen in the unbelievable productivity of American agriculture. By contrast, something as simple as altering planting techniques may violate jati dharma in India. By making custom holy, Indian caste dharma is an obstacle to economic progress. There is an old Hindu saying that it is better to do one's own dharma badly than another's well. This idea helps keep India frozen in poverty and economic backwardness.

Westerners are seemingly compelled to strive for accomplishments that will distinguish them from the crowd. Because transcient success essentially defines the individual, failure to achieve such goals in the West can be a tremendous source of frustration and anxiety. Traditional Hindus do not suffer from this form of identity crisis. They are more or less content with merely "having their being," as they are prone to put it. There are fleeting moments in an American's life when he or she feels what traditional Hindus feel most of the time--that one's social role is more important than individual personality. For example, a young woman in the role as the "bride" knows this feeling. Temporarily, she is not just herself but rather an archetypal figure, timeless and immortal. The young American man as the "football hero" also has experienced this. The Hindu as a member of a jati knows a sense of being that endures beyond a fleeting stage in one's lifetime. A Hindu's dharma constitutes a compass that gives his life direction. Lest the caste system be idealized here, it must be reemphasized that no world view is without penalty. This is true in India as well as in the United States. India is in the throes of poverty, encouraged by the caste system, while individual Americans wrestle with a psychological trauma alien to good Hindus.

Some psychologists have described what they call the underdeveloped Indian ego, which they ascribe to the caste system. In India, one's jati dharma does more than provide a sense of brotherhood and belongingness. It defines the individual completely. In the caste system, interpersonal relationships are codified. The need for individual judgment is thereby reduced. The ego is made passive. Consequently, a personality is molded that is ideally suited to transcendental meditation and the bliss that accompanies the losing of self.[38]

Some examples of the rules that bind a Hindu's life have been given. They involve whom one may marry, what occupation one may pursue, what one may eat, when one may travel, among the scope of concerns. These rules also involve what one should do during the various stages of life. These stages, which apply to those allowed to participate in Vedic rites, are: student life, householder life, retired life and renounced life. The dharmas associated with these four stages have always been considered optional, in contrast to required jati dharma. If the latter is considered duty, the dharma of the four stages of life is thought of as ideal.

After a Hindu male undergoes a coming-of-age rite, he enters the student phase of his life. This begins at different ages depending on his varna: eight years old for a Brahmin, 11 for a Kshatriya, and 12 for a Vaishya. Those undergoing this experience are called "twice born." Shudras are excluded from this process as are women of all castes. During his student stage, the young Hindu is trained in sexual abstinence. As the sex drive is recognized as the most binding material desire, the Hindu learns to control his sexual appetite during this first stage. This celibate period devoted to religious study ends at about 16 years of age, when the young Hindu enters householder life. After the twice-born male concludes his studies, he should get married and raise a family. Christianity and Buddhism would encourage some of their faithful to become celibate monks and nuns. Hinduism prescribed a different ideal. It urged celibacy during the first, third and fourth stages of life but taught that if one tried to suppress the sex drive completely good karma would not result. Only by developing a detached attitude toward sex in the controlled environment of marriage could the maturing man eventually escape sexuality's worldly snare.

When a man first sees the son of his son, it is time to enter the third stage, that of retired life. In this stage, husband and wife are to discontinue sexual relations. Ideally, the husband should live alone in the forest during this stage, although it is acceptable for his wife to accompany him as an assistant. The devotee is then to spend his time meditating and developing a detached attitude toward everything. When he feels that death is not many years away, the seeker should enter the stage of renounced life. Here, he leaves his wife and becomes a wandering beggar. When this occurs, his wife officially becomes a widow. So far as society is concerned, the Hindu in the renounced stage is no longer in and of the world. A poet wrote how the aged, wandering ascetic should view life and death: "He should not wish to die, nor hope to live, but await the time appointed, as a servant awaits his wages."[39]

Some do not wait until late middle age to renounce worldly pleasures and assume a mantle of celibate austerities. Morarji Desai, a prime minister of India in the 1970's, once boasted that he last experienced sex when he was 28. By that time, he had five children, and so took this step earlier than prescribed. The example of Desai suggests that the ideal of renunciation weighs heavily on the Hindu mind. The ideal of spiritual liberation spurs some Hindus to violate even the social norms of dharma. These extreme seekers of moksha are called sadhus, or saints. In breaking with the dharma system, they are viewed as walking dead and without caste. Consequently, they are impurity in the absolute and are socially ostracized. At the same time, sadhus are revered, for they have dedicated their lives to mystical union with the Absolute and consequently are living symbols of Hinduism's highest ideal. A sadhu's only possessions should be a staff and a bowl for alms. He is not allowed to beg for food until evening, after the villagers have all eaten. He may beg only once a day, should wear a simple, orange-colored garment and must never cut his hair or beard. From a material standpoint, most sadhus lead truly wretched lives. The sadhu provides a striking exception to the rules of the Hindu social order. Perhaps a social system as authoritarian and rigid as prescribed by Hinduism had to develop such an escape hatch for the more intractable souls within it. In this context, it is interesting to note that sadhus have not always acted as saints. Some have been known to travel in groups, [40] behaving as bandits and preying on society.

In recent years, free spirits wishing to reject Hindu social norms have not had to don the orange robes of the sadhu. A more affluent alternative has been provided by the Indian city, a monument to the British value system. Yet caste weakening influences emanating from Indian urban centers are more than mere holdovers from British imperialism. In fact, they are promoted by the Indian government itself and derive their ultimate authority from no less than Mahatma Gandhi, the father of the Indian independence movement. During his early life, Gandhi concluded that the caste system, by dividing Indian society into mutually jealous compartments, allowed the British to maintain their conquest. Accordingly, he made social unity among the Indian peoples his highest objective. Symbolically, he made the untouchables, the lowest elements in Indian society, the special recipients of his concern. He renamed them Harijans, or people of God. Upon winning independence, the Indian government continued his cause, building into its new constitution special privileges due the Harijans. All of this was done to dissolve the societal disunity promoted by the ancient caste system. [41]

In the past, caste dharma had preserved Hindu culture in spite of foreign overlords. Protected in the compartments of caste, Hinduism survived into the 20th Century. Some have wondered out loud whether this ancient culture can long remain intact with the force of the Indian government theoretically aligned against caste divisions. Others are sanguine that traditional Hinduism will endure. Despite influences from the Indian city, the caste system continues to thrive in the countryside. One of Gandhi's most respected biographers has noted that the great Indian leader made not "the slightest dent in the Hindu attitude toward spiritual pollution and untouchability." [42] Caste

72

spirit lives on in India's power centers as well, albeit to a lesser degree than in remote villages. Morarji Desai, who regards himself as one of Gandhi's disciples, forbade his daughter only a few years after the great man's death to marry into a different caste, a decision which drove her to suicide. And caste ties continue to dominate Indian politics. Even the communist party selects its candidates for regional elections from the politically dominant castes.[43]

Nevertheless, the caste system is weaker today than it was 100 or even 50 years ago. While it is far from dissolving, there is much evidence that even in rural areas caste segregation is not practiced with the rigidity that was once common. The weakening of caste has somewhat encouraged Hindu proselytizing efforts abroad. While India's spiritual outreach to the West is at least as old as Swami Vivekananda's tours of the United States in the 1890's, it is only in our own day that its potential is being realized. To date, the primary beneficiary of this success has been the Hare Krishna sect.

Several traditional concepts are reinterpreted by these caste-free purveyors of Hinduism in the West. Hare Krishna spokesmen define varnas as any number of occupational categories to which one may be temperamentally suited, and dharma is defined as "worldly or occupational duty." In Hare Krishna, general norms of correct behavior receive primary emphasis, and jati dharmas are forgotten.[44] As with Judaism, Hinduism enjoys many variants in the modern world. The more traditional versions continue in the villages of India. There, the many rules of the Hindu social order still discourage the assimilation of outsiders. Elsewhere, Hindu principles are taught more or less free from the ancient strictures of caste.

## The Divinities of Hinduism

Hinduism is perhaps the most complex of the world's great religions. To one casual observer, it appears as polytheism or a belief in many gods. To another, Hinduism may represent strict monism or the belief that ultimate reality is indivisible. To both, it may appear as pantheism or the view that God is in everything. In fact, it is all of these and more. Some may argue that this author is presumptuous in even attempting to define a solitary religion called Hinduism. What the West popularly labels Hinduism is in fact a myriad of often conflicting tenets and practices. In spite of this, Hinduism is held together by several factors, one of which is the caste system, which was just reviewed. Another unifying force in Hinduism consists of the high degree of doctrinal toleration found among its believers. According to some in the West, those unable to accept Christian doctrine are denied salvation. By contrast, there is no official Hindu creed.

The tolerance that characterizes Hinduism is best explained by the Hindu parable of the blind men and the elephant. Once upon a time, the story goes, a king called the blind men of his region together for the purpose of describing the characteristics of an elephant. Arranging themselves around the beast, the various blind men felt those parts of the elephant closest to them. The man near the elephant's head claimed that the animal was shaped like a pot. The man holding the trunk announced that the elephant was shaped like a plough. The blind man beside the elephant's leg said that the beast was shaped like a pillar. Their disagreement quickly became a violent quarrel. The meaning of the parable is clear. We mortals are as blind men, face to face with an eternal reality beyond our understanding. Consequently, to assume that we clearly can see ultimate truth is to reveal only our own arrogance and blindness.[45]

Ramakrishna, a Hindu holy man in the 19th century, exemplified Hindu toleration in matters of religious doctrine. Ramakrishna was a devotee of Kali, the divine Mother, one of the principal deities in the Hindu pantheon. Early in his life, he experienced the direct presence of God in the female form of Kali. Later, he experienced God through worship of first the male god Krishna, and later the Muslims' Allah and the Christians' Christ. In addition, he regarded the historic Buddha as an incarnation of God. God's truth is indeed in all faiths and was found by the tolerant Ramakrishna. "'As one can ascend to the top of a house by means of a ladder or a bamboo or a staircase or a rope,'" Ramakrishna declared, "'so diverse also are the ways and means to approach God, and every religion in the world shows one of these ways.'"[46]

As Hinduism has developed new religious perceptions through the ages, it has not discarded older truths in the process. Hindu religion encompasses beliefs that span from primitive animism on one extreme to highly intellectualized philosophical monism on the other. The contrast with Judaism could

74

not be more striking. We have seen that the Baal cult of ancient Canaan possibly influenced Judaism in positive ways, but any reader of the Torah knows that Judaism firmly rejected Baal. Had a Hindu degree of toleration existed in Judaism, Baal, Yahweh and Christ would today all be accepted for purposes of Jewish worship. Each would be viewed as rungs on a ladder leading to God.

The Hindu Godhead is not a jealous god. To the contrary, He welcomes every form of creed. Accordingly, Hinduism has many faces and many gods. Devotees desirous of specific things are encouraged to pray to the demigod that most appropriately suits one's immediate needs. A farmer wanting rain will pray to Indra, who is no longer considered among the most important gods of India. Agni, the ancient Vedic fire god, is now petitioned by those wanting increased effectiveness in interpersonal relationships. A person wanting knowledge worships the goddess of learning; another seeking a beautiful wife worships still another goddess. Hindus regard this pantheon, as well as humanity and creation in general, as merely emanations from the Supreme Godhead. Such a belief system can easily be interpreted as either monism, pantheism or polytheism. Any particular emphasis depends upon which part of this complex theological elephant is being examined at any one moment.[47]

In addition to worshipping specific deities, Hindus hold a special reverence for certain animals, namely cows and snakes. The cause of this is lost in the ancient past. We know that while there was some feeling in ancient Vedic religion against the killing of cows, it was not then a strict taboo, as it has been in recent memory. Whatever its source, the sacredness of cows in India has long been a reality. Traditional Hindus believe the natural wastes of the cow to be purifying. Indeed, Morarji Desai was reported to have drunk cow urine for its purifying qualities during his tenure as India's prime minister. Cow dung has been used to disinfect residences contaminated by ritually unclean foreigners. A Hindu passing by a urinating cow might stop, put his hands into the stream and wet his forehead and clothing,[48] much as a Roman Catholic would do with holy water.

India's snakes are only slightly less regarded than cows. This reverence for snakes is demonstrated in the mythology surrounding the god Shiva, one of the principal deities of Hinduism. Snakes are unique in suggesting the human phallus while also occasionally serving as agents of death. Accordingly, in the Shiva cult, snakes symbolize the link between disintegration or death and regeneration or life. In our world of constant change, life and death are defined only in relation to one another. Without the fear of death, "life" would not have the emotional definition commonly given it. In samsaric existence, life and death are bound together in the flow of time. This meaning is embodied in the snake.[49]

We have already seen that in ancient India many gods were worshipped and that the Aryan religion was subsequently refined by the authors of the <u>Upanishads</u>. The next major development came roughly a century before Christ, when Shiva and Vishnu emerged as Hinduism's two major gods. As noted above, Shiva was associated with the disintegrating aspects of life, the constant destruction and rebirth that accompanies the passage of time. Hence, he was named the "destroyer." On the other hand, Vishnu represents the joy of life. While Shiva is commonly portrayed as an ascetic, naked to the world except for being smeared with ashes from the funeral pyre, Vishnu is shown bedecked in fine clothes and jewels. Vishnu is a god to celebrate the good things of life; Shiva, to acknowledge that they are not constant. The cults surrounding both gods drew upon the Aryan religious heritage. In Vedic times, Vishnu had been a minor deity associated with the sun, a common symbol of life's hopeful aspects. For his part, Shiva built upon the legends of the Vedic god Rudra, who had also been called the "destroyer." Both the Shiva and Vishnu cults drew upon pre-Aryan, native, Indian religions as well. This was especially clear in the worship of Shiva. To this day, Shiva's temples enclose a phallic symbol called a lingam, upon which devotees pour clarified butter as a reverential act. The modern-day worshipper performs this rite without sexual feeling. Nevertheless, the fertility ceremonies of pre-Aryan religions are commonly identified as contributing to this aspect to Shaivite worship.

While Vishnu's devotees regard Him as the "preserver," they believe that Shiva's qualities are in Him as well. Shiva's followers likewise see their God as encompassing Vishnu's characteristics. A Vaishnavite (a devotee of Vishnu) sees his God as the Supreme Godhead. A Vaishnavite will acknowledge the existence of Shiva as a subordinate deity but in no way sees him as equivalent to the Godhead. Conversely, a Shaivite (a worshipper of Shiva) views Vishnu as merely

76

an emanation of Shiva, the Supreme Lord. The duality of these gods is mainly in the minds of those attempting to make sense of Hindu mythology. To their worshippers, each alone is the Godhead, embodying all divine attributes.[50]

The emergence of Vishnu and Shiva a century before Christ represented the amalgamation of Aryan and native religion in the crucible of Upanishadic philosophy. Seven to eight centuries later, another important development occurred with the emergence of the Shakti cult. Those relating more easily to a mother goddess than a male deity were drawn to the Shakti cult presided over by Shiva's consort. Known by a variety of names, this goddess is most commonly represented as Kali, a black hag embodying all of the fearsome aspects of existence. If one can worship a divinity associated with death and destruction, perhaps liberation from all worldly attachments can more easily result. In any case, the worshipper of Kali is not overly concerned with Her mythological image. For him, Kali is simply the divine Mother bringing religious solace to Her devotees.[51]

Shiva, Vishnu and Kali are Hinduism's principal gods. Nevertheless, Hindu mythology identifies a slightly different trinity: Shiva, Vishnu and Brahma, or Destruction, Preservation and Creation. Brahma, not to be confused with the impersonal Brahman of the Upanishads, is not of equal stature to Vishnu or Shiva. Brahma is a minor god, whose only role is to create the cosmos and expire with its destruction. Unlike Vishnu, Shiva or Kali, Brahma is not immortal, though his life-span is quite lengthy. No cult surrounds Brahma. He exists only in Hindu folklore, and even there his role as creator is tightly defined.[52] In short, he exists only as a servant of the Most High.

Each of Hinduism's main deities is portrayed with four arms, the symbol of absolute dominion. Interestingly, this is also the meaning of the cross as a Hindu yantra or graphic symbol. While the origins of the Christian cross are obviously not related to Hinduism, its meaning is close to that of the four arms of Vishnu, Shiva or Kali.[53] The avatar concept in the Vishnu cult also is similar to the Christian view of Jesus of Nazareth as God incarnate. In Christian theology, Jesus came to redeem mankind from sin and death. In Vaishnavite religion, Vishnu has periodically incarnated himself to save mankind.

77

An avatar is a complete incarnation of the Supreme Godhead. It is generally accepted that Vishnu has had nine such incarnations to date. One is yet to occur. These incarnations are identified. The first avatar was a giant fish that saved mankind at the time of the great flood. The story of the flood is fairly universal. In Judaism's version, the flood occurs because of God's anger over human sin. In the Indian story, the reason for the flood is unexplained. It just happens. Vishnu in the form of a fish advises Manu, who in Hinduism plays roles similar to both Adam and Noah, to build a ship. Manu does as the Fish commands and is saved. Another important incarnation of Vishnu is Krishna, the eighth avatar and the one most Vaishnavites relate to most easily. He is worshipped as fully god and fully man, much as is Christ in Christianity. Buddha was the ninth avatar, the last incarnation of Vishnu to date. Buddha's role, according to Vaishnavite mythology, was to lead Kshatriya philosophers astray, thus returning the Vedas to their rightful masters, the Brahmin priest caste. The tenth avatar, named Kalkin, is yet to come. Generally recognized spiritual leaders, such as Jesus or Mahatma Gandhi, are considered by some Hindus to be partial incarnations of the Godhead, but they are not listed among the ten avatars of Vishnu.

It is written that Kalkin will come to save the faithful during the age of Kali. According to Hindu cosmology, the Kali-yuga or age of Kali is a dark age terminating each cosmic cycle. It is a time when men abandon caste and overthrow established standards. Foreigners dominate during that age, and religious rites are ignored. Eventually, Kalkin arrives to restore the rightful place of the Brahmins and Vedic practices. The similarity between the hopes surrounding Kalkin and Western eschatological themes most probably derives from a common Zoroastrian source. While no longer a thriving world religion, Zoroastrianism continues indirectly to shape the expectations of worshippers both East and West.[54]

One may dwell on certain similarities between Eastern and Western religions, yet their differences are just as striking. For example, Judaism allows for one creation only, whereas Hindu cosmology notes innumerable creations. The Jewish account of creation is simple and easily remembered. By contrast, the Hindu mind, which glories in theological intricacies, has given a most complex story of the process of creation. Brahma, the creator, has a life-span of 100

78

divine years. Each of his days constitutes 4,300,000,000 earthly years. Each of his nights is of equal length. One of his months consists of 30 divine days and nights, and one of his years comprises 12 divine months. In short, his life-span is 309,600,000,000,000 earthly years. At the end of each divine day, Brahma absorbs his entire creation back into his being. During the night he sleeps, only to create the universe anew the next day. This cyclical process of creation goes on and on but not for eternity. At the conclusion of Brahma's life-span, all emanations, including Brahma himself, return to the Godhead. The Supreme God, whether it be Shiva, Kali or Vishnu, then rests, ultimately to re-create Brahma and start creation's process into motion once again. Therefore, the age of Kali comes not once as does the end of days in Judaism or Christianity. It comes again and again at the end of each of Brahma's divine days. In our own cycle, the age of Kali reportedly began in 3102 B.C. and is still with us.[55]

Hinduism's descriptions of samsaric existence, as the cosmology described above amply demonstrates, invariably reminds us of the insignificance of our own petty, worldly lives. After all, what do we amount to when compared to even one of Brahma's days? All of Hindu religion seems intent upon raising such questions in hopes that we may seek any one of the developed paths to moksha. At this point, the differences between the Shaivite and Vaishnavite religions need to be reemphasized. Worshippers of Shiva tend to seek loss of self through ascetic detachment from the world. By contrast, Vaishnavites seek liberation through joyful love of God.

The Shaivite path originates with the twin identification of the sex impulse as the predominant worldly attachment and Shiva with the death of lust. Adorned with skulls, Shiva symbolizes the destruction of worldly ties of every sort, especially those of a sexual nature. Hindus typically seek to control sexual energy, which if not mastered can easily enslave the spirit of man. Accordingly, Shiva's Lingam, ever erect, is always under the Supreme Lord's control. Shiva's mount, a white bull named Nandi, also symbolizes the sexual impulse which Shiva dominates.

Shiva's image as the supreme ascetic appeals to those who aspire to conquer the samsaric manifestations of sex and death. In a somewhat different manner, Vaishnavite folklore also makes abundant use of sexual

79

themes. For example, Krishna engages in numerous amorous adventures with cowherd girls. When he departs, the girls feel the agony of separation, symbolic of what we feel when God is absent from our lives. How can we be free from this worldly prison of self? "Love God," the Vaishnavite would reply; "lose yourself in devotion to Him." "Be as God," the Shaivite might answer; "as God is not bound by the chains of mortal self, rise above human limitations by means of rigorous mental and spiritual meditation."[56]

The polytheistic images of Hindu folklore appeal to different aspects of human personality. Each Hindu god and goddess portrays a different face of divine truth. As a cut diamond shows many flat surfaces, each of which has definition only in its relationship to the larger gem, so the many portrayals of God are united in Hindu polytheism. Hindus recall the parable of the blind men and the elephant in relating to their respective deities. Accordingly, they are tolerant of rival sects, acknowledging that each of them embodies a spiritual truth. However, disagreement occurs regarding which of these variants represents the highest insight.

## Shankara and Chaitanya

Western feminists have complained that the God of Judaism and Christianity traditionally has been given a male personality. Not content with mere protest, one American woman leader once advised a follower to pray to God and noted that She would provide. We have seen that while Hinduism generally portrays God as a male personality, it is also open to the idea that God is female. Kali, the Divine Mother, is worshipped by millions of Hindus as the Supreme Godhead. By contrast, the Muslim's Allah is a male figure, and, according to Christianity, God incarnated Himself as a male human being to communicate more fully His redemptive message.

This worldwide concern over God's gender has raised an important question: Is it appropriate to conceive of God in such anthropomorphic terms? One version of Hinduism has argued that it is not. We have seen that as early as the Upanishads, the Hindu mind conceived of God as beyond both personality and gender. The God of Atman/Brahman was defined as Tranquility and Bliss rather than as Father, Mother or Son. This impersonal conception of God waited until the end of the 8th century A.D. for its full development on the

Indian subcontinent. At that time, a philosopher named Shankara would construct a system based on Upanishadic thinking. It would describe not only the nature of God but also of ourselves and all of God's creation. The name of Shankara's philosophy is Advaita Vedanta.

Vendanta means the "end of the Vedas," or ultimate knowledge; advaita means philosophical monism, or the notion that reality cannot be divided into this or that, or you and me and God. Shankara argued that all that exists is God, and that the only part of us that really exists is God, and is called Atman. Hindus had earlier conceived of the individual soul, which they called the jiva. The jiva or soul has both personality and consciousness of its separate existence. The Atman has neither of these attributes and remains unrealized as long as the individual identifies with his jiva. The jiva is the bundle of karma that transmigrates from body to body as long as the individual is mired in samsara. The Atman is what is realized when the seeker approaches moksha and leaves the illusion of samsara behind.

Shankara taught that the jiva, or what is called personality, is a most transitory thing, changing from decade to decade, year to year, and even moment to moment. Accordingly, he noted, it has no more real existence than a passing dream. Just as our physical bodies are in a state of constant change, whether due to growth or deterioration, our personalities also have no permanent existence. Therefore, Shankara preached that the notion of a permanent jiva or soul is an illusion that blocks true understanding. While our bodies and our personalities are not eternal, Shankara argued that deep within each of us is a divine spark, the Atman, beyond personality and individual consciousness, and that this spark is equivalent to God. Atman is Brahman.⁵⁷

Forms of Vedanta, other than Shankara's system, developed that allowed for a personal God. But Shankara's Vedanta became the most well-known, both in India and in the West. Consequently, the common definition of Vedanta came to be philosophical monism, or Advaita Vedanta. One idea central to this system is maya, a word deriving from the sanskrit root matr, meaning "to measure." Our words meter, material and matter have developed from this ancient Aryan word. The most simple definition of maya is "illusion," or the world of matter as an illusion. Shankara said that the world of this and that, of you and me, is maya.

What he meant was that the phenomenal world of our human perceptions, a world of divided, measured and separate realities, is not true.

Shankara built his philosophy on the obvious fact that nothing in this world has an independent existence. Every "thing," including our own selves, has definition only in relation to other things. Am I rich? I am, if compared to a community of landless, exploited peasants. I am not, if transported into the inner circles of American capitalism's most exclusive clubs. The definition of my social and economic status is thereby dependent upon others. Were this single example multiplied concerning every aspect of my existence, it could be demonstrated that the entity called "me" is in fact illusory, for there is no "me" apart from my surrounding environment. "No man is an island," said the poet. Consequently, can we say that any person really is?

Shankara taught that we live our day-to-day lives assuming that things, ourselves included, really have independent existence. Every selfish craving is founded upon this misconception. We strive for individual happiness, irrespective of whatever misery others may suffer around us. We believe that each is separate and exists apart. This separateness is an illusion, yet we behave much as a man at twilight dimly mistaking a coiled rope for a snake. For us the illusion is real. Our very language demonstrates this fundamental ignorance. It differentiates between this and that and you and me and God. We refer to waves, as if they are separate entities, and yet we know that they have no independent existence apart from the ocean. In fact, a wave is a most transitory (even illusory) entity, yet the separateness of the word used to describe that oceanic phenomenon subtly persuades us that waves do in fact exist in and of themselves. Shankara emphasized that we have no real existence apart from God and that each jiva is no more independent from God than a wave from the ocean.

Using another analogy, Shankara taught that every seemingly definable aspect of reality is no more independent from God than a slip knot is from the rope used in making it. Correspondingly, as the rope is the only substantial part of a slip knot, Atman is the only substantial or real part of ourselves. The rest is maya. A traditional Jew or Christian might see the Vedantist identification of God and man as blasphemous. On the other hand, Vendantists view the Western

82

conception of God as an entity separated from mankind as idolatrous. While the conception of God as a male personality (or a female personality for that matter) may be only a mental idol, it is an idol nonetheless. A Vendantist sees no sharp differences between worshippers of a personal God and primitives bowing before a golden calf.

Why is it so difficult to see reality as Shankara described it? Intellectually, we can understand that seemingly separate objects are ultimately bound together in a total scheme, yet our "common-sense" perceptions are otherwise. What explains this discrepancy? Shankara provided no easy answer. He did not hold Brahman responsible for the pain of samsara; that, he saw as our fault, our ignorance, our karma. Yet, why were we created ignorant? A Vedantist would note that this very question is based on the false assumption of God as a divine personality existing apart from beings of His own creation. In an uncharacteristic moment, Shankara unwittingly encouraged such a conception by calling Brahman the great magician, the creator of maya. This vision contradicts the main thrust of Shankara's teaching, which portrays Brahman as intentionless, pure knowledge. According to Vendanta, pain is maya or not ultimately real. To find who or what created something that is non-existent constitutes an empty search. Rather, our guide lies in gaining understanding of God's true nature. No rational person would pray to a mathematical equation for its solution. Similarly, Vedantists argue, people of a religious bent should not seek gifts from heaven. Rather, they should think through that which constitutes ultimate reality. The necessary process is one of intense meditation and mental concentration, not wordy supplications to a heavenly monarch.

A careful examination of language is important in training the mind out of ignorant habits. Vendantists are often called monists, yet they object to the term, preferring to be called non-dualists. The word "monist" suggests oneness or one. Correspondingly, one suggests two, and two implies yet a third number. Before we are aware of what is happening, our use of the word monist teases our minds to think in terms of differentiated, divided reality, or maya. By contrast, the negating quality of the word "non-dualist" leads the mind away from its tendency to define and measure. Hopefully, through such careful word choice and intense mental effort, the seeker comes to realize that there is no difference between the understander and the understanding, between subject and object, and that Atman/Brahman is all in all.[58]

Most Hindus have trouble accepting Shankara's Vedanta, which appeals only to those of a strong intellectual and contemplative bent. Accordingly, wide circulation is given to stories that mock Vedantist theology. One such tale concerns the maya concept. Once upon a time, the story goes, a Vendantist guru taught a powerful prince about maya. The prince was skeptical and decided to test his master's convictions. One day, when the guru was strolling through the palace grounds, the prince released a wild elephant in his vicinity. Upon seeing the charging elephant, the holy man ran for his life, ultimately climbing a tall tree to escape. Later, the prince asked his teacher why he ran, if the elephant was just an illusion. The guru replied that everything that the prince saw was maya, including the guru running for his life.

Another Indian tale, this one ridiculing the Atman/Brahman concept, proceeds as follows: Once upon a time, a Vedantist guru inspired his student with the notion of Atman/Brahman. The student left with a new wonder that he had God within him. Walking into the street, he saw a herd of elephants coming toward him. He told himself, "I have nothing to fear; I am God; the lead elephant is also God; God would not hurt God." Just then, the elephant herder interrupted his musing by shouting, "Get out of the way, you idiot!" The lead elephant then hit the student with his trunk, throwing him to the side of the road. Later, the student asked his guru why the incident occurred if the conception of Atman/Brahman was true. The holy man responded: "Why did you fail to heed the word of God telling you to get out of the way?"[59]

Lest we dismiss Shankara's thought with cynical smiles, it should be emphasized that Advaita Vedanta does not try to prove that we, as distinct and fallible personalities, are God. Rather, Shankara's Vedanta seeks to reduce ego until the latter ceases to obstruct God. For the Vedantist, moksha, or final liberation consists of the merger of individual consciousness into Supreme Consciousness or Brahman, similar to a drop of water returning to the ocean. The Vedantist teaches that my world of self has no independent existence and therefore is not ultimately real. All that exists is God or Brahman.

All of the world's great religions seek to minimize self or ego. The way of Shankara's Vedanta is through intellectualizing upon abstract principles. For most people, this is not a satisfying path. Most people, East or West, can attack the problems of self only by engaging emotions, which reach to the very core of human existence. Consequently, the Hasidic Jew fervently praises God with every daily act; the devout Christian loves Jesus for having saved his life; and the devotee of Lord Krishna chants ecstatic praises to the Supreme Godhead. Most people need to worship a God separate from themselves to reduce their own sense of self-importance. For most people, the painful world of self can be overcome only through adoration, or emotion directed away from self.

Representative of this more common religious expression in Hinduism is bhakti, or devotional worship of a personal God. Bhakti's most famous expositor was Chaitanya, who lived in Bengal from 1486 to 1530 A.D. As Shankara based his religious philosophy upon the ancient Upanishads, Chaitanya was inspired by the Bhagavad-gita, a Sanskrit treatise from the second century B.C. The Bhagavad-gita consists of a dialogue between Krishna, an avatar of Vishnu, and a human devotee named Arjuna. Their conversation concludes with the insight that the easiest way for most persons to find God is through worship of Him as a being apart from themselves, a being with personality. Chaitanya agreed. His soul cried out in devotional worship, and he and his disciples sang and danced ecstatically. They rolled on the ground, laughed, cried, and became senseless in a sea of emotional, religious fervor. The object of their devotion was Lord Krishna, the Supreme Personality.[60]

Bhakti is most closely associated with worship of Vishnu (Krishna), although Shaivite bhakti expressions are not unknown, especially in southern India. Shankara's Vedanta—cold, abstract and austere in comparison to Chaitanya's faith—is commonly regarded as an intellectual offshoot from the Shaivite tradition. While generally tolerant of each other, bhakti Hindus and Advaita Vedantists do disagree which of the two represents the highest truth. We have already reviewed the Vedantic critique of the portrayal of God as a divine personality. For their part, Bhaktas (followers of bhakti) see potential danger in Shankara's philosophy. Specifically, they fear that it misleads some to an enhanced egoism, which results from the idea that God is within them. Chaitanya agreed with Shankara that we are not independent of God. But rather than claiming identity with Him, Chaitanya argued that we are dependent, as an adjective is dependent upon a noun. Krishna's creation is dependent upon Him. Consequently, we have no meaning apart from Him. Chaitanya acted out his theology, keeping in nearly constant communion with Krishna's life-giving love.

Because of bhakti's emphasis upon love and salvation, some scholars have speculated that possibly it was inspired by Christianity. Others have criticized this thesis, noting that the Bhagavad-gita antedates Christianity.[61] Nonetheless, a case can be made for Christianity's influence, albeit an indirect one, on the full flowering of bhakti worship in India. All scholars acknowledge the influence of Sufism, or Islamic devotional mysticism, upon Chaitanya and his bhakti movement. This contact resulted from Islamic military penetration of the Indian subcontinent, which began in about 1000 A.D. Within Islam, Sufism was greatly inspired by the example of Jesus of Nazareth. Accordingly, through Sufism, Jesus's love indirectly encouraged the further development of bhakti within Hinduism. It should also be acknowledged that Sufism was enriched by its interaction with Hinduism. Similarly, charismatic Christianity in our own day owes much of its inspiration to the example of Hare Krishna bhakti devotees. All in all, human religious development owes a debt to each of the world's great religions.

With the introduction of Islam into India, many low caste Hindus and untouchables converted to the new faith if for no other reason than to enjoy higher social status. Hinduism responded to this challenge in several ways. One was to retreat behind caste barriers. Interestingly, the rigorous systematizing of caste law occurred only after Islamic proselytizing threatened to undermine traditional caste dharma. A Hindu response leading in quite the opposite direction was the blossoming of bhakti itself. Chaitanya found the Muslim emphasis on the brotherhood of all believers attractive. Accordingly, he taught that as all persons are united with God in love, there should be no distinctions among them, and he refused to observe caste discriminations.[62] This fact has encouraged the export of his brand of Hinduism in modern times. It is known in the West as Hare Krishna, the first example of Westerners celebrating oriental religion on their cities' streets since the decline of the Roman empire.

In disregarding the caste system, Chaitanya was faced with a philosophical challenge. How would he treat the karma theodicy, the traditional justification of caste differences? In many ways, the karma concept is at the core of the Indian world view, yet it ran counter to the essential thrust of Chaitanya's teaching. For Chaitanya, the ultimate cause of salvation was not one's works, or karma, but rather God's grace, called prasada by Bhaktas. Prasada is an act of divine love. Karma is the result of individual merit. Bhaktas have attempted to combine the two ideas, much as St. Augustine did with free will and predestination in Christianity. For example, some of Chaitanya's followers have argued that God saves humans from samsara as a mother ape carries its young: A mother ape holds its offspring that simultaneously clings to its mother. In short, one can contribute to his own salvation by earning good karma, yet that salvation could not occur without the grace of God. This ape analogy has been popular among the Bhaktas of northern India. On the other hand, those of southern India have conceded the unresolvable nature of the conflict between karma and prasada. Consequently, they use the analogy of a cat carrying its young: A mother cat carries a kitten by the scruff of its neck, with no assistance from its offspring. In short, their view is that salvation is the work of God alone.[63]

As noted earlier, tolerance helps bind contradictory ideas such as karma and prasada to the same ancient tradition. The Hindu mind has a talent for resolving seemingly unresolvable differences. For example, the Hindu poet Tulsidas once wrote: "There is no difference between the Personal (Krishna) and the Impersonal (Brahman)....He who is impersonal, without form and unborn becomes personal for love of His devotees. But how is it that the Impersonal could become Personal? Just as water transformed itself into ice."[64] Despite often holding contradictory religious perceptions, Hindus appreciate their common goal: moksha, or liberation from samsara, the endless cycle of rebirths. Further, all of Hinduism's different forms of expression devalue the world to a greater extent than do Western religions. The latter tend to emphasize this world as a battleground between the forces of good and evil. By contrast, Hindus ultimately look beyond the human categories of good and evil to God.[65] To Western observers, this often appears socially irresponsible or escapist. To traditional Hindus, their religion is oriented to

87

spiritual truths, in contrast to what they see as the
materialism of the West.


NOTES


1. A.C. Clayton, The Rig-Veda and Vedic Religion,
With Readings from the Vedas (London, 1913), p. 3;
Zenaide A. Ragozin, The Story of Vedic India, As
Embodied Principally in the Rig-Veda (New York, 1895),
p. 72; Max Weber, The Sociology of Religion (New York,
1958), pp. 169-173, 177; J.L. Brockington, The Sacred
Thread, Hinduism in its Continuity and Diversity
(Edinburgh, 1981), p.7.

2. Weber, The Religion of India (New York, 1958),
pp. 132-133, 152; V.S. Naipaul, India, A Wounded
Civilization (New York, 1976), p. 191; James A. Kirk,
Stories of the Hindus, An Introduction Through Texts
and Interpretation (New York, 1972), p. xiv; Jean
Varenne (Derek Coltman, trans.), Yoga and the Hindu
Tradition (Chicago, 1976), pp. 19, 179.

3. Clayton, Rig-Veda, pp. 51, 77; R.C. Majumdar,
ed., The History and Culture of the Indian People (11
vols.; Bombay, 1951-1969), I (The Vedic Age), 365;
Ragozin, Vedic India, p. 167; A.L. Basham, The Wonder
That Was India (New York, 1954), pp. 233-235.

4. Majumdar, ed., The Vedic Age, p. 368; Ragozin,
Vedic India, p. 146; Weber, Sociology of Religion, p.
26; Basham, Wonder That Was India, p. 241.

5. Nirad C. Chaudhuri, Hinduism, A Religion to
Live By (New York, 1979), p. 76; Majumdar, ed., The
Vedic Age, pp 331, 375-379; Sir William W. Hunter, A
Brief History of the Indian Peoples (Oxford, 1907), pp.
101-103.

6. Ragozin, Vedic India, p. 174.

7. Clayton, Rig- Veda, p. 85; Basham, Wonder That
Was India, p. 239; Ragozin, Vedic India, pp. 179-185,
388, 391, 393.

8. Chaudhuri, Hinduism, pp. 152-153; Majumdar,
ed., The Vedic Age, pp. 229, 447, 472-473, 498; Paul
David Devanandan, The Concept of Maya, An Essay in
Historical Survey of the Hindu Theory of the World With
Special Reference to the Vedanta (London, 1950), pp.

31-32.

9. Christopher Isherwood, ed., Vedanta for the Western World (Hollywood, 1948), p. 163; Robert E. Hume, ed., The Thirteen Principal Upanishads, Translated from the Sanskrit (Madras, 1931), pp. 142-144, 366-369; Donald H. Bishop, ed., Indian Thought, An Introduction (New York, 1975), pp. 38-39; Basham, Wonder That Was India, pp. 250-254.

10. Alain Danielou, Hindu Polytheism, (New York, 1964), pp. 174, 350, 353; Robert E. Ornstein, The Psychology of Consciousness (New York, 1977), pp. 163, 165, 171; John Blofeld, The Tantric Mysticism of Tibet (New York, 1970), pp. 88-89; Ajit Mookerjee and Madhu Khanna, The Tantric Way: Art, Science, Ritual (Boston, 1977), pp. 34-35.

11. Varenne, Yoga, Hindu Tradition, p. 19.

12. Ibid., p. 47; Geoffrey Parrinder, Upanishads, Gita and Bible (New York, 1962), pp. 63-64.

13. Louis Renou, ed., Hinduism (New York, 1962), p. 117.

14. J.H. Hutton, Caste in India, Its Nature, Function, and Origins (London, 1969), pp. 126-127; Ananda K. Coomaraswamy, The Dance of Shiva (New York, 1957), p. 13; Bishop, ed., Indian Thought, p. 66; Michael Edwardes, A History of India, From Earliest Times to the Present (New York, 1961), pp. 254-255; Naipaul, India, p. 142; Weber, Religion of India, pp. 144-146, 172.

15. Chaudhuri, Hinduism, pp. 198-199, 205-206; Weber, Religion of India, p. 43.

16. Clayton, Rig-Veda, pp. 13-14; Hutton, Caste in India, p. 158.

17. Erik H. Erickson, Gandhi's Truth, On the Origins of Militant Non-Violence (New York, 1969), pp. 110, 120-122; Varenne, Yoga, Hindu Tradition, p. 65; Vern L. Bullough, Sexual Variance in Society and History (New York, 1976), pp. 255-273; Cornelia Dimmitt and J.A.B. van Buitenen (eds. and trans.), Classical Hindu Mythology, A Reader in the Sanskrit Puranas (Philadelphia, 1978), pp. 258-262; Isherwood, ed., Vedanta, p. 331; Mookerjee and Khanna, The Tantric Way, p. 9; Philip Rawson, Tantra, The Indian Cult of Ecstasy

(New York, 1973), pp. 7-30; R.C. Majumdar, ed., The History and Culture of the Indian People (11 vols.; Bombay, 1951-1969), IV (The Age of Imperial Kanauj), 315-316.

18. Celestin Bougle (D.F. Pocock, trans.), Essays on the Caste System (Cambridge, England, 1971), p. 91; Sarvepalli Radhakrishnan and Charles A. Moore, eds., A Source Book in Indian Philosophy (Princeton, 1957), p. 180; Basham, Wonder That Was India, pp. 146-147, 166-167, 182; Weber, Religion of India, pp. 41-42.

19. Clayton, Rig-Veda, pp. 12-13; Edwardes, History of India, pp. 128, 255; Zaehner, Hinduism, pp. 146-147, 199; M.N. Srinivas, Caste in Modern India and Other Essays, (Bombay, 1962). p. 47; Basham, Wonder That Was India, p. 188.

20. Varenne, Yoga, Hindu Tradition, pp. 64-65.

21. Chaudhuri, Hinduism, pp. 201-203; Mookerjee and Khanna,Tantric Way, p. 120; Naipaul, India, p. 119; Basham, Wonder That Was India, p. 490.

22. Renou, ed., Hinduism, p. 128.

23. Majumdar, ed., The Age of Imperial Kanauj, p. 356; Basham, Wonder That Was India, p. 243; Huston Smith, The Religions of Man (New York, 1958), p. 27.

24. R.C. Zaehner, Hinduism (London, 1962), pp. 77-78; Isherwood, ed., Vedanta, pp. 11-12.

25. Bhagavad-gita, 3:33; Coomaraswamy, Dance of Shiva, pp. 11, 130; Blofeld, Tantric Mysticism, p. 80; Bishop, ed., Indian Thought, pp. 202, 349, 382; Hermann Hesse, Siddartha (New York, 1951), pp. 80-81; Smith, Religions of Man, p. 17; Weber, Religion of India, pp. 183-184; Brockington, The Sacred Thread, p. 3.

26. Danielou, Hindu Polytheism, pp. 313, 369-370; Matthew 5:27-28; Zaehner, Hinduism, p. 217; Heinrich Zimmer, Philosophies of India (New York, 1951), pp. 38-39; Basham, Wonder That Was India, pp. 170-171, 361-362.

27. Jules H. Masserman and J.L. Moreno, eds., Progress in Psychotherapy (5 vols., New York, 1957), II, 199; Louis Renou, ed., Hinduism (New York, 1962), p. 197; Isherwood, ed., Vedanta, p. 95.

28. Will Durant, The Story of Philosophy, The Lives and Opinions of the Great Philosophers of the Western World (New York, 1926), p. 172.

29. Varenne, Yoga, Hindu Tradition, p. 67; Bishop, ed., Indian Thought, pp. 270, 364-365; Weber, Religion of India, p. 121; Smith, Religions of Man, p. 68; Naipaul, India, pp. 19, 57; K.N. Jayalilleke, The Message of the Buddha, (New York, 1974), pp. 142-195; Parrinder, Upanishads, Gita and Bible, p. 108.

30. Alan Watts, Nature, Man and Woman (New York, 1958), pp. 51-52; Bishop, ed., Indian Thought, pp. 222, 265; Isherwood, ed., Vedanta, pp. 61, 348.

31. Zimmer, Philosophies of India, pp. 441, 444-445; G.S. Ghurye, Caste and Race in India (Bombay, 1969), p. 89; Varenne, Yoga, Hindu Tradition, p. 67; A.C. Bhaktivedanta Swami Prabhupada, ed., Bhagavad-gita As It Is (New York, 1968), p. 60.

32. Andre Beteille, Castes: Old and New, Essays in Social Structure and Social Stratification (Bombay, 1969), pp. 40-43; Hutton, Caste in India, pp. 2, 47, 149; Edwardes, History of India, p. 27; Majumdar, ed., The Vedic Age, p. 454; Basham, Wonder That Was India, p. 137.

33. Ghurye, Caste and Race, pp. 172-173; Chaudhuri, Hinduism, p. 82; Zaehner, Hinduism, p. 142.

34. Hutton, Caste in India, p. 191; Bougle, Essays, p. 103.

35. Srinivas, Caste, pp. 7-8, 54-55, 57, 65-66, 69; Beteille, Castes, p. 116; James Silverberg, ed., Social Mobility in the Caste System in India, An Interdisciplinary Symposium (The Hague, 1968), pp. 33-34, 72-73, 91, 99, 122; Ghurye, Caste and Race, p. 176; Weber, Religion in India, p. 16.

36. Bougle, Essays, pp. 20, 150; Hutton, Caste in India, pp. 71-72, 88, 136, 139; Chaudhuri, Hinduism, p. 195; Bishop, ed., Indian Thought, p. 198; Srinivas, Caste, pp. 66-67, 153; Beteille, Castes, p. 91; Coomaraswamy, Dance of Shiva, p. 16.

37. Sir William W. Hunter, A Brief History of the Indian Peoples (Oxford, 1907), p. 98; Srinivas, Caste, p. 70; Naipaul, India, pp. 187-188; Weber, Sociology of Religion, pp. 42-43.

38. Bishop, ed., Indian Thought, pp. 364-365, 375; Bougle, Essays, p. 165; Coomaraswamy, Dance of Shiva, p. 51; Heinrich Zimmer, Philosophies of India (New York,1951), pp. 172-173; Weber, Religion of India, p. 122; Naipaul, India, pp. 107-109.

39. Zaehner, Hinduism, pp. 145, 148-150; Radhakrishnan and Moore, ed., A Source Book, pp. 174-191; Hutton, Caste in India, p. 93; Srinivas, Caste, p. 152; Bishop, ed., Indian Thought, p. 206; Basham, Wonder That Was India, pp. 137, 158-159, 161, 175; Satsvarupa dasa Gosvami, ed., Readings in Vedic Literature, The Tradition Speaks for Itself (Los Angeles,1977), pp. 66, 68-69; Weber, Religion of India, p. 61

40. Varenne, Yoga, Hindu Tradition, pp. 94-97, 134-135, 181; Chaudhuri, Hinduism, pp. 142-143; Majumdar, ed., The Age of Imperial Kanauj, p. 358.

41. Erikson, Gandhi's Truth, p. 166; Zaehner, Hinduism, pp. 241-245; Basham, Wonder That Was India, p. 483; Naipaul, India, pp. 169-173, 182.

42. Ved Mehta, Mahatma Gandhi and His Apostles (New York, 1976), pp. 249-250; Bougle, Essays, p. 131.

43. Srinivas, Caste, pp. 72, 75; Beteille, Castes, p. 145; Newsweek, April 4, 1977, p. 35.

44. Beteille, Castes, pp. 94, 129; Hal Bridges, American Mysticism, From William James to Zen (Lakemont, Georgia, 1970), p. 73; Edwardes, History of India, p. 346; Renou, ed., Hinduism, pp. 228-229; Newsweek, January 30, 1978, p. 57; San Bernardino Sun-Telegram (California), Dec. 11, 1976, A-14; Prabhupada, ed., Gita As It Is, pp. 74-75, 165-166, 208-209; Gosvami, ed., Vedic Literature, p. 192.

45. Chaudhuri, Hinduism, pp. 146, 148-149; Bishop, ed., Indian Thought, pp. 95, 350; Zaehner, Hinduism, pp. 2, 10-11; Danielou, Hindu Polytheism (New York, 1964), p. 13.

46. Bishop, ed., Indian Thought, pp. 350, 379.

47. Gosvami, ed., Vedic Literature, p. 41; Prabhupada, ed., Gita As It Is, pp. 79-80, 135-136; Zimmer, Philosophies of India, p. 396.

48. Majumdar, ed., The Vedic Age, pp. 396, 465; Clayton, Rig-Veda, p. 9; Basham, Wonder That Was India, p. 195; Weber, Religion of India, (New York, 1958), p. 28.

49. Danielou, Hindu Polytheism, pp. 217-218; Basham, Wonder That Was India, pp. 307, 319; Brockington, The Sacred Thread, p. 28.

50. Danielou, Hindu Polytheism, pp. 149, 159, 214; Varenne, Yoga, Hindu Tradition, pp. 27-28; Dimmitt and van Buitenen, eds., Classical Hindu Mythology, pp. 149, 152; Chaudhuri, Hinduism, pp. 150, 230; Bullough, Sexual Variance, p. 248; Coomaraswamy, Dance of Shiva, p. 73; Prabhupada, ed., Gita As It Is, p. 101; Majumdar, ed., The Vedic Age, p. 191; Renou, ed., Hinduism, pp. 36-38, 167; Weber, Religion of India, pp. 298, 302-307, 311; Basham, Wonder That Was India, pp. 298, 301-304, 311-312.

51. Danielou, Hindu Polytheism, pp. 256, 273-274; Zaehner, Hinduism, p. 112; Chaudhuri, Hinduism, p. 150-151; Isherwood, ed., Vedanta, p. 15; Zimmer, Philosophies of India, pp. 378, 413.

52. Basham, Wonder That Was India, pp. 309-312.

53. Danielou, Hindu Polytheism, p. 272.

54. Zaehner, Hinduism, p. 139; Chaudhuri, Hinduism, p. 255; Danielou, Hindu Polytheism, pp. 180-181; Basham, Wonder That Was India, pp. 302-307, 371; Renou, ed., Hinduism, pp. 84-85; Prabhupada, ed., Gita As It Is, p. 69; Ainslee T. Embree, ed., The Hindu Tradition, Readings in Oriental Thought (New York, 1966), pp. 220-224; Brockington, The Sacred Thread, p. 68.

55. Prabhupada, ed., Gita As It Is, p. 154; Edward J. Thomas, The Life of Buddha as Legend and History (London, 1927), pp. 3-4; Basham, Wonder That Was India, pp. 85, 320-323; Weber, Religion of India, p. 121; Gosvami, ed., Vedic Literature, p. 33; Geoffrey Parrinder, Upanishads, Gita and Bible, A Comparative Study of Hindu and Christian Scriptures (New York, 1962), pp. 22-24, 29.

56. Danielou, Hindu Polytheism, pp. 217-220; Dimmitt and van Buitenen, eds., Classical Hindu Mythology, pp. 103-105, 150-151; Weber, Religion in India, p. 322.

57. Devanandan, Concept of Maya, pp. 85-86; Poola Tirupati Raju, The Philosophical Traditions of India (London, 1971), pp. 181-182; Eliot Deutsch and J.A.B. van Buitenen, eds., A Source Book of Advaita Vedanta (Honolulu, 1971), pp. 164, 176, 179-180, 191-192; Frederick H. Holck, Death and Eastern Thought, Understanding Death in Eastern Religions and Philosophies (New York, 1974), pp. 14-15.

58. Danielou, Hindu Polytheism, pp. 20-21, 29, 53-54; Zaehner, Hinduism, pp. 9, 96; Martin Buber (Maurice Friedman, ed., and trans.), The Origin and Meaning of Hasidism (New York, 1960), p. 185; Alan Watts, The Way of Zen (New York, 1957), pp. 39-41; Fritjof Capra, The Tao of Physics, An Exploration of the Parallels Between Modern Physics and Eastern Mysticism (Berkeley, 1975), pp. 88, 161, 202-203; Raju, Philosophical Traditions, p. 223; Varenne, Yoga, Hindu Tradition, p. 19; Isherwood, ed., Vedanta, pp. 5, 117, 187-188, 341; Bishop, ed., Indian Thought, pp. 157, 180-181, 294; Alan Watts,. Psychotherapy East and West (New York, 1961), p. 5; Weber, Religion of India, pp. 168-169; Parrinder, Upanishads, Gita and Bible, pp. 44-45; Zimmer, Philosophies of India, pp. 362-363, 575.

59. Zimmer, Philosophies of India, pp. 20, 22, 420.

60. Zaehner, Hinduism, pp. 127, 129-130; Devanandan, Concept of Maya, p. 175; Chaudhuri, Hinduism, pp. 257, 291; A.C. Bhaktivedanta Swami Prabhupada, ed., and trans., Sri Caitanya-Caritamrta of Krsnadasa Kaviraja Gosvami, Antya-Lila (5 vols., New York, 1975), V, 126-129; A.C. Bhaktivedanta Swami Prabhupada, ed., and trans., Sri Caitanya-Caritamrta of Krsnadasa Kaviraja Gosvami Madhya-Lila (9 vols., New York, 1975), I, 207-213; Radhakrishnan and Moore, eds., A Source Book, pp. 143-145; Smith, Religions of Man, pp. 36, 39; Gosvami, Vedic Literature, pp. 52-53, 57.

61. R.C. Majumdar, ed., The History and Culture of the Indian People (11 vols., Bombay, 1951-1969), VI (The Delhi Sultanate), 552-554; Zaehner, Hinduism, pp. 173, 182, 191; Srinivas, Caste, p. 157; Basham, Wonder that Was India, p. 330; Weber, Religion of India, p. 299.

62. Edwardes, History of India, p. 130; Zaehner, Hinduism, pp. 143, 180, 192-193; Bishop, ed., Indian Thought, pp. 280-281; Majumdar, ed., The Delhi Sultanate, p. 574.

63. Weber, Religion of India pp. 187, 309;
Parrinder, Upanishads, Gita and Bible, p. 98; Basham,
Wonder That Was India, p. 333.

64. Renou, ed., Hinduism, p. 220; Gosvami, ed.,
Vedic Literature, p. 24.

65. Zaehner, Hinduism, p. 217; J. Duncan M.
Derrett, Religion, Law and the State in India (New
York, 1968), p. 69; Parrinder, Upanishads, Gita and
Bible, pp. 56, 120-121; Prabhupada, ed., Gita As It Is,
p. 101.

## The Founding of the Middle Way

Buddhism began in India in the 6th century B.C.,
at the end of the Upanishadic period. Its founder was
of the Kshatriya caste, as were most of the authors of
the Upanishads. Like them, he found unsatisfying a
religion devoted to animal sacrifice and the
ritualistic consumption of soma. Like them, he thought
that common perceptions of "reality" are based on human
ignorance. More clearly than they, he exposed the
sources of that ignorance. In developing his system,
he rejected much of the terminology and categories of
the Upanishads. For example, his teaching would not be
couched in terms of Atman/Brahman. Nonetheless, his
view of ultimate truth, which he called nirvana, was
quite close to that of the Upanishadic reformers, so
much so that his own teaching may be seen as a
culmination of their efforts.[1]

The Buddhist nirvana, similar to the Upanishadic
Atman/Brahman, would necessarily lack precise
definition. It too would be described as "without
attributes," yet be characterized as "ultimate
tranquility and bliss." Unlike Atman/Brahman it would
not be translated as "God." Rather, nirvana would
represent a state of mind that one could achieve after
following a systematic, mind-clearing regimen. In
stark contrast to Vedic tradition, Buddhism would have
no room for speculations on the nature of God. At
least this would be so during the first centuries of
the new religion. Billed as more practical and
down-to-earth than either primitive Vedic religion or
its Upanishadic refinement, Buddhism's sole and direct
concern would be the elimination of human suffering.
During its first thousand years, the new religion would
out-compete traditional Indian religion for the best
minds of the subcontinent. In so doing, it would
contribute to the development of Hinduism itself, a
process that would finally result in the teachings of
Shankara.

[4] Similar to Christianity and unlike Hinduism,
Buddhism was founded by an historical individual. His
name was Siddartha Gautama of the Sakya clan. As a
prince of his people, he lived in luxury during his
formative years. According to legend, when he was born
in northern India in about 500 B.C., a seer predicted
that he would grow to be either a great king or a

97

religious leader.  His father, wanting to insure that
his son would never take an otherworldly path,
encouraged the boy to indulge in a life of pleasure.
He also tried to shield Siddartha from all ugliness, so
that his young mind would stay fixed in worldly
grooves.  Ironically, these efforts had the opposite
effect, for when as a young man Siddartha finally did
see examples of old age, sickness and death, they had a
shattering impact upon him.  Once introduced to these
realities, he could not again return to pleasure
seeking with a carefree heart.  He now found worldly
enjoyment as mere sugar coating to the pain and sorrow
that he saw as the essence of life.  And so, one night
he left his palace, bade a silent farewell to his
sleeping wife and young son, and went off to live in
the forest.  Twenty-nine years old, he began his search
by following the way of the Jains.[2]

At that time, a new religion was capturing the
imagination of northern India.  This faith, called
Jainism, was founded by an older contemporary of
Gautama named Vardhamana Mahavira.  Like Gautama, he
was a Kshatriya who had been raised in luxury in a
royal family.  Like Gautama, he had renounced pleasure
and sought enlightenment, which he found after
practicing severe asceticism for 12 years.  He was
proclaimed to be a Jina, or "conqueror," as he had
conquered ignorance and death.  Accordingly, his
followers were called Jaina, or "followers of the
Jina."  Jainism, which today has a scant million and a
half adherents, preaches that each of us has an eternal
soul, or jiva.  Unlike Hinduism, Jainism denies the
existence of any god, whether personal or impersonal.
Its program for enlightenment involves exhausting the
soul's karma through rigorous asceticism.  Some Jain
monks went naked in all seasons until the British
overlords of India outlawed this practice in the last
century.  To this day, the highest virtue that a Jain
can perform is slowly starving himself to death.  This
practice supposedly destroys all karma and frees the
soul to ascend to the highest heavens, there liberated
from the cycle of rebirth and death.

The Jains rejected the authority of the Brahmin
priests and regarded Vedic horse sacrifices as
producing bad karma.  Indeed, ahimsa (or non-violence
to all sentient beings) was carried to new extremes by
them.  Not only were horses not to be killed; special
care was to be taken not to harm even the smallest
insects.  To this day, Jains may be seen in India
gently sweeping a path before themselves as they walk,

so as not to step inadvertently on tiny unseen creatures. Jains have established hospitals for crickets with broken legs, and they drink water through a filter so as not to swallow and destroy microscopic beings. Clearly, the Jains take extreme positions in regard to their own ascetic practices and their unique interpretation of ahimsa.[3]

It was axiomatic in Gautama's day that if one were indeed serious in religious matters, he would follow the discipline of the Jains. The Brahmin priest caste had lost temporarily its moral authority by exhibiting signs of loving pleasure too much. Their practice of providing religious services primarily for the rich, those with sufficient resources to fund the horse sacrifices and soma ritual, had branded them as corrupt. Accordingly, Gautama chose the Jain path. For six years, he mortified his flesh, only to find himself no closer to enlightenment than when he began. Consequently, he renounced asceticism, but some of the Jain influence would remain with him even after he formed a rival religion. Specifically, Gautama would reject the authority of the Brahmins, would preach ahimsa (albeit a less thorough-going form than the Jains), and would pay no heed to the existence of personal or impersonal gods. Unlike the Jains, he would reject the concept of an eternal soul.[4]

Almost dying from his ascetic ordeal, Gautama concluded that this path was as false and superficial as the way of luxury in which he had been raised. Thereupon, he came to his first realization. Story tellers say that one day after having suffered acutely from his Jain regimen, he heard the following song: "'The string o'er stretched breaks, and the music flies; the string o'er slack is dumb and music dies; tune us the sitar neither low nor high.'" The message was clear: Neither self-mortification nor self-indulgence leads to enlightenment. Henceforth, Gautama would advocate what he would call "the middle way." His moderate system would allow the seeker sufficient energy to pursue truth while avoiding the snares of a pleasure-filled life.

Legend reports that one day Gautama sat beneath a tree and vowed not to budge until he received enlightenment. As he sat there in the lotus position, spiritual tempters in various forms tried to keep him from his goal. Fear of death appealed to his sense of self-preservation. Visions of beautiful women danced in his imagination, tempting him to return to worldly pleasures. All these obstacles were overcome, and that night he experienced the loss of ego which all of the world's great religions associate with ultimate truth. Thereafter, Siddartha Gautama would be known as the Buddha, or the enlightened one. In Sanskrit, the word budh means "to wake, to rise from sleep, to come to one's senses or regain consciousness." He would also be called Tathagata, or "one who has trodden" the path to truth.[5]

For his remaining 45 years, the Buddha encouraged others to follow his program of self-realization, which he described in terms of the Four Noble Truths and the Eightfold Path. The Four Noble Truths served as the foundation of his teaching. Simply stated, they proclaimed that 1) life is suffering, 2) craving is the cause of suffering, 3) elimination of craving brings an end to suffering, and 4) the way to overcome one's cravings is to follow the Eightfold Path.

As one student of Buddhism has written, "birth is suffering; age is suffering; death is suffering; contact with what we dislike is suffering; separation from what we like is suffering; failure to attain what we crave is suffering--in brief, all that makes bodily existence is suffering." Ancient Judaism, with its communal focus, taught that one should not covet his neighbor's goods. By contrast, the Buddha taught that one should not covet, irrespective of community good feelings or a presumed divine command to behave in a prescribed manner. He preached that coveting only brings sorrow to him who covets. Covetousness or craving is essentially insatiable. Alexander the Great conquered his known world but was not satisfied and yearned for more. Happiness is fleeting. The glow of a past accomplishment quickly fades as we set our goals higher still. An old Buddhist saying claims that "there is no fear for him who hath no wants." Buddha taught that total acceptance of what has been, what is, and that which shall be will eliminate suffering. Accordingly, he instructed his followers to be <u>bhikkus</u> or beggars living on alms, desiring no worldly goods or status.[6]

Buddhist teaching may be viewed as timid or noble, depending upon the perspective of the observer. For example, Sir Francis Bacon once commented on those who, like the Buddha, lived by the maxim, "Use not that you may not wish, wish not that you may not fear." Such cautious souls, he wrote, "make the life of man little more than a preparation and discipline for death, [and] it is impossible but the enemy must appear terrible when there is no end of the defense to be made against him." Christianity seeks to overcome fear of death with love. In contrast, the Buddha sought to conquer fear by eliminating its cause, not with the help of a divine savior but through the power of the mind to correct its own faults. The Buddhist enlightenment experience, called nirvana, literally means "to blow out" fear and its accompanying emotions of lust and hatred. It is to be achieved through a mental detachment from all human desires, including even those involving hearth and home. The Buddha taught that attachments to others (to mother, father, wife, husband, son and daughter) are to be avoided, for they breed sorrow. There is a story of a woman who came to the Buddha for comfort when her grandson died. The Buddha asked her if she would like to have as many grandchildren as there were people in a great city of that day. She eagerly replied that she would. He pointed out that every day of her life would then be filled with grief, for several were sure to die every day. He then gave her the following precept: "'Those who have a hundred dear ones have a hundred woes; those who have ninety dear ones have ninety woes...; those who have one dear one have one woe; those who hold nothing dear have no woe.'"[7]

We have seen that Hinduism also taught renunciation, albeit postponing its more extreme consequences until the latter stages of life. The Buddha's regimen was more thoroughgoing. His followers were to maintain lifelong celibacy in order to avoid the snares of both sexuality and family attachments. Consequently, the Buddha's teachings have been characterized as encouraging caution and safety to an excessive degree. On the other hand, his precepts may be seen as encouraging noble independence. Too often, dependency relationships and selfish motives masquerade as love and service to others. The Buddha recognized this and sought to attack the sorrow underlying all manifestations of human desperation. Similar to the Stoicism of the ancient West, his message was that life's challenges should be met with heroic independence.[8]

The Buddha's program was free of the superstition and irrationalities that he saw characterizing the Vedic religion of his day. He summed up his own view in his parable of the arrow: The only concern of a man pierced by an arrow should be to extract it. He should not waste precious time speculating on the identity of the person who shot it. Rather, he should directly confront the problem immediately at hand. The Buddha did not deny or affirm the existence of God or gods; he saw debate concerning their existence to be irrelevant for those caught in the pain of samsara. Here, like the Jains, he broke with Vedic tradition, albeit the Jains were more definite in their atheism. Also like the Jains, he rejected the secretiveness, luxury and corrupt privilege of the Brahmin caste. Again, as with the Jains, he opposed the Vedic sacrifices of horses as a cruel and barbaric ritual, and the success of his movement ultimately forced an end to this ancient practice. The Buddha also abandoned the Brahmin habit of using Sanskrit as the only language of religion. Sanskrit was largely unintelligible to the people. Accordingly, he insisted that his teachings be transmitted in the popular vernacular. He welcomed women as well as men as followers, and some of the former became nuns in his order. Buddhism would later incorporate much of Hinduism's prejudice against women, but to this day there is still room for nuns in Buddhist sects.

Buddhist monks were instructed to dress in simple ochre-colored garments, this being the traditional garb of criminals and social outcastes. This clothing signified that the monks were dead to the traditional social hierarchy and worldly values in general. As such they were freed from the world's limitations and attached to nothing. Having the attitude of leaving to the world that which was worldly, Buddhism was not oriented to reform the caste system. Accordingly, the Brahmanic system survived the era of Buddhist dominance in India. However, in one sense, Buddhism's approach to caste did bring significant social change. Buddhism, rather than Hinduism, became a successful, proselytizing religion largely because of the former's liberation from the bonds of caste. Buddhism became the first of the world's great religions to communicate its message effectively to peoples far from the boundaries of its native land. Indeed, today the world center of Buddhism is Japan, a fact due to the Buddha's attitude toward caste as much as any other single cause.

The Buddha told his followers, "Be ye lamps unto yourselves." By this he meant that they should not look to the heavens for their salvation but rather into the dynamics of their own thought processes. Eventually, some forms of Buddhism would later deify the Buddha and worship him as God dispensing grace.

102

Had Buddha himself been able to witness this subsequent transformation of his teaching, he surely would have scorned it as a perversion. He had founded a system of spiritual self-help, clearly a religion of works and not of faith. Nevertheless, upon his death in his eighties, the Buddha's ashes were distributed to various stupas or burial shrines. Buddhist devotees made pilgrimages to these shrines. It was then but a short step to deifying the object of these pilgrimages. Nonetheless, this development had not been encouraged by the historical Buddha, who had preached that salvation did not derive from any supernatural source. He had sought to found a "middle way," between the poles of luxury and asceticism, and between secularism and theism as well. His way was utilitarian, concentrating solely on the source of psychic pain and the means to overcome it.[11]

## A Program for Enlightenment

Siddartha Gautama spoke in terms of Four Noble Truths and an Eightfold Path. His Four Noble Truths identified envy, covetousness and craving as the sources of human suffering. His Eightfold Path showed the way out of such misery. He advised his followers that a proper supporting environment was needed to implement this program for enlightenment. Just as a wild elephant is tamed by being yoked to a trained elephant, the Buddhist novice learns the eight steps to enlightenment under the direction of a master in the sangha or Buddhist monasterial order. The Buddha taught that those wishing to follow his program should become monks or nuns, shave head and eyebrows to begin the necessary relinquishment of this world's vanities, and don the ochre-colored robes of an outcaste. Thereupon, training for enlightenment could begin.

He called the first of his steps "right knowledge." By this, he meant that the novice must first intellectually accept the truth of the Buddhist program. He did not want his followers to accept his teaching on blind faith. Rather, they should first weigh the utility of this program as a rational, objective endeavor. Along these lines, the Buddha taught the parable of the elephant seeking its escape. When an elephant finds himself in danger, he cautiously tests whether an apparent path of escape will bear his weight. He does not rush blindly forward. An elephant never acts upon untested faith, and the Buddha urged that we operate in a similar manner.

Lest the dichotomy of faith and reason be overdrawn, it should be noted that elements of faith were indeed present in the Buddha's program. For example, he taught that human nature is essentially flawless, perfect and whole. Indeed, fully realizing this "truth" in one's own life is what constitutes the Buddhist enlightenment experience. Clearly, Buddhist belief on this score is in stark contrast to Christianity's darker portrayal of humanity. Similar to all other great religions, Buddhism does posit certain assumptions which neither can be scientifically proven nor disproven. At the outset of the Buddhist program, the novice is asked to ponder the Buddhist assumptions, weighing their validity on the scales of personal experience. As the Buddha taught that each person was a lamp unto himself, no external authority is called forth to proclaim the truth of Buddhist teaching. In Buddhism, that authority can only come from within each believer. [12]

As soon as one has decided that Buddhism makes good sense, then he should set his heart on accomplishing enlightenment. This commences the second step of "right aspiration." The Buddha knew that great achievements never occur unless one strives for the goal with firm determination. And so, while the first step amounts to thinking the matter over, the second step consists of resolving to undertake the Buddha's program. In turn, the program only truly begins to be acted on with the third step of "right speech." The Buddha taught that we largely define ourselves by our speech. If we gossip or lie, we are negatively shaped by that behavior. Conversely, reforming negative habits of speech can create a new reality. He taught that speech should be true. He also insisted that it should be useful and that one should not engage in idle chatter. The Buddhist program advocates that when one has nothing to say that will contribute to his own or another's enlightenment, he should practice silence. "Learn this of the waters," said the Buddha, "loud splatters the streamlet, the ocean's depths are silent." [13] In teaching "right speech," he began to advocate the sober behavior that would be more fully developed in subsequent steps of his ego-reduction program.

In the fourth step of "right behavior," the Buddha urged his followers not to be lazy, to spend a minimum of time sleeping, to eat only one meal a day, and to invest most of their time in meditation. His purpose here was to starve and exhaust human selfishness. To

104

outward appearance, a Buddhist monk leads a very drab life. He must do nothing frivolous, such as dancing or listening to music. As we have seen, he should spend much of his day in silence. If one so alters his behavioral patterns, the Buddha taught, he will find his mind gradually transcending all worldly concerns. Experience shows that for better or worse, one is transformed by his own overt behavior. The young man who unthinkingly performs illegal acts comes to think like a criminal and is hardened into this mold. On the other hand, a person who chooses to perform deeds of a selfless nature is gradually uplifted by that behavior.[14]

The Eightfold Path consists of various groupings of steps. Specifically, the first two steps of "right knowledge" and "right aspiration" are concerned with intellectual understanding of the Buddhist program, whereas the next several steps are devoted to moral training. This latter purpose characterizes "right speech" and "right behavior," as well as the fifth step of "right livelihood," which in fact is little more than an extension of "right behavior." In this fifth step, Buddhism urges that occupations that serve to retard spiritual progress be avoided. The Buddha was especially concerned that his followers not raise livestock. He did not worry that they might be musicians or dancers, as he had earlier forbidden access to these professions. On the other hand, members of his order might have unthinkingly raised livestock among their daily chores unless otherwise instructed. Consequently, the Buddha warned of the bad karma resulting from the slaughter of animals. However, he taught that his followers could eat meat if donated by faithful laymen without negative karmic effect. Jains saw this as hypocrisy, but the Buddha viewed it as simply another facet of his "middle way" which avoided behavioral extremes.[15]

As the first two steps are concerned with intellectual understanding, and the next three, moral training, the remainder of the Eightfold Path involves meditation techniques. The first step in this last grouping is that of "right endeavor." Here the Buddha urged focusing the mind upon the goal of enlightenment so that this objective might govern every waking moment. Indeed, even when asleep the Buddhist should not lose sight of the desired end. In this step, the Buddha stressed that steady effort, not momentary, quick spurts, leads to enlightenment. The placement of this step is significant, for it follows in progression those which involve modification of one's external behavior and immediately preceeds the most difficult step of all, that of controlling one's very thoughts. The Buddhist needs to resolve to steady effort before undertaking this next most difficult step, that of "right mindfulness."

Imagine yourself having ventured through the first six steps of the Eightfold Path, having mastered your speech and, indeed, all outward behavior. Nevertheless, you know secret cravings that betray your real condition. Now in the step of "right mindfulness," you must directly confront these remaining passionate thoughts. One Buddhist method of doing so is that of concentrating the mind on those things that frighten, disgust and attract one the most. For example, there are "meditations on the foul," which involve sitting beside rotting human remains in order to overcome all craving associated with bodily appearances. The purpose of such meditations is to realize experientially that any and all objects of desire have no real permanence. Consequently, to suffer in hopes of possessing that which cannot truly be possessed is the height of ignorance. This is the essence of Buddhist teaching.[16]

The transitory quality of existence may be quickly accepted on an intellectual level. Each of us knows that death awaits us, that the appealing image of one who now attracts us will fade with time, that the accomplishments we strive for will not ultimately satisfy. Yet, we continue to live our daily lives dominated by the false assumptions that earthly immortality is ours and that we will live happily ever after if we achieve the current object of our desire. Buddhists use different metaphors to describe our foolish orientation: We "chase shadows" or "try to catch water in a sieve." The human body is a "burning house," yet we regard it as an eternal monument.[17] "Right mindfulness" consists of concentrating on the fluid character of those very forms which our ignorant egos claim are permanent. We define things or events as absolutely "good" or "bad" depending on our momentary perspective. These definitions too must dissolve under the glare of "right mindfulness."

Buddhist scripture reports: "All that we are is the result of what we have thought." One Buddhist story tells of two monks who were arguing one day about the nature of a pennant blowing in the wind. One claimed that the flag was in motion, while the other insisted that the wind was truly the active agent in the scene. A third monk then intervened and disclosed that the only things in motion were their minds. The goal of "right mindfulness" is to enable one to comprehend fully the truth of this story. Many of the teachings of Jesus of Nazareth are in harmony with the insights of "right mindfulness." For example, Jesus said that if one lusted in his mind to commit adultery it was as if he had performed the act itself. It appears that Jesus agreed with the Buddha that all that we are is what we think in our most private moments.[18]

The final step in the Buddha's program, that of "right absorption," represents the calm that follows the storm of confronting and defeating one's own, craving ego. This step is the Buddhist nirvana, a mental state of perfect equanimity. When asked to describe nirvana, the Buddha instead told his parable of the blind man. How could a sighted person, he said, describe color to a man who had been blind from birth? Accordingly, how can one mired in ignorance conceive of a state of consciousness in which all mental cravings have been extinguished? Nevertheless, sketchy descriptions of nirvana, which literally means "to extinguish," do exist. Some of these portray it as living completely in the present moment, without feelings of either anxiety over what might occur or regret for what has been. Nirvana is a state completely free from fear. The person in nirvana accepts everything, just as it is. He is conscious but is without a sense of his own individuality. He is marked by a sweetness of disposition and a gentle gaiety. He is not on his guard and is completely indifferent to his own personal comfort. For the person who reaches this awareness, the question of what happens after death is completely irrelevant, for he knows that the supposed entity called himself has no more existence than an illusory circle of flame made by a whirling torch.[19]

On one occasion, a sick, old man came to the Buddha seeking a cure for his physical ailments. The Buddha informed him that physical degeneration and suffering are inherent in the nature of material existence. However, he urged the old man to follow the Eightfold Path to become mentally whole. "Wherefore thus should you train yourself," the Buddha advised his petitioner: "Though my body is sick, my mind shall not be sick."[20] Look not to gods or God for your salvation, said the Buddha. Seek not life after death and survival of the ignorant ego, but rather discover life under your nose at this very moment. Complete peace is at hand. Follow the Eightfold Path and awaken to find a consciousness beyond craving and sorrow. This was the Buddha's message to the world.

## Buddhist Metaphysics

The Buddha emphasized the practicality of his program and scorned all theology as contributing not one whit to the easing of human suffering. Yet he could not avoid metaphysical speculation. Right mindfulness stressed the transitory character of life with the corollary that it makes no sense to crave that which has no real existence. This metaphysical view was designed to train the mind away from thoughts that inevitably breed sorrow and pain. The Buddha called his metaphysical position the dhamma, the Pali language's translation of dharma, a Sanskrit term. In Hinduism, dharma is defined as law or duty, and it is tied to the requirements of the caste system. Dharma or dhamma does not have this meaning in Buddhism.[21]

The Buddha's dhamma was his law of transitoriness. It did not teach that things are. Neither did it teach that things are not. Nor did it teach that they neither are nor are not. Any one of these possibilities was an extreme view in the Buddha's eyes and inharmonious with his "middle way." Everything, he claimed, is in the process of becoming; life is process, not substance; everything is impermanent, including the supposed substance called "me." We habitually think of ourselves as surviving from moment to moment, from year to year, and from decade to decade. Of all of our habits of mentally dividing and categorizing reality, we hold most dear the concept that self, ego, or soul does have real existence. The Buddha identified this mental habit as the root of our sorrow, and he offered his followers a different view of reality, which he taught in his parable of the chariot. The ignorant mind, he said, considers the self "to be" in the same sense that an unthinking glance at a chariot might convince one that this machine too is an entity. But, upon closer examination, one finds that this is not so. In truth, the chariot is a composition of bolts, wheels, an axle, springs and pieces of wood and metal of varying shapes. As a composition, it has no independent existence. The Buddha claimed that the human ego is like that chariot. It is composed of feelings, ideas, traits and values. Each component part, the Buddha proclaimed, alone has real existence. The composition of these various

108

entities is constantly being modified as new qualities are added and old ones discarded.

Which of us has maintained the same feelings, ideas, traits and values over a lifetime, let alone a year or a day? The Buddha taught, even with his dying breath, that "all compound things decay." With each of us, the Buddha emphasized, every moment sees a new composition, which is ignorantly referred to as "me" or "you," suggesting a continuity which in fact does not exist. By this view, what is death? If we accept the Buddha's dhamma, death certainly changes its definition, for he claimed that the composite entity that we wish to maintain after death in fact dies every second. This view is supported somewhat by modern biology, which informs us that not one of the cells composing any of our bodies seven years ago is still alive. Physically, each of us is a completely new creation every sabbatical year.[22]

We perceive that a river exists. Yet, at any one spot, a river does not contain the same drops of water from moment to moment. A river, similar to the supposed being called "me," is in an ever-changing state of becoming something new. The Buddha described how this process works in human life. First, an individual's thoughts and deeds cause karma, which in turn alter that person's character. The new man thus created makes new karma. And so the process goes, analogous to a river flowing to the sea. According to the Buddha's vision, an individual's consciousness and physical regeneration end with physical death, but his karma remains, much as Shakespeare's reference to the evil that men do that lives after them. At physical death, karma is passed as a flame is passed from one candle to another. What we commonly refer to as death, said the Buddha, does not stop the process of becoming, for death is as much a part of samsara as is birth. Death is not moksha, or liberation from sorrow. The craving that inevitably accompanies karma keeps human suffering alive. In this negative sense, the buddha saw survival after physical death. He rejected the Hindu and Jain notions of a jiva or soul surviving physical death to be housed in a new physical body. He saw no transference of such a substance at death. Rather, he described a process of causation that characterizes samsaric existence. One cannot speak of a flame burning on a new candle as being the same substance as that which burned on the candle that passed it. Accordingly, the soul of a dying man is not passed to his grandson. His karma alone is passed to his survivors in the form of shared values and traits.[23]

If craving is passed from life to life, what happens when desire is finally extinguished and nirvana is attained? The Buddha was disappointed by such questions, as they reflect an attachment to ego concerns that characterize the human problem. Accordingly, he refused to answer them. His metaphysical speculation about life being process rather than substance was designed to help his followers break ego attachments. His refusal to answer some speculative questions, while engaging in others, did not necessarily derive from his ignorance concerning the former. Rather, he refused to reinforce human craving by his own behavior and speech. He delved into metaphysical questions only to the extent that this activity might help his followers gain enlightenment. In his parable of the arrow, he urged mankind to focus attention on the problem at hand, that being the arrow of sorrow buried deep in human consciousness, causing daily grief. He cautioned against purposeless philosophizing about how the arrow got there, but rather urged work on its extraction. In his parable of the raft, he taught that any metaphysical speculation should be for practical purposes only. A man, he said, uses a raft to cross a river and then abandons it upon reaching the other shore. Similarly, he intended his speculations on the nature of being to be merely functional instruments used during the step of "right mindfulness." He considered of little import whether or not his metaphysical conclusions were eternally true. They were useful in helping to create the proper frame of mind to break the hold of ego on human thought. This utilitarian attitude would persuade later Buddhists to engage in metaphysical speculation contrary to the Buddha's if it promised to aid in the quest for enlightenment.[24]

A spiritual innovator named Nagarjuna, who lived in India roughly 700 years after the Buddha, was encouraged by Buddhism's utilitarian approach to metaphysical issues. Accordingly, he proposed a new metaphysical view of the nature of being which he claimed was truer to Buddhist goals than the metaphysical position ascribed to the Buddha himself. The Buddha had held out the goal of enlightenment and urged his followers to seek their own salvation. Here was an incongruity that did not miss the penetrating eye of Nagarjuna. How could a religion dedicated to the obliteration of selfishness advocate with such single-mindedness that its practitioners seek their own well-being to the exclusion of all others? Similarly, how could a religion dedicated to the elimination of human craving achieve its objective by encouraging a craving for enlightenment?

Nagarjuna realized better than perhaps even the Buddha himself that the metaphysical means used in the quest helped determine the end result. He began his effort to eliminate all traces of selfishness and ego-craving from Buddhist thought by emphasizing the relativity of all things and beings. Everything in existence, he taught, is without independent definition. This is an obvious truth, but one that the ego-oriented mind likes to suppress. In fact, nothing has definition apart from its context in relation to the whole. On our increasingly ecologically conscious planet, we know that an action in one part of the world often has unforeseen consequences elsewhere. In our own individual lives, we may also witness the interconnectedness of events. The husband who decides to devote most of his energies to his career later finds his marriage in trouble. Any one thing cannot be accomplished without consequences. Everything is interconnected. That which I call "myself" is not an independent disassociated entity. A primary goal of most sects of modern Buddhism is to have their followers experientially realize this perspective. This result may be credited largely to Nagarjuna.

The Buddha himself had sought to demolish self-centeredness by stressing that only the traits, values, ideas and feelings that contribute to the composite called ego have real existence. Nagarjuna took the opposite tack, seeing the reality only of the entire cosmos. In his metaphysical view, ego has no more existence than in the Buddha's system. In short, both metaphysical perspectives come to the same conclusion. However, by orienting the mind to the whole of life, Nagarjuna promoted brotherly love. Unfortunately, the Buddha's metaphysics had subtly encouraged a denial of the needs of others. Nagarjuna sought to change this pattern. Accordingly, he held up the spiritual progress of all of mankind as the proper goal of the seeker of enlightenment. As an individual has no independent existence, Nagarjuna thought of liberation from ignorance as having meaning only in relation to the spiritual emancipation of all sentient beings. After Nagarjuna, the goal of nirvana would be altered for most Buddhists.

The Buddha had preached a practical metaphysics, and Nagarjuna was true to his master's utilitarian attitude. Indeed, Nagarjuna's philosophical exploration into the nature of being was even more likely than the Buddha's own system to inspire the selflessness that is the essence of nirvana. He transformed the Buddhist concept of identity to include all of existence. Once achieved, this consciousness is naturally expressed as universal love. It freely accepts everything and everybody. It does not discriminate between this and that, between that which is desirable and undesirable. It sees everything as wondrous and of equal value. Such a consciousness sees samsara as equivalent to nirvana. Nagarjuna's thought inevitably led to this radical conclusion. Setting nirvana apart from ignorant existence, as the Buddha himself had done, made nirvana a goal, an object of craving, and therefore productive of sorrow. Accordingly, Nagarjuna eliminated this flaw in Buddhist logic.[25]

Nagarjuna's philosophy even made rejection of Buddhist teaching itself the highest expression of Buddhism. Craving is always manifested by attachment to a desired object, and one characteristic common to religious persons everywhere is their clinging to holy writ. Nagarjuna realized that this attachment was perhaps the most subtle of all. Zen Buddhism, which is in harmony with Nagarjuna's teaching, has urged its students to burn Buddhist scripture and destroy Buddhism's holy relics. In the fourth stage of life, Hinduism made rejection of its own norms the highest religious act. Indeed, any religion that truly devalues ego ultimately ends in seeking release even from its own teaching. The Buddha himself foresaw this possibility in his parable of the raft, in which he clearly stated that the means used for salvation were just that, and should never be confused as ends in themselves.[26]

Nagarjuna described the essence of reality as the Void. By this he meant that each thing is empty unto itself and is without independent definition. Yet, he said, the entire universe is contained in a single blade of grass, for everything is interconnected with it, ourselves included. Therefore, everything is simultaneously empty and full. The word used by Buddhists to describe this condition is tathata, "suchness," which connotes the identity of everything with myself and vice versa. The Buddha had used a word

112

with negative connotations, nirvana (meaning to extinguish), to describe ultimate reality. Nagarjuna described it as suchness or non-dualistic wholeness. The shift in emphasis was profound. Up until Nagarjuna, Buddhism justly could be charged with being escapist in nature. With Nagarjuna, it became incorporative, stressing that there is nothing in reality from which we can stand apart. All things and beings are interdependent, and all of life has only one identity and one life.[27]

In pure mind, said Nagarjuna, there is no difference between the knower and the known. His scheme had no room for subject or object or, for that matter, any divisions of any sort. The Hindu thinker Shankara later borrowed many of Nagarjuna's ideas, translating them into Upanishadic terminology. Both men preached a rigorous non-dualism. Nagarjuna spoke in terms of suchness, a concept that dissolved the differences between this and that. In turn, Shankara described the world of this and that, of subject and object, as maya or illusion. Nagarjuna saw the Buddha nature in all sentient beings, whereas Shankara saw the divine spark of God (Atman/Brahman) in every being. Living some six centuries after Nagarjuna, Shankara's revitalized Hinduism would help drive Buddhism from India. In part, this would happen by virtue of Shankara absorbing Buddhism's most refined metaphysical expression into the body of Hindu thought. With some justice, Shankara would be described by his enemies as merely a Buddhist in disguise.[28]

Nagarjuna found ultimate reality in the entire life of the cosmos. Lesser minds in the story of Buddhist development defined this abstract notion in terms of a deified Buddha. Indeed, even in the centuries before Nagarjuna, Buddhism was slowly transforming itself into a theistic religion. Greek influences, following Alexander the Great's invasion of the Indian subcontinent, encouraged this drift. Specifically, statues in the Greek style began to abound in India at the outset of the Christian era. Representations of the Buddha, along with those of Shiva and Vishnu, were openly worshipped as gods. Originally, portrayals of the Buddha's image had been regarded as sacrilegious, a belief encouraged by his teaching that the "self" has no real existence. However, this restriction was gradually forgotten. Subsequent centuries of pilgrimages to stupas, or shrines housing portions of the Buddha's ashes, heightened devotional feeling. Accordingly, in

113

Nagarjuna's day, which was in the second century of the Christian era, the Buddha began to be worshipped as a savior-god.[29] A popular religion oriented to the masses emerged. It drew upon Nagarjuna's speculative philosophy but was not confined to it. Nagarjuna had refined the metaphysical means necessary for the Buddha's original utilitarian purpose. The theistic, myth-ridden, devotional faith that would characterize much of Buddhism after Nagarjuna would have less in common with Buddhism's earliest message. However, this new form of Buddhism would influence greater numbers of the human family than had been reached heretofore. To that story, we now turn.

## Buddhism for the Masses

Theravada and Mahayana constitute the two principal Buddhist groupings in the world today. The Buddha's own metaphysical position is commonly associated with Theravada, which means "the way of the elders." By contrast, Nagarjuna's philosophy is identified with Mahayana, which means "the large raft." The names Theravada and Mahayana are symbolic. Theravada, "the way of the elders," suggests that it is the original, true version of Buddhism, the form practiced by the Buddha himself. The meaning of Mahayana, "the large raft," takes a little more explanation. In ancient India, bridges were non-existent. As mighty rivers cut the Indian landscape, ferryboats or rafts were an indispensable means of transportation. Interestingly, the Buddha referred to his own teaching as a raft that would take his followers from ignorance to enlightenment. The term Mahayana suggested that, unlike Theravada, Mahayana was big enough to carry most of mankind.[30] In any case, each of the two schools alone claimed to represent the Buddha's true intent.

Siddartha Gautama had taught that his followers should be bhikkus or wandering monks, resorting to the safety of a monastery only during the rainy season. A monk was to have few possessions, in fact, only a saffron-colored robe, a girdle, razor, needle, water strainer and a bowl with which to beg food. He was not to perform any priest-like functions, such as administering sacraments. His only goal in life was his own salvation. After the Buddha's death, bhikkus engaged less in wandering and increasingly became attached to monasteries, a development which came to characterize Theravada Buddhism. Theravada maintained the experiential aspect of the Buddha's message that

114

only those who live the Eightfold Path can achieve salvation. Oriented to the practicing monk, Theravadin existence is devoted to minimizing contact with the outside world. The role of the laity in this path is mainly to support the monks with gifts of food. However, Theravadin laymen often spend short periods in the monasteries to experience Buddhist teachings.[31]

Theravada developed strict rules to guide the life of a monk. These stated that a monk shall refrain from 1) harming living beings, 2) stealing, 3) sexual activity, 4) lying, 5) drinking alcohol, 6) eating after midday, 7) engaging in frivolous activity such as listening to music, dancing or attending the theater, 8) wearing perfume and/or jewelry, 9) sleeping in a comfortable bed and 10) receiving gifts of gold or silver. These rules apply equally to all within a monastery. Each Theravadin monastery identifies one monk as chief administrator, but he has no special privileges or binding authority over his brother monks. All monks are equal in that each seeks his own salvation alone. Their only real authority is the collection of guidelines, rules and precepts which they proudly trace back to the Buddha himself.[32]

Buddhism underwent minor changes in the first two centuries after the Buddha's death. Then, in the third century B.C., the religion caught the attention of Ashoka, king of all of India. Ashoka ascended the throne in about 270 B.C. and proceeded to unify virtually all of India by the sword. This bloody experience drove him in despair to become, temporarily at least, a Buddhist monk. Back on his throne, he proceeded to make Buddhism the favored religion in the land. True to the doctrine of ahimsa, he banned animal sacrifice, which had been a traditional part of Vedic practice. He also discouraged the slaughter of animals for food, giving vegetarianism a tremendous boost on the subcontinent. As Constantine the Great would later make Christianity the religious arm of his state, Ashoka demanded conformity in religious doctrine and punished dissenting monks by forcing them to wear white robes. Here was high irony. Saffron-colored robes had originally been chosen as these were the traditional garments of criminals and outcastes. This symbolism had communicated that Buddhists were beyond all worldly authority. Ashoka now bound Buddhism to that authority. Before Ashoka, nirvana had been Buddhism's highest goal, but the reclusive life of a Buddhist monk obviously could serve no state interest. As a worldly ruler, Ashoka wanted good citizens. Accordingly, he made the goal of a higher rebirth in the next round of samsara the chief Buddhist aim. This would encourage his subjects to lead ethical lives while remaining in the world. Apparently, the fact that this objective made no sense in Buddhism did not create a serious obstacle.

While compromising his adopted religion, Ashoka was intent on broadcasting his form of the Buddhist message throughout all of India and, indeed, the known world. He sent Buddhist missionaries as far west as the Mediterranean. Throughout India, he erected many more stupas, or shrines devoted to the Buddha, and further subdivided the Buddha's ashes among them. Buddhist laity and monks alike were encouraged to make devotional pilgrimages to these shrines. Rather than attempt to crush Hinduism, Ashoka pacified it. He commanded that Hinduism's Brahmin caste be shown reverence, even though such an edict had no foundation in Buddhist teaching and even contradicted it. Having thus flattered Hindu leadership into acquiescence, Ashoka sought to capture the public imagination for Buddhism. In addition to encouraging the stupa cult, he made cuttings from the fabled tree under which the Buddha achieved enlightenment and had them planted as far away as Ceylon (Sri Lanka).[33]

Less than a century before Ashoka, Alexander the Great had introduced Greek sculpture to the subcontinent. This art form would grow in popularity and later supplement Ashoka's efforts to popularize Buddhist religion. Several centuries after Ashoka, icons of the Buddha would be worshipped by India's masses. With these various influences, Buddhism was acquiring attributes that certainly would have been offensive to the historical Buddha. This new, devotional, theistic Buddhism would come to be called Mahayana.

Mahayana Buddhism came to be characterized by the following: 1) It deemphasized the historical Buddha, replacing him with a transcendent being who came to earth more as an apparition than a man. 2) In many of its sects, worship of an eternal, heavenly Buddha was encouraged. 3) Many Mahayana sects tended to stress salvation by grace, dispensed both by the heavenly Buddha and earth-bound holy men called bodhisattvas. 4) Belief in heavenly or hellish domains was also encouraged. 5) Finally, Mahayana promoted an eschatology that holds that Maitreya, an incarnation of the Buddha, will return at the end of time and inaugurate a new world.

Some forms of Mahayana, such as Zen, seem closer to Theravada in retaining the goal of achieving enlightenment in this life by disciplined, individual effort. Nonetheless, most Mahayanists are more oriented to otherworldly concerns typically associated with Christianity or Islam. It is possible that some western influences affected Mahayana belief and practice. On the other hand, much in Mahayana can be seen deriving from India's Hindu tradition, especially the bhakti developments associated with the composition of the Bhagavad Gita several centuries before Christ. Most people, the world over, have typically yearned for a salvation not earned through difficult effort but granted as a free gift. Mahayana, along with bhakti Hinduism, Christianity and Islam, has been most successful in addressing this need. Accordingly, Mahayanists have called Theravada "Hinayana," or the small raft, to indicate that this earlier form of Buddhism is capable of carrying only a limited portion of mankind. Nevertheless, Theravada remains the primary Buddhist expression in some countries, namely Sri Lanka, Burma, and other parts of southeast Asia.[34]

Mahayana came to full flower in India in the seventh century and remained dominant there until the death of Indian Buddhism in about 1300 A.D. Subsequently, it also became the principal form of Buddhism in China and Japan. Typically, Mahayana sects conduct a mission to help the poor, comfort the grieving and offer hope to the downtrodden. Mahayana's monks and nuns, while basically following Theravada's monastic precepts, are called to an additional role, that of serving the needs of mankind. Nagarjuna's metaphysics served to justify Mahayana's popular orientation to help those in need, as he had taught that an individual monk's self realization has no real meaning when viewed within the context of a suffering world. Instead of striving for nirvana, Mahayanist monks have typically aspired to the bodhisattva ideal. In Mahayanist terminology, a bodhisattva is one who in his search for enlightenment becomes a suffering servant for mankind. As a Mahayana seeker nears enlightenment, he should realize his identity with all of life, and from this awareness step back from entering nirvana to help all sentient beings toward the path of liberation. In this way, he becomes a bodhisattva. By contrast, a Theravadin aspires to be an arhat, or one who has achieved nirvana. Theravadins argue that when one successfully travels the Eightfold

117

Path, the process of retraining the mind out of its worldly ruts leads inexorably to nirvana. In short, it is impossible to step back from the brink of nirvana as Mahayanists allege. While Theravada leads its monks and nuns away from the world, Mahayanists are encouraged to go the opposite direction. Along these lines, Mahayana monks and even bodhisattvas might marry and sire children. Mahayanists do not shrink from life's experiences as the cautious Theravadins are prone to do. Acknowledging this violation of traditional Buddhist practice, one Mahayana apologist has written that "celibacy is not the whole of Buddhism."[35]

A bodhisattva may transfer his own surplus merit, earned in years of struggle toward enlightenment, to those in need. Nagarjuna provided the intellectual justification for this apparent violation of the karma concept. As the individual has no real definition in Nagarjuna's view, karma is not the sole possession of an individual. In short, karma has meaning only as an accumulation belonging to all of life. From this non-dualistic, metaphysical position, some Mahayanists extracted the idea that good karma or surplus merit may be transferred to others. All that is required of the beneficiary of this surplus merit is faith. Here Mahayana is strikingly different from Theravada, which is far more rationalistic in its message. Some Mahayana sects emphasize faith in a deity as well as in the powers of earthly bodhisattvas. Amitabha or the Amida Buddha, the heavenly Buddha, is worshipped as God in one of the more prominent Mahayana sects. If His devotees have faith in Him and His heavenly Pure Land, or the Western Paradise as it is also known, they will be saved. Accordingly, the laity of this Pure Land sect are encouraged to think of salvation not in terms of final liberation that will come when all sentient beings are ultimately freed from samsara, but rather of a heavenly afterlife. A concern for one's own preservation is thereby fostered. This creates a problem, as Nagarjuna's metaphysics supposedly eliminated all possibility for selfish thought in Mahayana.[36]

As a theistic faith, the Pure Land sect describes the godhead in terms of a trinity, the Three Bodies of Buddha: namely, the human Siddartha Gautama who walked the earth, the divine person represented by Amitabha, and absolute knowledge and compassion or the impersonal and absolute unity of the cosmos. The similarity of this to the Christian Trinity of the son, the father and the holy spirit is striking. Some have speculated that both Christianity and Pure Land derived their concepts of God from a common Gnostic source. In any case, when modern Christian missionaries entered China they found that Mahayana had prepared their way. "I hold," one of them proclaimed, "that in its Mahayana form, [Buddhism] is not an enemy to the Christian missionary, but a friend, for it has familiarized the Chinese mind with ideas essential to the right appreciation of Christianity."[37]

Mahayana is also similar to Christianity in that it has an eschatology. Four thousand years after Siddartha Gautama, Mahayana affirms, the returned Buddha (Maitreya) will inaugurate a new and beautiful world in which mankind will live for 80,000 years.[38] However, the parallels between Christianity and Mahayana can be overdrawn. In one important aspect, Mahayana is quite different from Christianity. In the latter faith, there is only one Christ, and none can hope to reach his station. In Mahayana, one may aspire ultimately to become the Buddha himself. Mahayana teaches that all sentient beings have the Buddha nature and that fully realizing this constitutes enlightenment. This is similar to the Vedantist notion of Atman, the divine spark within each of us which is equivalent to Brahman or God.

Mahayana teaches that all may aspire to become bodhisattvas. The code of the bodhisattva is expressed in language that sounds strangely Christian: "I take their suffering upon me. I must bear the burden of all beings. I give myself in exchange. I agree to suffer as a ransom for all beings." There have been many bodhisattvas, and there may be many more. All persons have the potential to become bodhisattvas, and bodhisattvas are on their way to becoming one with the Buddha. Mahayana teaches that ultimate reality is non-dualist in nature. Accordingly, the last word in the Mahayana world view cannot allow for a god separate from his devotees. Even the Pure Land sect, with its emphasis on individual survival after death, must admit that the ultimate goal is to become one with the the bliss that constitutes the third body of the Buddha. This blending of all of reality into a unity of consciousness violates the traditional Christian view of God as a being apart from ourselves. Perhaps, Mahayana Buddhism is closer to Hinduism than to Christianity. Similar to Hinduism, Mahayana includes both a popular theism and a refined metaphysics that identifies the individual with God. It popularly

119

teaches the survival of the soul after death, a view denied by Nagarjuna's philosophy which constitutes Mahayana's highest intellectual achievement. Including these apparent contradictions, Mahayana may be compared to Hinduism that counts both Shankara and Chaitanya in its ranks.[39]

Theravada claims to represent the purest form of the Buddha's original teaching, yet Mahayanists argue that they have been truer to the master's intent. Mahayanists note that while the earthly Buddha achieved enlightenment when still a fairly young man, he spent the rest of his long life helping others grow spiritually. He did not retire into tranquil inactivity and disassociate himself from humanity, as Theravadin monks do. Mahayanists claim that the Buddha set the pattern for all the bodhisattvas who would follow. This view would lead the novelist Hermann Hesse to claim of the Buddha that "his deeds and life are more important...than his talk; the gesture of his hand is more important...than his opinions."[40] Theravada would memorize the Buddha's words and follow them to the letter. Mahayana, appealing more to the bulk of humanity, would look for a deeper meaning in the Buddha's life.

## China's Religious Heritage

After reaching out to influence the religious perspectives of peoples as far away as China and Japan, Buddhism all but vanished in its founder's homeland between 700 and 1300 A.D. Several factors explained this demise. Over the ages, popular Buddhism had become so encrusted with myths and deities that it had largely lost the qualities that had once distinguished it from Hinduism. A second reason involved a revival of Hindu theology in India under Shankara in the 8th and 9th centuries. Shankara blended the Buddhist Nagarjuna's metaphysical concepts with the vocabulary of the ancient Vedic Upanishads to appeal to the best in both traditions in the name of Hinduism. As a result, Hinduism was intellectually revitalized at the expense of Buddhism. Third, as Hinduism revived, Indian princes increasingly came to show it official favor to the detriment of Buddhism. Just as Indian rulers, primarily the great Ashoka, had earlier advanced Buddhism, they now encouraged its decline. A fourth reason, and the one most commonly given for the death of Indian Buddhism, is the Muslim invasion of the subcontinent which began about 1000 A.D. In the eyes of the earliest and most fanatic Muslim conquerors, both Buddhists and Hindus were polytheists and deserving of destruction. Later, Muslim overlords would restrain their zeal but not until Buddhism had been virtually wiped out in India. Revitalized Hinduism, firmly rooted in the Indian villages, withstood and survived the storm. Flabby, degenerate Indian Buddhism, localized in luxurious monasteries, invited Islamic religious vandalism. Accordingly, Buddhism disappeared in India, surviving only in Ceylon (Sri Lanka) to the south and in Nepal along India's northeastern frontier.[41]

Buddhism's world center would now be China, where the religion had been since the first century A.D. As we have seen, Indian Buddhism had interacted with Hinduism, taking onto itself many of the latter's attributes. In China, a similar process occurred, albeit between Buddhism and China's endemic religious heritage--Confucianism, Taoism and the yin-yang concept. Accordingly, the influence of China's native religions on Buddhist development will now be examined, commencing with Confucianism.

Confucius lived in the 6th and 5th centuries B.C., in a time of political and social chaos in China. In his day, society seemed to be disintegrating. Confucius's solution for this disorder called for virtuous behavior from those who govern the state. He taught that virtue is contagious and that if the elite would curb their own thoughts and actions collective well-being would result. Once the head of the powerful Chi family asked Confucius how thievery might be brought under control in his domains. Confucius answered, "If you, sir, had no improper desires, they wouldn't steal if you paid them to." The advice was typical, as shown in the Confucian saying that "a highly virtuous ruler conditions a highly virtuous people." "He who brought virtue to the task of government," said Confucius, "could be likened to the North Star, fixed in its constant place, with all the constellations clustered round it." Later Confucians would elaborate upon this belief and construct a theodicy that explained even natural disasters such as wind storms and earthquakes as resulting from the misdeeds of the emperor and his minions. This view would encourage revolution when otherwise unaccountable disasters befell the land. Under such adverse conditions, an emperor was said to have lost the mandate of Heaven.[42]

In pre-Buddhist days, the Chinese concept of

God was rather limited. The emperor alone sacrificed to Shang Ti, a personal god of the state. However, the masses looked to T'ien or Heaven, which corresponded to a cosmic, impersonal balance of nature. Confucius's own attitude was that focus should be on this life, here and now. Heaven should be respected, and proper sacrifices should be made to ancestors, but inordinate amounts of time should not be devoted to the spirit world. Confucius once scolded an otherworldly disciple by remarking, "You are not able to serve man; how can you serve spirits?" The disciple persisted with a question about death, and Confucius answered, "You do not yet understand life; how can you understand death?" Nevertheless, the Chinese masses hungered for knowledge of the spirit world, and by the time that Buddhism began to flower on Chinese soil Mahayana had become a faith replete with 32 heavens.[43]

The otherworldly orientation of Mahayana Buddhism would earn it contempt from Confucians, who also could not abide Buddhist renunciation of all family and social ties. On this latter count, Buddhism would face a powerful challenge from China's religious heritage. Traditional Chinese mores highly valued filial responsibility. Accordingly, Buddhism adjusted to this fact and ultimately encouraged its monks to pray and sacrifice for the congregation's departed ancestors. These added priestly functions made Buddhism somewhat useful to Chinese society. Nevertheless, Confucians would charge down through the centuries that Buddhist monastic life and celibacy were anti-social and unproductive. One 9th-century Confucian attack on Buddhism reads: "When one man does not farm, others suffer hunger, and, when one woman does not weave, others suffer from the cold."[44]

Interestingly, Confucianism and Buddhism both taught the benefits of rigorous introspection, as demonstrated by Buddhism's Eightfold Path and Confucianism's emphasis on li. Clearly, self-discipline was needed to complete the Eightfold Path. Li demanded a similar emphasis on behavior control. All Confucian virtues balance opposing behaviors into a kind of behavioral golden mean--the essence of li. For example, Confucius taught that the virtuous man must be magnanimous yet inspiring respect, gentle yet firm, honestly direct yet sensitive to others' feelings, peaceful yet bold, upright yet easy-going, generous yet discriminating, unwavering in purpose and yet cautious, and strong yet just. The tendency to value a balance of opposites was deeply ingrained in the Chinese character. Such balance did not come without serious self-analysis and constant self-discipline. Accordingly, Confucian self-control helped condition China for the entry of Buddhism, which, while oriented toward non-Confucian, otherworldly values, was also characterized by stern self-discipline and behavior control. [45]

Nonetheless, Buddhism had far more in common with Taoism than Confucianism. Indeed, the similarity was so close that Taoists held that Lao Tzu, the semi-mythical founder of their religion, was in fact also the founder of Buddhism. Lao Tzu, which literally means "the old fellow," was supposedly an older contemporary of Confucius. Scholars know that his cryptic sayings, transcribed in the Tao Te Ching ("The Way and Its Power"), were in fact not composed until some three centuries after Confucius. However, Taoists were motivated to claim that their religion was slightly older than both Confucianism and Buddhism in order to give it the prestige of seniority among China's competing faiths. Accordingly, they speculated that after the venerable Lao Tzu successfully refuted the emerging world view of the young Confucius, he traveled to India where he became known as Siddartha Gautama, the founder to Buddhism. [46]

Taoism and Confucianism represent different faces of China's religious heritage. An old Chinese saying relates: "In office a Confucian, in retirement a Taoist." Confucian advocacy of the active, worldly life may be contrasted with Taoist quietism. Taoism emphasizes living naturally, without effort, whereas Confucianism emphasizes the need for self-improvement through education. Taoism denigrates academic learning and instead advocates wu-wei. Wu-wei, meaning "no effort," is the principle whereby one does not strive beyond his own natural abilities. Taoism teaches that one should blend in with nature rather than struggle against it. Chinese art reflects this perspective in typically portraying a tiny, insignificant human being surrounded by the grandeur of a natural setting. A Taoist poem expresses the view that things should be accepted as they are: "What is spontaneously so, and not made to be so, is the natural. The roc can fly in high places, the quail in low ones." A Taoist story tells of a man who tried to make corn grow by pulling at the ears of grain, which were ruined as a result. Let it alone, and it will grow naturally. Accept your natural self. Do not strive to become something that you are not. Let a bucket of muddy water alone, and it

123

will clear.  This is the message of Taoism.[47]

The wisdom of wu-wei is seen in daily life.  A childless couple struggles to conceive a child of their own without result.  Ultimately, they adopt a child and finally relax.  Within a year, the adoptive mother is pregnant.  A man strives to remember a forgotten word to no avail.  Then, after having given up the effort, the word comes to him.  The sleepless woman can find no rest, though she devotes all of her energies to falling asleep.  Not until she stops trying does sleep come.  And we all know that the more you push people, the harder they resist.

Some critics have said that only a dead man can be a good Taoist.  This is ironic, for early Taoists advocated inactivity to preserve life.  Their belief was that struggle consumes personal energies and shortens life.  Lao Tzu supposedly lived for more than 200 years because he practiced wu-wei.  Early Taoists claimed that when their masters seemingly died, their real bodies flew away to a heavenly realm made possible by their lives of inactivity.  Their quest for immortality would evolve into this philosophy of life: Peace of mind results by letting the natural self emerge through inactivity.  Strip the clutter from your life, taught the Taoist, and you will find bliss.[48]

One student of Taoism has written that the sage "transcends the distinction between the self and the world, the 'me' and the 'non-me.'  Therefore, he has no self.  He is one with the Tao....The Tao does nothing, and therefore has no achievements."  The Tao is the undifferentiated whole of life, which is very hard for neurotic, self-centered and confused human beings to realize.  The Tao is absolutely indivisible.  While life is always in flux, the totality of it is always the same.  The Indian Buddhist Nagarjuna had stated this same idea in highly metaphysical language.  Taoism would accept Nagarjuna but not rely upon his thought.  Taoism had taught that "knowledge" and "learning" inevitably trains the mind to think in terms of discrete things or fragments of the whole.  Accordingly, Taoism would be suspicious even of philosophy that supported its world view, as was the case with Nagarjuna's thought.  Opposed to the mental striving of scholarship, it urged that we become "quiet" and calmly realize the whole that cannot be expressed in words.  Lao Tzu's most famous aphorism emphasized this point:  "Those who know do not say, and those who say do not know."[49]

124

Interestingly, Buddhism itself would be reinterpreted through the perspective of Taoism. Ch'an (Zen) Buddhism would result. Sounding very much like a Taoist, the 6th-century founder of Ch'an Buddhism would proclaim: "You cannot find Buddha in books. Look into your own heart, and there you will find him." The sayings of this new school of Buddhism would also sound very Taoist. Take, for example, this Zen teaching: "Clay is molded into a vessel, but the empty space is the useful part." Taoism would gradually degenerate into magic and sorcery, claiming that its practitioners could walk on water, raise the dead, and be immune to fire, water and even bullets. But this would not occur until philosophical Taoism had imparted its most sublime truths to Zen Buddhism.[50]

China's ancient yin-yang concept also contributed to the development of Chinese Buddhism. Yin and yang are commonly represented symbolically in the T'ai Chi, a circle within which are dark and light areas intertwined with one another. Yang is the light portion, whereas yin is the dark. In addition, yang is usually associated with heat, activity, good fortune, masculinity and that which is primary; whereas yin represents coldness, receptivity, misfortune, femininity and that which is secondary. Both yin and yang are bound together. Neither has definition without the other. However, yang and yin cannot be understood unless we search for a deeper meaning. Each of us, whether man or woman, has both male and female characteristics, which the psychologist Carl Jung referred to respectively as animus and anima. From what was said above, one might deduce that a woman's animus (male characteristics) would be regarded as yang. Interestingly enough, such is not the case. As a secondary set of personality traits, a woman's animus is yin. This example demonstrates the most important teaching of the yin-yang concept: Nothing has any definition in and of itself. Contextual relationships alone define traits, people, events or anything else that the human mind identifies.[51]

The Chinese fable of the farmer's runaway horse illustrates the yin-yang perspective. This tale begins with a farmer's horse running away, which the farmer initially regarded as yin or misfortune. Then the horse returned with a herd of wild horses, which were corralled by the farmer. This was yang, or good fortune, and the farmer realized another aspect to the initial act of his horse running away. The next day, his son was thrown while riding one of the wild horses. Unfortunately, his leg was broken in the fall. This caused the farmer again to rethink the initial act of his horse running away. Again, he saw it as yin or misfortune, for the boy would never have broken his leg had the horse not run away and returned with the wild horses. The next day, a roving conscription unit from the army rejected the farmer's son for military service because of his broken leg. Again, the initial act of the horse running away appeared to the farmer as yang or good fortune. In short, the event of the farmer's horse running away contained in the perspective of time elements of both yang and yin. The message of the story is that all values are relative.[52]

In the yin-yang mentality, there is no existence without both good and evil. Therefore, to seek the destruction of evil is naive. According to this view, good and evil are not at war in the Zoroastrian sense that has typically dominated Western thinking. Rather, good and evil are mutually interdependent and complementary. The yin-yang conception is organic, ecological and ultimately non-dualistic. Through this perspective, everything is interconnected and nothing has meaning apart from the whole. In contrast to the activistic European mentality, this view encourages a passive acceptance of life. Accordingly, Westerners have labeled it "fatalistic." Indeed, any philosophy of life that stresses the relativity of all values will seem fatalistic to those who hold absolute values, for the former view belittles the consequences of choice.[53] Yin-yang relativism conditioned the Chinese mind for Mahayana Buddhism. As we have seen, Mahayana also taught that nothing in the phenomenal world is independent or absolute and that humanly defined beings or objects have meaning only in relation to the undifferentiated whole of life.

Despite its many similarities to native Chinese religion, Buddhism had to endure the handicap of being a "foreign" religion on Chinese soil. China's hard times frequently were blamed on "foreign" Buddhism which preached otherworldliness and "social irresponsibility." Taoism's similarity to Buddhism tended to be overlooked at such times because of the former's native credentials. Ironically, this stigma benefited the growth of Buddhism in China. Foreign conquerors regularly took advantage of China's weaknesses and seized the reigns of government. Regarded as barbarians by Confucians and Taoists, these overlords found comfort in "foreign" Buddhism.

Consequently, Buddhism prospered from the patronage of China's many foreign conquerors.[54]

Native Chinese religion had prepared the way for Buddhism. Confucianism opened the Chinese mind to the Buddhist emphasis on behavior modification and thought control. In turn, Taoism harmonized nicely with Buddhist mysticism and detachment from worldly cares. Additionally, the yin-yang concept supported Mahayana's view that the dualistic world of self does not represent ultimate reality. With the help of official patrons, Buddhism prospered in China which would remain the religion's world center until 1948. Then the weight of communist, totalitarian government would repress all religion in China, and the focus of Far Eastern Buddhist development would shift to Japan.

## Zen

Some think that Zen is synonymous with Japanese Buddhism. However, this is a mistaken view. To begin with, Zen is not of Japanese origin. As we have seen, it arose in the crucible of Chinese culture. More importantly, Zen has never claimed any but a minority of Japanese Buddhists. Unlike Pure Land Buddhism, which is a far more popular form of Japanese Buddhism, Zen has no god to worship, no heavens, no hells, and no souls to be saved. By contrast, Zen's vision is simple--so simple that it cannot be adequately described with words. This is the major source of its appeal.[55]

Zen began in sixth-century China. There, it was called Ch'an, a Chinese phonetic rendition of the Sanskrit term "dhyana," which means meditation. In turn, when Ch'an migrated to Japan in the 13th century, it was pronounced "Zen" by the Japanese. The story of Zen or Ch'an begins with one Bodhidharma. In about 520, Bodhidharma arrived in China from India. He supposedly was the 28th Patriarch, in other words the 28th direct spiritual descendant of the Buddha. Zennists emphasize this detail and claim that Bodhidharma merely brought the Buddha's true teaching to China. In short, they propose that the Buddha himself was the real founder of Zen.

A more realistic view is that Bodhidharma, trained in Nagarjuna's metaphysics and further inspired by Taoist simplicity, was the true founder of Ch'an. His new sect advocated radical experiential religion. Zen's ideal is "suchness" or simply reality as it _is_

127

and not categorized, divided, and ripped asunder by the abstractions which we call words. Bodhidharma taught that words and their accompanying thoughts create substitutes for reality. They do not comprise reality itself. At worst, they fool us into mistaking mental pictures for reality. We have seen that the ancient Jews kept the name of their God mysterious, for classifying Him with a word would limit His power and majesty. Zen has much the same attitude towards existence itself.[56]

One may question proceeding with this word description of Zen, for by Zen standards it must fail in its purpose. Nonetheless, there are Zen scriptures. Also, Zen has become known to the Western world primarily through the writings of one Daisetz T. Suzuki. Professor Suzuki, himself a Zennist, has amusingly confessed himself to be a "great sinner, ...destined for hell" due to his use of words to spread Zen's message. "But it is not a bad thing to go to hell," Suzuki adds, "if it does some good to somebody." The Buddha himself taught that a man travelling across a wide river discards his raft once the far shore is reached. Zen writings are like that raft. After they have convinced the searcher that words cannot lead to enlightenment, they are to be discarded.[57]

Zen rejects symbols. Zen is direct. It values the primitive and discards the derivative. It seeks to make the mind as barren of preconceptions as an infant's. It is iconoclastic. Zen monks have burned Zen scriptures as graven images. They have spit upon statues of the Buddha. "The Buddha is a dried piece of dung of the barbarians," a Zen master once proclaimed. Having developed an attitude in which all craving is absent, the Zennist views reality without discrimination or preference. Accordingly, the Buddha is equal to a piece of dung. Everything is worthless, and everything is important. The enlightened Zennist has no likes and dislikes. Feeling that he possesses everything already, he has no cravings. A person who has reached this point has experienced satori, which has been described as "an awareness of the undifferentiated unity of all existence." For a fleeting eternity," said one who recalled his first satori experience, "I was alone--I alone was." "What an immense relief," said another, "to discover that just as I am I lack nothing!"[58]

Some have said that Zen glorifies animal existence, which is characterized in part by acceptance of what is. Animals easily adapt to their environment and seldom try to improve upon that which is given by nature. Were they able to justify their existence, animals might quote Jesus of Nazareth: "Take...no thought for the morrow: for the morrow shall take thought for the things of itself." Zen advocates that we experience reality, rather than read or think about it. Zen does not say that we should "understand" ourselves; that is too objective, intellectual and detached for Zen. Zen asks something more direct--that we plunge into experience totally. A famous Zen master once said of his first satori experience: "When I heard the temple bell ring, suddenly there was no bell and no I, just sound." Zen wants the subject and the object involved in any particular experience to dissolve into a total engagement of the experience itself. The accomplished Zennist knows a sense of wonder with each passing moment, a state of mind that sees the world as being created every moment. There is a story of the Buddha teaching his disciples which Zennists like to tell. Asked to convey his most sublime teaching, the Buddha simply held up a flower. No words were uttered. No principles were expounded upon. Merely a flower. Nothing more.[59]

Zen says: Live entirely for the moment. Have no goals. Totally experience the process of living. In living for the moment, Zen insists that we not try to hold on to it, to grasp it, but rather let life flow through us, as electricity flows through a light bulb. The Buddha taught that suffering comes from trying to possess partial aspects of life. Zen agrees. We have seen that Theravadin monks avoid everyday experiences in hopes of eliminating sorrow. In contrast, Zennists do not preach otherworldly detachment. Zen totally accepts the world, just as it is. One Zennist has described this attitude in poetic language: "Things are beautiful but not desirable; ugly but not rejected; dirty, but ourselves no cleaner." Zen cannot be accused of timidity, as it relishes every experience; it looks upon even the moment of death as something to be experienced with undivided attention.[60]

The samurai, the warriors of feudal Japan, were attracted to Zen because of its advocacy of courageous encounter with life. A soldier's life is one of split-second decisions. Either he responds successfully to the demands of the moment, or he is gone. Zen's emphasis on dealing with such crises instantaneously and spontaneously, without conscious thought, appealed to the samurai. They developed Zen's powers of concentration, called joriki, for dealing with the sudden and unexpected situations of their profession. Zen also taught the samurai the beauty present even in death. Japanese culture typically values those things that are fleeting: cherry blossoms, the thin crust of snow that disappears in the morning sunlight, mists fading on a hill side. The ephemeral is equated with the beautiful. Finding its purest expression in the teachings of Zen, this attitude does not seek permanency, but finds greatest joy in the spontaneous flow of life and death.$^{61}$

In the 1950's, American "beatniks" justified much of their libertine behavior in the name of Zen's appreciation of the spontaneous moment. Their understanding of Zen was shallow. Properly understood, Zen is highly disciplined. Zen novices are placed under the tutelage of an accomplished master and put through a regimen that exhausts both physical and mental reserves. To some, there might seem to be a contradiction in this, as Zen supposedly advocates living spontaneously. The justification for Zen discipline is that old mental habits have to be broken by rigorous effort before life can be experienced afresh. Only after this process is completed can the Zennist meaning of spontaneous living be known.$^{62}$

Zen discipline begins with zazen or seated meditation. After the student has adjusted to the physical discomfort of long periods of zazen, he is given a koan, which on the surface appears to be a nonsensical riddle. "What is the sound of one hand clapping?" is one famous koan. "Why is the Western barbarian (the Caucasian) beardless?" is another. One initially thinks, "This is ridiculous. One hand cannot make a clap, and everyone knows that white men grow luxurious beards." Nonetheless, the student seats himself in the lotus position and meditates on his koan. Hours pass. A Zen monk armed with a stick strolls behind a row of students deep in zazen. Occasionally, the monk strikes a student to help his mind break through the mental barrier of the koan. Then a student says he is ready to explain the meaning of his koan. Typically, he provides his master with an intellectual answer in harmony with Nagarjuna's metaphysics. For example, one hand clapping mocks the dualistic world of words. All sounds, all thoughts, all words, and all events are created in dualism. In the world of dualism, relative fragments are misperceived as independent and absolute entities. In reality, fragments have no existence. All is suchness, the undifferentiated whole of life. This is the realm of one hand clapping. The answer is rejected by the master. It is too slick, too intellectual and too pat. The student receives a blow on his shoulder and returns to zazen to wrestle with his koan.

Intense mental and physical fatigue drives the student to the breaking point. The intellectual answer did not suffice. What is the way out of his dilemma? He feels as if his mind is trapped in a straitjacket. All his effort is for naught. He knows he will never find enlightenment. He is totally defeated, utterly devastated, and yet he is close to victory, for that which is being exhausted is the old self of dualistic conceptualization. A new Self, undifferentiated from the entire cosmos, is about to be born. An old Chinese saying relates: "When you are in an impasse, there is an opening." Christians express the same idea by saying "man's extremity is God's opportunity." This is the purpose of the koan: to create the impasse, to drive the dualistic mind to its own destruction. And finally it comes. Zttt. Coming as a total surprise, satori is realized, sometimes coming after years of intense struggle. Now the student runs to his master and in joy and sobbing tells him the answer to the koan. It may be phrased in a way that seems nonsensical to the unenlightened or it might be a rehash of the intellectual answer given above. What is distinctive in the answer is the student's bearing, the look in his eye. The master has seen it before. He now knows the student has achieved satori.[63]

The new consciousness of one who has experienced satori sometimes appears quite bizarre. One example involves two Zennists at dinner. Striking up a conversation, one asked his companion a question, and he replied by tipping the table over, spilling the food on the floor. The next evening, the scene was repeated, driving the offended party to comment upon his companion's rudeness. The accused man instantly retorted: "In Buddhism, there is neither rudeness nor politeness. What a blind fellow you are!" Another story tells of two men who simultaneously visited a Zendo, a Zen monastery. One of them was a government official who cared nothing about enlightenment but was required to go to the Zendo for political reasons. The other visitor was a Zen master. The Roshi, the monastery's director, treated the official with complete deference and the visiting Zennist with utmost contempt. Later on, the Zen visitor asked the Roshi to explain his behavior. The latter replied: "To show deference is to show contempt and to show contempt is to show deference." Thereupon, the visiting Zennist hit the Roshi in the nose and said, "To hit is not to hit, and not to hit is to hit."

Living in a mental state that rejects dualistic thought patterns commonly prevalent in society, Zennists can often appear slightly crazy. This was the face of Zen seen by the beatniks. Unfortunately, they did not understand Nagarjuna's metaphysics that underscores such behavior. Also, the beatniks did not realize that these playful anecdotes do not represent the most meaningful expression of Zen. Self-centered and hedonistic, the beatniks could not see Zen's appreciation of the inseparable bond among all beings. In Nagarjuna's world view, which Zen borrows, the entity called "me" has no meaning divorced from other beings. Such a vision cannot condone self-centeredness.[64]

The koan discipline, used to prepare a student for satori, is commonly associated with the Rinzai school of Zen Buddhism. By contrast, Zen's Soto school, and the larger of the two, suspects that koans merely feed the grasping, craving nature of the dualistic mind. It scorns what it calls Rinzai's "artificial satori," which it compares to the good feeling one gets when he stops hitting his head against a stone wall. Soto students are not to strive for anything, including satori. Rather, Soto advocates motiveless, purposeless action such as walking just to walk or sitting just to sit. Rinzai, which in the West is commonly thought to be synonymous with Zen, belittles Soto for exchanging mere self-control for satori as a goal. Soto stresses Zen in daily life, whereas Rinzai strives for the mountain-top experience of satori. In truth, most Zennists are eclectic, adopting elements from both schools.

Many think that Zen best represents the true spirit of the Buddha in the modern world. Similar to early Buddhism, Zen's orientation is toward the individual seeker of enlightenment. Unlike other forms of Mahayana expression, Zen does not offer the masses solace dispensed by a host of semi-divine saviors. One Zennist has commented on the lack of social action in Zen: "You can't begin to save anybody until you yourself have become whole through the experience of Self-realization." Certainly, the Zennist who has fully developed his new consciousness meets the world in a totally accepting manner, full of loving-kindness.

He is unlike the Theravadin who, afraid of temptation,
retreats from life. By contrast, the Zennist sees life
and wonder everywhere. Indeed, the unfathomed spirit
of Siddartha Gautama, awakened in India 2500 years ago,
lives on in him.[65]


## NOTES

1. Paul D. Devanandan, The Concept of Maya, An
Essay in Historical Survey of the Hindu Theory of the
World, With Special Reference to the Vedanta (London,
1950), p. 89; Heinrich Zimmer, Philosophies of India
(New York, 1951), p. 521.

2. A. Barth, The Religions of India (London,
1932), p. 142.

3. Louis Renou, Hinduism (New York, 1962), p. 15;
Edward J. Thomas, The Life of Buddha as Legend and
History (London, 1949), p. 205; Max Weber, The Religion
of India (New York, 1958), p. 199; Frederick H. Holck,
ed., Death and Eastern Thought, Understanding Death in
Eastern Religions and Philosophies (New York, 1974),
pp. 145-146, 149-151; Balwant Nevaskar, Capitalists
Without Capitalism, The Jains of India and the Quakers
of the West (Westport, Conn., 1971), p. 162; Donald
Bishop, ed., Indian Thought, An Introduction (New York,
1975), pp. 85-86; A.L. Basham, The Wonder that Was
India (New York, 1954), p. 292; George Foot Moore,
History of Religions (2 vols., New York, 1929), I,
282-283; Zimmer, Philosophies of India, pp. 278-279.

4. G.F. Allen, ed., The Buddha's Philosophy,
Selections From the Pali Canon and an Introductory
Essay (New York, 1959), p. 30; Moore, History of
Religions, I, 292.

5. Christopher Isherwood, ed., Vedanta For the
Western World (Hollywood, 1948), p. 120; K.N.
Jayatilleke, The Message of the Buddha (New York,
1974), p. 31; Thomas Berry, Buddhism, (New York, 1957),
p. 13; Zimmer, Philosophies of India, pp. 472-473;
Bishop, ed., Indian Thought, p. 115.

6. Moore, History of Religions, I, 285; R.C.
Majumdar, ed., The History of Culture of the Indian
People (11 vols., Bombay, 1951-1969), II (The Age of
Imperial Unity), 374; Archie J. Balm, Philosophy of the
Buddha (New York, 1958), pp. 41-42.

7.  Will Durant, The Story of Philosophy, The Lives and Opinions of the Great Philosophers of the Western World (New York, 1926), p. 88; J.B. Pratt, The Pilgrimage of Buddhism and A Buddhist Pilgrimage (New York, 1928), p. 30.

8.  Pratt, Pilgrimage of Buddhism, p. 33; Weber, Religion of India, p. 208; Jayatilleke, Message of Buddha, p. 238.

9.  Ananda Coomaraswamy, Buddha and the Gospel of Buddhism (Bombay, 1956), pp. 154-159; Beatrice Lane Suzuki, Mahayana Buddhism (New York, 1959), p. 75; W.E. Soothill, The Three Religions of China (Westport, Conn., 1923:1973), p. 142; Peter A. Gard, ed., Buddhism (New York, 1962), pp. 67, 100; Weber, Religion of India, p. 212; Basham, Wonder That Was India, p. 177.

10.  D.F. Pocock, trans., Essays on the Caste System by Celestin Bougle (Cambridge, 1971), p. 74; Jayatilleke, Message of Buddha, p. 26.

11.  Coomaraswamy, Gospel of Buddhism, p. 273; Weber, Religion of India, p. 206; Pratt, Pilgrimage of Buddhism, p. 95.

12.  Huston Smith, The Religions of Man (New York, 1958), p. 104; Pratt, Pilgrimage of Buddhism, pp. 185-186; Christmas Humphreys, Studies in the Middle Way (London, 1959), pp. 20-21.

13.  Allen, ed., Buddha's Philosophy, p. 51.

14.  Philip Kapleau, The Three Pillars of Zen (Garden City, New York, 1980), p. 159; Pratt, Pilgrimage of Buddhism, p. 44.

15.  Weber, Religions of India, p. 218.

16.  Holck, ed., Death and Eastern Thought, p. 134; Coomaraswamy, Gospel of Buddhism, p. 135; Christmas Humphreys, Concentration and Meditation, A Manual of Mind Development (Baltimore, 1971), pp. 11, 13; Basham, Wonder That Was India, pp. 270-271.

17.  Alan Watts, The Way of Zen (New York, 1957), pp. 40-42, 47; R.H. Blyth, Zen in English Literature and Oriental Classics (New York, 1960), p. 185.

18.  Humphreys, Studies in Middle Way, p. 122;

Pratt, Pilgrimage of Buddhism, p. 50.

19.   Bahm, Philosophy of Buddha, p. 79; Jayatilleke, Message of Buddha, pp. 117-127; Rune E.A. Johansson, The Psychology of Nirvana (London, 1969), p. 45; Berry, Buddhism, p. 28; Watts, Way of Zen, p. 47; John Blofeld, The Tantric Mysticism of Tibet (New York, 1970), pp. 67-68.

20.   Pratt, Pilgrimage of Buddhism, p. 41.

21.   Allen, ed., Buddha's Philosophy, p. 67.

22.   Coomaraswamy, Gospel of Buddhism, p. 167; Gard, ed., Buddhism, pp. 110-111, 114-116; Weber, Religion of India, pp. 211-212; Thomas, Life of Buddha, pp. 153, 202; Kenneth Ch'en, Buddhism in China, A Historical Survey (Princeton, 1964), p. 72; Holck, ed., Death and Eastern Thought, pp. 121, 130, 230.

23.   Ch'en, Buddhism in China, pp. 8-9.

24.   Weber, Religion of India, p. 209; Jayatilleke, Message of Buddha, p. 46.

25.   Pratt, Pilgrimage of Buddhism, pp. 25-26; Nalinaksha Dutt, Mahayana Buddhism (Calcutta, 1976), p. 265; Watts, The Way of Zen, p. 63; Arnold Toynbee, An Historian's Approach to Religion (London, 1956), pp. 293-294; Garma C.C. Chang, The Buddhist Teaching of Totality, The Philosophy of Hwa Yen Buddhism (London, 1971), pp. 69, 100-101; Bernard Phillips, ed., The Essentials of Zen Buddhism, Selected from the Writings of Daisetz T. Suzuki (New York, 1962), p. 359; Berry, Buddhism, pp. 122-123, 125; Watts, Way of Zen, p. 61.

26.   Berry, Buddhism, pp. 123-124.

27.   Beatrice Lane Suzuki, Mahayana Buddhism (New York, 1959), p. 36; Blofeld, Tantric Mysticism, p. 59; Coomaraswamy, Gospel of Buddhism, pp. 232-233.

28.   Poola Tirupati Raju, The Philosophical Traditions of India (London, 1971), p. 122; Coomaraswamy, Gospel of Buddhism, p. 199; Basham, Wonder That Was India (New York, 1954), p. 328.

29.   Majumdar, ed., History and Culture of the Indian People, II, 364, 518; Nirad C. Chaudhuri, Hinduism, A Religion to Live By (New York, 1979), pp.

90, 94; Basham, Wonder That Was India, pp. 367-368; Michael Edwardes, A History of India, From the Earliest Times to the Present Day (New York, 1961), pp. 66-67.

30. Zimmer, Philosophies of India (New York, 1951), p. 474.

31. Coomaraswamy, Gospel of Buddhism, p. 147; Allen, ed., Buddha's Philosophy, p. 85.

32. Basham, Wonder That Was India, pp. 281-283.

33. Ibid., pp. 54-55, 213, 263; Zimmer, Philosophies of India, pp. 158, 496-497, 501; Majumdar, ed., History and Culture of the Indian People, II, 385; Weber, Religion of India, p. 230; Holck, ed., Death and Eastern Thought, p. 123; Sir William Wilson Hunter, A Brief History of the Indian Peoples (Oxford, 1907), p. 80.

34. Ch'en, Buddhism in China, pp. 12-14; Gard, ed., Buddhism, pp. 68-69, 84; Weber, Religion of India, p. 247.

35. Majumdar, ed., History and Culture of the Indian People, V, (The Struggle For Empire), 413; Zimmer, Philosophies of India, pp. 534-535; Coomaraswamy, Gospel of Buddhism, p. 245; B. Suzuki, Mahayana Buddhism, p.75; Ch'en, Buddhism in China, pp. 241, 295.

36. Berry, Buddhism, pp. 103, 105; Geoffrey Parriner, Upanishads, Gita and Bible (New York, 1962), pp. 110-111; Ch'en, Buddhism in China, pp. 106-107; B. Suzuki, Mahayana Buddhism, p. xxxvii; Soothill, Three Religions of China, pp. 103-106.

37. Coomaraswamy, Gospel of Buddhism, pp. 238, 247-249; B.Suzuki, Mahayana Buddhism, pp. 37, 39, 41-43, 47; Basham, Wonder That Was India, pp. 276-277; Weber, Religion of India, p. 248; Soothill, Three Religions of China, p. 108.

38. Pratt, Pilgrimage of Buddhism, pp. 227-228; Gard, ed., Buddhism, p. 93; Basham, Wonder That Was India, pp. 264, 274.

39. Basham, Wonder That Was India, p. 275; Zimmer, Philosophies of India, pp. 545-546; B.Suzuki, Mahayana Buddhism, pp. 50-51; Ch'en, Buddhism in China, pp. 46-47, 117-118, 129.

40.   Hermann Hesse, Siddartha (New York, 1951), p. 119.

41.   Devanandan, The Concept of Maya, p. 89; Majumdar, ed., History and Culture of the Indian People, IV (The Age of Imperial Kanauj), 356, 360; M. N. Srinivas, Caste in Modern India and Other Essays (Bombay, 1962), pp. 159-160; Ch'en, Buddhism in China, pp. 399-400; Holck, ed., Death and Eastern Thought, p. 16; Edwardes, History of India, pp. 80-84; Chaudhuri, Hinduism, pp. 125-126; Pratt, Pilgrimage of Buddhism, p. 114.

42.   H.G. Creel, Confucius, The Man and the Myth (London, 1951), pp. 40, 85-86, 204; Soothill, Three Religions of China, p. 192; Shigeki Kaizuka, Confucius (London, 1956), p. 130; Liu Wu-Chi, A Short History of Confucian Philosophy (London, 1955), p. 125; Moore, History of Religions, I, 24-25, 168; Max Weber, The Religion of China (Glencoe, Ill., 1951), pp. 28-32, 152-153.

43.   Soothill, Three Religions of China, pp. 30-33, 122; Creel, Confucius, pp. 124-125; Ch'en, Buddhism in China, p. 396; Weber, Religion of India, p. 269.

44.   Pratt, Pilgrimage of Buddhism, pp. 273-274; Liu Wu-Chi, Confucian Philosophy, p. 137; Holck, ed., Death and Eastern Thought, pp. 216-217; Ch'en, Buddhism in China, pp. 143, 209, 231; Weber, Religion of India, p. 265.

45.   Ch'en, Buddhism in China, pp. 207-208; Liu Wu-Chi, Confucian Philosophy, pp. 77-78, 141-142; B. Suzuki, Mahayana Buddhism, p. 121; Derk Bodde, ed., A Short History of Chinese Philosophy by Fung Yu-Lan (New York, 1961), p. 45; Creel Confucius, p. 104; Gard, ed., Buddhism, pp. 152-153; Soothill, Three Religions of China, pp. 192-193.

46.   Ch'en, Buddhism in China, p. 24; H.G. Creel, What is Taoism? And Other Studies in Chinese Cultural History (Chicago, 1970), pp. 48-49; William McNaughton, The Taoist Vision (Ann Arbor, Michigan, 1971), p. 7; Holmes Welch, Taoism, The Parting of the Way (Boston, 1965), p. 152; Bodde, ed., Philosophy by Fung Yu-Lan, p. 241.

47.   Welch, Taoism, p. 158; Weber, Religion of

137

China, pp. 169, 182; Bodde, ed., Philosophy by Fung Yu-Lan, p. 229; Moore, History of Religions, I, 52, 61.

48. Welch, Taoism, p. 83; Watts, Way of Zen, p. 27; Creel, Taoism, pp. 4, 67; McNaughton, Taoist Vision, pp. 9, 19; Bodde, ed., Philosophy by Fung Yu-Lan, pp. 64, 67; Liu Wu-Chi, Confucian Philosophy, p. 53; Ch'en, Buddhism in China, p. 27.

49. Bodde, ed., Philosophy by Fung Yu-Lan, pp. 110, 254; Creel, Taoism, pp. 2-4, 27, 30, 42; Ch'en, Buddhism in China, p. 60; Welch, Taoism, pp. 26-27.

50. Liu Wu-Chi, Confucian Philosophy, p. 144; R.H. Blyth, Zen in English Literature and Oriental Classics (New York, 1960), p. 248; Soothill, Three Religions of China, pp. 44-76; Welch, Taoism, p. 129.

51. Richard Wilhelm, Lectures on the I Ching, Constancy and Change(Princeton, New Jersey, 1979), pp. 5-6.

52. Smith, Religions of Man, pp. 188-189.

53. Jung Young Lee, The I Ching and Modern Man: Essays on Metaphysical Implications of Change (Secaucus, New Jersey, 1975), pp. 29, 30-31, 62; Alan Watts, Psychotherapy East and West (New York, 1961); Watts, Way of Zen, p. 117; Moore, History of Religions, I, 53.

54. Liu Wu-Chi, Confucian Philosophy, p. 139; Ch'en, Buddhism in China, p. 426.

55. Phillips, ed., D. T. Suzuki, p. 10.

56. Bodde, ed., Philosophy by Fung Yu-Lan, p. 255; Soothill, Three Religions of China, pp. 94, 96; Coomaraswamy, Gospel of Buddhism, p. 255; Sohaku Ogata, Zen for the West (London, 1959), p. 24; Holck, ed., Death and Eastern Thought, p. 236; Watts, Psychotherapy, p. 80; Alan Watts, Nature, Man and Woman (New York, 1958), p. 57; Bishop, ed., Indian Thought, p. 142; Christmas Humphreys, ed., Studies in Zen by D. T. Suzuki (New York, 1955), pp. 192-193; Nakamura Hajime, "The Acceptance of Man's Natural Dispositions," The Japan Foundation Newsletter, VII (1979), 2; Hesse, Siddartha, p. 115.

57. Humphreys, ed., Zen by Suzuki, p. 142.

58. Zimmer, Philosophies of India, pp. 255-256; Pratt, Pilgrimage of Buddhism, pp. 623-624; Blyth, Zen in Literature, pp. 22, 59, 66, 223; Bodde, ed., Philosophy by Fung Yu-Lan, pp. 263-264; Humphreys, ed., Zen by Suzuki, pp. 134, 147; Phillip Kapleau, The Three Pillars of Zen (Garden City, New York, 1980), pp. 143, 150, 231, 239, 298; Phillips, ed., D.T. Suzuki, pp. 123-126, 154; Ch'en, Buddhism in China, p. 358.

59. Blyth, Zen in Literature, pp. 32, 403; Kapleau, Three Pillars of Zen, pp. 113-114; Matthew 6:34; Humphreys, ed., Zen by Suzuki, pp. 101, 191; Watts, Way of Zen, p. 120; Phillips, ed., D.T. Suzuki, p. xxi.

60. Blyth, Zen in Literature, pp. 278, 322; Phillips, ed., D.T. Suzuki, pp. xvi-xvii; Weber, Religion of India, p. 278.

61. Humphreys, ed., Zen by Suzuki, pp. 34-35; Kapleau, Three Pillars of Zen, pp. 49-50; Holck, ed., Death and Eastern Thought, pp. 232-233.

62. Phillips, ed., D.T. Suzuki, p. 337; Bodde, ed., Philosophy by Fung Yu-Lan, p. 261.

63. Humphreys, ed., Zen by Suzuki, pp. 55-57; B. Suzuki, Mahayana Buddhism, p. 81; Pratt, Pilgrimage of Buddhism, pp. 626-630.

64. Humphreys, ed., Zen by Suzuki, p. 126n; Blyth, Zen in Literature, p. 179; Bodde, ed., Philosophy by Fung Yu-Lan, p. 320; Kapleau, Three Pillars of Zen, p.18.

65. Kapleau, Three Pillars of Zen, pp. 8, 49, 51-52, 147; Watts, Way of Zen, pp. 106-107; Holck, ed., Death and Eastern Thought, pp. 236-237; Humphreys, ed., Zen by Suzuki, p. 28.

Chapter Four:    Christianity


## The Message of Jesus

Christianity's origins date the beginning of our
era.   Its inspirer, Jesus of Nazareth, was a Jew who
preached his message in Galilee at a time when his
people hoped that Israel's subservience to Rome would
be broken through divine intervention.   He instructed
his followers to love God completely and cherish their
neighbors as they did themselves.   Clearly, if one
succeeded at these tasks selfish ego would dissolve.
We have seen that the Buddha sought the same result
with an elaborate eight-step program.   Jesus did not
supply his followers with any comparable method.
However, he did provide them sufficient encouragement
by using the eschatological expectations of his time
and place.   He described the old worldly order as
ending and God's new Kingdom breaking in upon the old
reality.   Selfishness had no place in God's coming
Kingdom.   For this reason, surrendering all attachments
in love of God and neighbor made sense.

Jesus taught his message in the form of parables,
a technique that required much involvement on the part
of the learner.   His attitude was to provide a teaching
only for those who had "ears to hear."   Several
generations later, his message was recorded in
narratives called gospels, or good news.   These books
are not of a matter-of-fact sort.   Their biographies of
Jesus include no trivial detail.   They do not even
describe how he looked, for they were designed to serve
religious rather than merely historical purposes.   The
gospels were intended to teach by means of poetic
analogies.   Elements from the Jewish Torah were
repeated in the patterns of Jesus's life story for
those who had "ears to hear."[1]

An example of the gospels' teaching style is
called for.   An analogy concerning the birth of John
the Baptist will suffice.   John the Baptist had
immediately preceded Jesus in proclaiming the coming
Kingdom of God.   He had urged repentance and frequent
baptisms in preparation for the new order.   Indeed, in
the course of his ministry he had baptized Jesus
himself.   Subsequently, John was arrested and executed
for criticizing the private life of Herod Antipas, the
ruler of Galilee.   Jesus had replaced John as the
preacher of the coming Kingdom, yet many continued to

regard John as primary and Jesus as only a substitute created by unfortunate events. The gospel story of John's birth was designed to address this early challenge to Jesus's authority.

According to the gospels, John was born of aged parents. This was analogous to the birth of Isaac, a story from the Torah. Isaac's birth to the aged Abraham and Sarah had symbolized the growing covenant relationship between God and His chosen people. The message of John's similar birth suggested the beginning of a new covenant relationship between God and man. Even more was implied. Isaac was a secondary figure in the Jewish story. He was clearly not on a par with the likes of Moses and David. Similarly, the gospels described John as not fit to untie the footwear of Jesus, who would fulfill God's new covenant. Also, the miracle of John's birth could not compare with being born of a virgin, which is how the gospels describe the birth of Jesus himself. A Greek translation of the book of Isaiah had said that Immanuel, or "God with us," would be born of a virgin. The gospels proclaimed that this prophecy was fulfilled in Jesus's birth. In these introductory stories, Jesus was elevated above the popular Baptist.[2]

Historical writing of the present day bears little similarity to the style of the gospels. The canons of modern scholarship require that written history report only that which can be documented. While not without its benefits, this approach to recording history tends to skim only the surface of human events. It consumes an inordinate amount of attention on accidental details at the expense of more profound truths. By contrast, the gospel historians were poetic artists, who allowed their inspired imaginations to address fundamental issues of human existence. The fact that much in the gospels can be identified as Midrash, or folkloric elaboration upon ancient Jewish themes, does not negate their story as history. What it does require is that we, as modern persons, appreciate the value of historical literature as it was crafted in ancient times.

Modern, secular historians concede that Jesus walked the earth, that he preached for a brief period in Galilee and that he was executed while on a Passover visit to Jerusalem in 29 A.D. Christians accept that he rose from the dead shortly following his execution, although gospel accounts are somewhat confusing on the incidental details of his resurrection. Whether the resurrected Christ appeared before his disciples in Jerusalem or Galilee or both is left unresolved in the gospels. The fact remains that shortly after Jesus's death his followers experienced something profound upon which they based their subsequent lives. Accordingly, they sought to communicate the depth of what they had experienced by drawing upon familiar analogies from the Torah.

Jewish eschatological expectations were varied during Jesus's day. Some held that Moses or Elijah would inaugurate God's Kingdom, while others saw a return of the lost Davidic monarchy at the end of days. Accordingly, the gospel narratives connected Jesus to these expectations. The transfiguration scene (Matthew 17:1-3) portrays Jesus as a luminous being together with Moses and Elijah. Clearly, Jesus was neither Moses nor Elijah, but he was certainly in league with them. The gospels identified Jesus as of the house of David, although the genealogies of Jesus offered in Matthew and Luke differ concerning which of David's sons carried Jesus's line. The discrepancy is unimportant, as the message that Jesus was the messenger of the long-expected Kingdom of God was clearly made in the Davidic claim.[3]

Other events in the gospel history of Jesus clarified his relationship to the coming Kingdom. As he approached Jerusalem on his last journey to that city, Jesus apparently prearranged his entrance to coincide with prophecy from Zechariah 9:9-10:

Rejoice greatly, O daughter of Zion:
Shout aloud, O daughter of Jerusalem:
Lo, your king comes to you;
triumphant and victorious is he,
humble and riding on an ass,
on a colt the foal of an ass...,
and he shall command peace to the
nations; his dominion shall be from
sea to sea, and from the river to the
ends of the earth.

Matthew's gospel narrative harmonizes with the above account in describing Jesus as simultaneously riding both an ass and a colt into Jerusalem. Again, the incidental details were not important. The religious message was. Jesus was proclaimed as the foretold king of the Jews. Zechariah 14:21 had prophecied that "there shall no longer be a trader in the house of the Lord of hosts on that day [the end of days]."

Accordingly, Jesus threw the money changers from the Temple, an event that apparently contributed to his subsequent arrest and execution. In any case, in tying his story to the prophesies of Zechariah, the authors of the gospels had cryptically described Jesus as the long-awaited eschatological Messiah of Judaism.

The Christian New Testament would refer to the crucified Jesus as the Passover Lamb of God. Here again, the gospel historians relied on an Old Testament religious theme. Exodus describes that when Moses failed to persuade the Pharoah to liberate the Hebrew people, God visited his wrath on Egypt by killing the first-born males of every household. The Israelites were spared by smearing an unblemished lamb's sacrificial blood on the doorposts of their dwellings. Thereby, God's angel of death knew to pass over the Hebrew homes. This was the symbolism of the Jewish Passover that would be transferred to the Christian Easter. Easter would be a celebration of God's deliverance of his new chosen people from the power of death through the self-sacrifice of Jesus Christ, the new Passover lamb of God.

It was normal Roman practice to break the legs of crucifixion victims to keep them from propping themselves up and renewing the circulation of blood through their bodies. Gospel says that this was not done in Jesus's case. Here was another analogy. Exodus 12:46 had proclaimed: "No bone of the Paschal lamb shall be broken in the Passover feast." In the story of Jesus, the Jewish Passover was transferred to an immortal plane. Those who would share in Jesus's sacrifice would have eternal life. Death would have no permanent power over them.[4]

Over the centuries, Judaism's ancient emphasis on blood sacrifice had evolved into the belief that suffering confers divine power. Chapter 53 of Isaiah exhibited the culmination of this development in Jewish scripture. It described "a man of sorrows,...familiar with suffering," who bears the sufferings of the multitude. "On him lies a punishment that brings us peace, and through his wounds we are healed....Yahweh burdened him with the sins of all of us....Yahweh has been pleased to crush him with suffering.... He offers his life in atonement." Here was the ultimate sacrifice. It did not involve a lamb, dumbly taken from its flock for unknown purposes. Rather, here was the element of self-sacrifice, made with foreknowledge of the suffering. Here was the model for Jesus on the cross. Some historians have speculated that Jesus was motivated not to defend himself as he deliberately sought the sacrifice of Isaiah's suffering servant. In any case, after the crucifixion, his followers saw the connection with Isaiah 53. It explained his execution and indeed made it necessary.[5]

The story of Jesus did not end on Golgotha, his execution site. On the third day of his entombment, he rose from the dead. Why was this necessary? Why did a man bearing the power of God have to sacrifice himself on a cross? What was to be gained by self-sacrifice and suffering? Here was the essential mystery of Christianity. Mystics have explained that God can only be known when the natural human ego's defenses against Him are broken, a process which inevitably involves suffering. Irenaeus of Lyons, living in the second century, cryptically noted that Jesus Christ "became as we are that we might become as he is." A more precise theological exposition of the meaning of Jesus's sacrifice would await Anselm of Canterbury, who lived in the 11th century. His formula began by proclaiming the infinite weakness of man who is unable to overcome his condition by human effort. God alone, he noted, can remake mankind. Yet, as this weakness was the result of man's sin, it is man, not God, who must provide satisfaction. Hence, there was a need for a man-God, who alone could both provide the power and yet atone for the sins of man. Despite Anselm's intellectual explanation, the Church remains devoted to the essential mystery of the atonement wrought by Jesus Christ. Understanding of it can occur only on an existential level by personal participation in both Christ's suffering and forgiveness.[6]

Jesus's resurrection indicated that, to some degree, the Kingdom of God was beginning. This belief was reinforced by the experience of his disciples at the Jewish holiday of Pentecost, occurring 50 days after the second day of Passover. In Judaism, Pentecost celebrates the establishment of God's covenant relationship with the Hebrew people during Moses's time. We have seen that the meaning of the Christian Easter is linked to the story of the Jewish Passover. Similarly, the meaning of the Jewish Pentecost would be transferred to a Christian story. As God had earlier created a covenant with Moses, He would do likewise with the followers of Jesus on the first Pentecost following the crucifixion and resurrection. The result would be a new covenant, the establishment of the Christian Church.

145

The book of Acts reveals that Jesus's disciples were in Jerusalem for the first Jewish Pentecost following their master's execution. Jews from many foreign nations were there also, but they could not receive the redemptive message of Jesus Christ for they understood only foreign tongues. Then the Apostles were filled by the Holy Ghost "and began to speak with other tongues, as the Spirit gave them utterance." In this way, many visiting Jews heard and believed. This story played upon several Old Testament themes. One was a prophecy in Joel that God would pour out His spirit upon all flesh, causing young men to see visions. Indeed, this reference was directly acknowledged in the Christian account of the Pentecost story. Another theme in the Christian Pentecost was the destruction of all language barriers. Genesis 11:1-9 had described the origin of human language differences in God's wrath over human arrogance accompanying the construction of the Tower of Babel. Ever since that time, people had been divided into groups of mutual hatred and distrust. But with the creation of the Christian Church was born a new community, within which all human barriers fell away. This was the intended religious meaning of the Christian Pentecost story.

The early Christians had a clear sense of their purpose and mission: Christ's Church must be engaged with the world. It must suffer as the living body of Christ. The victory over death, witnessed in Christ's resurrection, was not yet complete, yet God's intention was now clear. No one knew when in God's time the Kingdom itself would come and Christ would return to judge all who have ever lived. During the interim, the Church must preach the gospel among all the nations of the earth. Indeed, the gospels state that this is a necessary prerequisite before the Kingdom of God may be established.

The early Christians knew the meaning of their faith. In modern times, some of this confidence has been shaken. For the last two centuries, much has been made of the fact that the gospels are not historically accurate. Atheists have revelled in this knowledge, while Christian Fundamentalists have desperately insisted, in spite of numerous problems of historical evidence, that the gospels are literally factual. The Fundamentalists' problem results in part from a misconception of the guiding philosophy of history in the ancient world. Two thousand years ago, historical

146

writing was not expected to be concocted solely of scientifically verifiable facts. At that time, one wrote history not to impart relatively sterile information but rather to communicate a certain religious or ethical view of life. In the ancient world, any good historical work necessarily involved much poetic imagination. A poet is concerned not only with what has happened but also with what may happen. He seeks to express that which is universal and eternal, whereas the modern historian is tied merely to that which is particular and relative.

It was not so long ago that historians freely used poetic imagination in the crafting of their stories. All Americans are familiar with the inspiring tale of young George Washington who chopped down a prized cherry tree, thereupon confessing the act to his father. "I cannot tell a lie," young Washington was reported to have said. This story was created by Mason Weems, who wrote a biography of Washington in the early 19th century. He got the idea from an event within his own family's history. Was Weems's account not historically accurate? The Weems's story is flawed only from the standards of modern historical scholarship. The main point that Weems was trying to relate, that being that Washington was a person of noble personal character and integrity, was true. Washington's modern biographers support this conclusion. Yet Weems's folkloric elaboration upon the Washington legend communicated this fact to his countrymen far better than "scientific" history subsequently has done.

Similar to Weems, early Christian writers exercised a flexible hand when working with historical fact, for their highest value was not modern historical objectivity but rather their Christian faith. Similar to Jesus himself, they taught by frequent use of allegories. Whereas Jesus used timeless parables to carry his teaching, the New Testament authors drew upon analogies in the Torah to show that Jesus represented the fulfillment of Judaism. Jesus had said: "Know the truth, and the truth shall make you free." The gospel writers sought to convey this truth--that man can be at one with God and his neighbor, that death can lose its sting by complete surrender to God through service and sacrifice for others and that man can rise above selfishness that brings only meaninglessness and despair. This was the way of Jesus of Nazareth. It was his message to the world.

147

## The Early Church

The earliest followers of Jesus of Nazareth did not call themselves Christians, a title deriving from "Christos" (a Greek word meaning Messiah, deliverer). Rather, they were known as Nazoreans. Nazorean meant maintainer or preserver, and its implication was that Jesus's followers were the guardians of Israel's true faith. Jerusalem was their base of operations. Peter, the disciple whom Jesus himself had chosen to found his movement, was their leader. Then in 42 A.D., some 13 years after the crucifixion, he relinquished his primacy to James, Jesus's kinsman. An eruption of orthodox Jewish hostility toward the Nazoreans apparently persuaded Peter to play a safer, secondary role.[10]

Paul soon joined Peter and James as a leader in the early Church. Beginning as an agent of the Jewish persecutors, Paul had followed Nazoreans to Damascus in 36 A.D., fully intending to do them harm. However, on the way there, he was blinded by a heavenly light, and he heard a voice calling: "Why do you persecute me?" He saw no human figure, but he would remember the event as his personal encounter with Jesus Christ. After a period of relative inactivity, needed by Paul to digest what had happened, he entered upon his career as the most successful Christian missionary of all time. Having known Christ in the spirit but not in the flesh, he claimed to be Christ's apostle to the Gentiles.

Paul quarreled with James, an event which divided the early Church. In Antioch, Paul allowed Gentile converts to avoid the difficult and generations-long adjustment to Jewish law. Meanwhile, James insisted that all converts adhere to essential Jewish traditions. For awhile, it appeared that a compromise between Paul and James was possible. However, this hope was short lived. Interestingly enough, the dispute that led to an open break between them involved Peter, who had come to Antioch and shared meals with Paul's Gentile converts. When James heard of this, he was furious, as Jewish law forbade dining with Gentiles. Peter contritely consented to commit no future transgressions. Paul thought differently. Leaving Antioch, he travelled to Anatolia (Turkey) and from there to Greece. Far from James's authority, Paul was free to preach what he called Christianity. Peter probably also grew tired of James's restrictive hand, as he moved to Rome. Both he and Paul would end their lives there, most likely victims of the Emperor Nero.

Christianity survived, while the Nazorean sect perished. In 62 A.D., James was stoned to death by a Jewish mob. Several years later, Jerusalem was destroyed in the first Jewish war with Rome. The Nazoreans were dispersed. Remnants were later found in Syria, but they would never again serve as the fount of Jesus's message. That honor would belong to the branch established by Paul.[11]

Paul's Christian theology was shaped by the nature of his own conversion. It had been instantaneous. He had not sought it. His salvation had not been earned by good works. He had not studied or trained for his unique knowledge of Jesus Christ. Instead, his insight had come as an undeserved gift, from God's grace. Judaism emphasized the importance of works, specifically adherence to the 600 and some laws prescribed in the Torah. For a traditional Jew, one could not hope to win God's favor without great effort. According to Paul, God had given Jewish law to sinful man as a means of external control. However, God's grace empowered by Christ's sacrifice on the cross, cancels the power of sin. Consequently, a person who received Christ's redemptive love was born anew with righteousness written on his heart. For Paul's converts, God's will was internalized in the believer. Accordingly, divine authority no longer had to be in the form of external, controlling law.

Paul conceded that even after one is born again in Christ, he experiences an on-going struggle against his own sinful, human nature. As he put it, his mind and heart were won over by Christ, while his flesh remained in bondage to sin. This situation required constant vigilance. Jews accused Paul of being an antinomian, one who advocates libertinism and freedom from moral law. This was unfair. Paul's Christians were not free to violate essential laws, such as the Ten Commandments of Moses. As for other Jewish requirements, such as painful circumcision and inconvenient dietary restrictions, Christ's redemption made them no longer necessary.[12]

Christianity was more appealing than Judaism to the Gentile world. For centuries, Judaism had struggled to win converts. These efforts had been somewhat successful, in spite of the fact that it took a proselyte family three generations to win full acceptance as Jews. Paul's religion was based on Judaism. Indeed, it claimed to have fulfilled Jewish

149

prophecy. But Christianity was far easier on converts than traditional Judaism. Paul's doctrine of salvation by grace allowed a believer quick entree to the Christian community. Accordingly, many Gentile Jews-in-training switched to Christianity. Paul can be viewed as denationalizing and universalizing Judaism, adding to it the redemptive message of Jesus Christ. Pharisaic Judaism could not effectively compete with Paul's message, and the former would eventually surrender its missionary role as a result.

Christianity also competed with other religions in the Roman world. These rivals like Christianity promised eternal life and featured gods who rose from the dead. Yet significant differences separated Christianity from other so-called mystery religions. The latter were outlandishly mythological in character, whereas Christianity was grounded in a human story. They were also lacking in ethical content. They were colorful and dramatic in their rites, so much so that Christianity appeared drab by comparison. Nevertheless, certain similarities linked Christianity to these religions in the popular mind. Christianity's Eucharist bore a rough resemblance to a ceremony of the Myth of Dionysus wherein devotees ate the flesh of a freshly slain bull in hopes of achieving personal immortality. The Virgin Mary, whom the Church would give attributes of a mother goddess, bore an increasing similarity to the goddess Isis, a central figure of another mystery cult. The calendar of the sun god Sol Invictus eventually helped determine the dates of Christmas and Easter. But these facts in no way altered the essential character of the Christian faith.[13]

Gnosticism, a religious movement at least as old as Christianity, posed a graver threat. The word gnosticism derived from the Greek word gnosis, meaning knowledge. Gnostics believed that they possessed special knowledge about the source of eternal life. They treated this knowledge as a secret gift. Upon converting to Christianity, they attempted to redefine the nature of Christian redemption. They claimed that their special knowledge had been handed down to them, from teacher to disciple, originating with Jesus himself. They held that only a few humans possess a divine essence or spark, which at death is reunited with the highest God. Most men, they believed, have mortal souls, which dissolve at death, much as with animals. They believed themselves to be in exclusive spiritual company.[14]

Gnostics were characteristically inventive, imaginative and highly mythological in their theology. This trait led them in many different directions, often in conflict with even other Gnostics. Nevertheless, certain themes tended to predominate among them. First, they saw this world as utterly corrupt and irredeemable. Like the Greeks, they drew a sharp distinction between the higher, eternal world of the spirit and filthy corporeal matter. For Christian Gnostics, the world's creation was either an act of ignorance or evil. Most of them viewed the Creator as the Demiurge, a lesser deity than the highest God. The Demiurge, with Archons or Rulers as his spiritual assistants, was often identified as YHWH, the stern, punishing God of the Jews. They held that the highest God, representing divine love, seeks to liberate the Gnostics from all suffering. In primordial time, the divine sparks at the core of their souls had been lost from the domain of the highest God and had fallen into that of the Demiurge. Christian Gnostics saw Jesus Christ as sent by the highest God to redeem those sparks. For some Christians, this hope replaced that of the coming Kingdom of God.

Christian Gnostics tended to regard Jesus of Nazareth as a divine apparition. Their belief was known as docetism, a term deriving from the Greek word dokeo, meaning "I appear." This notion challenged the traditional Christian redemption concept that Christ had in fleshly form suffered and died to cancel human sin. The docetists' spiritualized Christ was beyond human suffering. Importantly, Gnostics themselves tended to avoid acts of martyrdom and suffering in the face of Roman persecution. They viewed such involvement as irrelevant to their salvation. Detachment from the world, rather than engagement in it, marked their approach to Christianity.[13]

Christian Gnostics threatened the sanctity of scripture. Early in the second century, the Christian word of God was the Jewish Torah and some uncompiled Christian writings elaborating upon its meaning. Gnostic Christians accepted some of these writings, discarded others, and edited still others to suit their purposes. The Torah, being the revealed word of the Demiurge, tended to be seen by them as a lower order of scripture. Some Christian Gnostics rejected it altogether. One of these was Marcion, the son of the Christian bishop of Pontus. Arriving in Rome in 138 A.D., Marcion quickly gained a following. He created his own bible, composed solely of an edited gospel of

151

Luke and the 10 principal letters of Paul  These he could harmonize with his own version of Gnostic Christianity.

This challenge could not be ignored. In combatting Marcion and other forms of Gnostic Christian expression, the Christian bishops throughout the greater Mediterranean area moved into action. As the leaders of organized Christian communities, they asserted their collective authority to define correct Christian teaching and interpretation. To silence Gnostic speculation, they declared that the last valid revelations were received by the apostles. The age of revelation was over. They began to select acceptable writings into a new and official Christian Bible. They also codified the Apostles's Creed as an instrument against Gnostic Christianity.

The Apostles's Creed was not a general exposition of Christian belief. Its focus was more specific, primarily addressing points at issue with Christian Gnostics. It declared YHWH, the creator of this world, to be the supreme and only God. Jesus was identified as his son. It emphasized Christ's humanity--his birth, suffering and death. The Nazorean conception of a fleshly resurrection at the end of days was reasserted. Paul's view that resurrected bodies would be of a spiritual nature had been used too readily by the Gnostics for their own purposes. The creed also stressed the Second Coming of Christ and the eventual establishment of God's Kingdom upon a reconstituted earth, traditional Christian beliefs that had been rejected by many Gnostics within the fold.[16]

By these means, Gnosticism was driven from visible and direct influence in the Church. However, a heavy price was paid for this victory. By restricting revelation to a past age, Christianity was robbed of some of its early vitality. This negative effect did not go unchallenged. About one generation after Marcion was driven from the Church, a new controversy began. This time, the issue was Montanism, named after Montanus, a charismatic Christian from central Asia Minor. While generally acceptable in his theology, Montanus claimed divinely revealed knowledge of the time and place of Christ's Second Coming. He urged all believers to abandon their worldly goods and concerns and await the approaching end. To many genuine Christians, his call was irresistible. The fervor of early Christianity had been growing stale with the delay of Christ's return, and the laity's moral standards had been declining as a consequence. Montanism served to reverse this trend, at least temporarily.

As with Paul's generation of Christians, Montanus's followers lived in Christian love and moral purity, encouraged by their belief that judgment day was near. Montanists spoke in tongues, a babble of religious ecstasy, as had the early Church fathers. Revelations came to Montanus while in a trance-like state. Clearly, if one had this kind of direct relationship with the Holy Spirit, one had little need for Church authorities. Predictably, in 170 A.D., the bishops declared Montanus to be an enemy of the Church. Montanus's claim to knowledge of the time and place of Christ's return was condemned. Thereafter, the official Church would regard belief in Christ's imminent return as foolish and extreme. As a result, the affairs of this world increasingly captured more of the Church's attention. The early Church's appraisal of the world as not worth reforming had only encouraged the drift toward Gnosticism. Now, with the Kingdom of God postponed, Christian suffering and witness in the world would receive greater emphasis. A new Christian ideal was taking shape, that being to remake the world in Christ's image. Unfortunately, as judgment day was pushed off into the distant future, the threat of punishment faded in the Christian message. Accordingly, moral laxity increasingly characterized the Christian congregation.[17]

By the third century, Christian belief was becoming standardized. An official creed and codified scriptures were in the process of development. The Church had successfully met threats both from within its walls and from without. Controversies concerning the meaning of Christ and his message would continue periodically to divide the Church. Sporadic persecution by the Roman state continued to shed the blood of the faithful. Nonetheless, the vibrant era of the early Church was over. It came to a close with the battles over Gnosticism and Montanism. A process had begun toward creating a uniform Christian theology. Moreover, the means to enforce conformity to official Christianity had been established and exercised.

## The Universal Church

Concern over the social and economic weaknesses of the Roman empire grew during the early centuries of the Christian era. The Roman economy suffered from a mounting inflation encouraged by a steady reduction of precious metals in the currency. Hard work no longer seemed to be valued. Fewer Romans were willing to serve in the army, which increasingly had to rely on recruits from outlying, semi-barbaric lands. The birth rate was also in decline among the Roman citizenry. Traditional Roman virtue was increasingly rare. Hedonism and self-gratification set the tone of society. Foreigners of every race and culture brought strange sounds and smells to Roman cities. They brought exotic religions that fed on the credulity of the masses. Faith in the traditional gods of the Roman state was crumbling. Something was terribly wrong.

Thoughtful Romans could identify symptoms of their societal malady. It was more difficult to prescribe an effective cure. Frustration in high places was increasingly apparent, and Christianity was often a lightning rod of this mounting anxiety. Christian behavior seemed to symbolize the problem. Christians did not seek wealth. They avoided military service. They produced few children due to their expectation of an imminent end to history. Rumors held that they ate the flesh and blood of kidnapped babies in their communion rite. It was known fact that they refused to sacrifice to the emperor. For these reasons, they were branded as "atheists" and "enemies of the human race."

Before the emperor Decius, who ruled from 249 to 251 A.D., anti-Christian persecution had been local and sporadic. Decius made this persecution active and general. He identified Christianity as a fundamental source of his empire's problems, as he embarked on a loyalty oath campaign to be administered to every man, woman and child. The crucial test was a sacrifice to the emperor and the traditional gods of the state. Those who refused to participate were killed. Of course, Christians viewed sacrificing to the emperor as idolatry. Jews did also, but they were exempt from participation by their treaty status as a conquered nation. Christians enjoyed no such waiver, a fact which resulted in many martyrs. Some were beheaded, a form of execution reserved for Roman citizens. Others were burned to death, suffocated in prison, or killed by wild animals for public spectacle.[18]

Christianity appeared to thrive under lash, fire and sword. Many a Christian welcomed the status of "martyr," a term deriving from a Greek word meaning "witness." As a persecuted minority, Christians showed a courage and willingness to die for a creed.

154

Ironically, this was the very quality which the old, tired Roman empire wished to restore. Perhaps this realization transformed Constantine, who became emperor in 312 A.D., into a Christian. He halted the persecution. Public funds were showered upon the Church. He selected Byzantium, renamed Constantinople, as his new capital and molded it into a Christian showplace. Henceforth, with only one brief interruption during the reign of Julian the Apostate, the empire would favor Christianity.

The Roman empire, heretofore held together only by fear of the army and the tax collector, desperately needed an effective state religion to bind its multi-ethnic citizenry. To serve this cause, Church unity was essential. Accordingly, beginning with Constantine, Roman emperors were most sensitive to theological disputes that threatened this important political purpose. The most significant example of this in Constantine's day led to the first general Church council, held in 325 A.D. at Nicaea, a suburb of Constantinople. This dispute centered on one Arius, a presbyter from the Alexandrian Church. He held that God had created Christ, which if true made the Galilean subordinate to God. Arius also claimed that Christ never possessed a corrupt, human nature. He described Christ as an intermediate deity between God and man. This view offended Athanasius, a deacon in the Alexandrian Church, for it threatened not only Christian monotheism but also the very basis of Christian redemption. For Athanasius, God and man were reunited in Jesus Christ, who accomplished this reconciliation through his sacrificial, atoning death. A view such as Arius's that separated Christ both from man and God was unacceptable.

The Nicaean council hammered out a creed that ruled against Arius. It stated that Jesus Christ was uncreated and of one substance with God. Likewise, it suggested his human nature by dwelling on his birth, suffering and death as a man. Arius and his followers, who refused to sign the creed, were sent into exile. However, this did not end the controversy. Emperor Constantinius, who favored the Arian position, later exiled Athanasius, and the Church continued the debate. Resolution would come at the Council of Chalcedon (451 A.D.) which finally laid the Arian tradition to rest.[19]

Needs of state required Christian uniformity. The vitality of the faith required continuing opportunity for Christian witness. The end of official persecution

155

led believers to seek new ways to carry one's cross in the world. Inspiration was found on the Egyptian desert. In the last years of Roman persecution, some Egyptian Christians had escaped there to live alone in prayer and meditation. The fame of their ascetic practices, which included celibacy, spread. Named "athletes of God," these ascetics inaugurated the monastic tradition within Christianity. They erected a new standard of martyrdom for Christians, involving denial of physical cravings. Pressures mounted for the Church's priests to measure up to this new model. In Greek-speaking lands, priestly celibacy would remain only an ideal, albeit it was required of bishops. In Latin speaking regions, celibacy became demanded of priests as well as bishops, although this requirement was frequently ignored.[26]

While the debates on Arianism and priestly celibacy were important concerns in the 4th century, a far more fundamental issue faced the Church of that day. Stated plainly, it was whether the established Church of the state should be catholic, universal, a church for the masses, or a church for the spiritually pure alone. Donatus, a North African who lived early in the century, argued for the latter. In his opinion, those Christians who had apostatized under the threat of death during the Roman persecution were beyond forgiveness and destined to eternal hell. Donatus's party questioned the validity of sacraments administered by priests who had collaborated with the persecutors to escape death. From the Donatist perspective, the Church should consist only of the pure and resolute. All across North Africa, the Church split into Catholic and Donatist congregations, whose mutual hostility often resulted in open acts of violence.

A century later, a British monk named Pelagius likewise argued that Christianity was not for the common sinner. Arriving in Rome, he was shocked by the low state of morals he found there. He blamed the practice of infant baptism for this scandal. In his mind, the important step of baptism should signify a conscious, adult decision to live a life of Christian purity. For Pelagius, free will was a divine gift allowing human beings to choose the Christian life. He was not lenient with Christians who sinned after they had been baptized. Clearly, if his position had won out, the Church would have been for a very small minority.

St. Augustine, who from 396 to 430 served as the Bishop of Hippo, attacked the exclusive notions of Donatus and Pelagius. In doing so, he restated and elaborated upon the traditional Church position concerning the sinful nature of man. Before Christian baptism, he said, all carry the stain of Adam's "original sin." This concept concerned Adam's transgression of eating from the tree of knowledge, which had the effect of alienating both the first man and all of his descendants from God. This idea, briefly noted in the Pauline epistles, was thoroughly developed by Augustine. As Christianity taught that reconciliation between God and man was possible only through Christian baptism, Augustine argued that original sin required infant baptism. Otherwise, an unexpected or accidental death coupled with an unrelieved original sin would sentence one to an eternity in hell. In this way, Augustine dismissed Pelagius's advocacy of adult baptism.

Similarly, he rejected Pelagius's idea that human merit or purity could earn salvation. Again he emphasized man's sinful nature: Even after baptism washed away original sin, man was still left with a predisposition to sin. He called this concupiscence, or craving (especially sexual desire). Given this reality of the human condition, he saw all talk of a spiritually pure Church as self-righteous nonsense. According to Augustine, man is not free from sin so as to be able to save himself without God's grace. Indeed, he stressed that God predestines those who will be saved. Augustine stopped short of denying the existence of free will, an act which would have contradicted some of his early writings. In his theory of divine concurrence, Augustine emphasized that human free will and divine predestination exist concurrently, a marriage that violates human logic. Nonetheless, he argued, on a divine level of understanding, they coexist. His theory of divine concurrence directly ridiculed the powers of human understanding and cast man as insignificant when compared to Almighty God. In this way, he even used free will to support his twin themes of divine omnipotence and human weakness.

Above all, Augustine's message was one of hope for the average Christian. Sinful man could receive God's grace through the Church's sacraments. Augustine rejected the Donatist notion that sinful priests could invalidate the sacraments that they administered. He described the Church as the body of Christ in the world and its sanctity as independent of the sinful nature of its membership. Here was hope that the power of the sacraments could not be called into question. Augustine also offered hope for those Christians who temporarily succumbed to concupiscence. Whereas Donatus and Pelagius were unforgiving concerning sins committed after baptism, Augustine stressed how the negative impact of such sins could be minimized through confession and penance. Centuries before Augustine, confessions of post-baptismal sins had to me made in the presence of the Christian community. In Augustine's time, a mix of public and private confessions, depending upon the sin involved, was allowed. Less than 30 years after Augustine, confession and penance became a completely private matter, shared between the sinner and a priest alone. Augustine encouraged this trend toward an easy forgiveness of sins.

According to Augustine, few Christians go to hell. He claimed that most go to a place called purgatory when they die. There they will suffer until they can be sufficiently purged of their sins. Then they will enter God's own realm. Only the few who commit heinous post-baptismal sins are lost to the eternal torments of hell. The implication in Augustine's description of the afterlife was that most Christians, while possessing a sinful nature, are among God's elect. Augustine's Catholics were reassured by his theology of hope.

Augustine defeated his opponents. The Church would be catholic. True to the nature of a universal church, those wishing to be a spiritual elite would not be excluded. Catholic monasticism would appeal to such souls. But most Catholics would not become monks and nuns. Most Catholics would rely on concepts developed and argued by Augustine. Nonetheless, the Church modified his thought somewhat. His extreme emphasis on divine omnipotence had been fashioned in the heat of fighting Donatists and Pelagians. His doctrine of predestination failed to serve Catholic interests after these battles were won. Church authorities saw an emphasis on free will as encouraging Christians to live upright lives more than a doctrine of predestination. Through its sacramental system, the Church would promote a religion of acquired spiritual merit and good works within which free will played a predominant role. A degree of Pelgianism would live on in the robes of Augustine.[21]

# Medieval Christianity

In Augustine's day, the Christian Church was unified in a rough sort of way. Today, of course, this is not the case. Christianity has no commonly recognized central authority. Three major traditions (Roman Catholic, Greek Orthodox and Protestant) divide the Christian family. The Protestant branch is of rather modern origin, being born in the 16th century, albeit it claims the true spirit of early Christianity. The Roman Catholic and Greek Orthodox traditions are more ancient in their organization. Their divergence occurred during the medieval era, which spanned from 500 to 1450. Originally, both of these systems grew from the religion established by St. Paul.

Before the ascension of Constantine in 312, in questions dividing the Church, Christians had tended to defer to the Pope, the bishop of Rome. His prestige was built upon several factors, namely Peter and Paul's roles in founding the Roman Church and the fact that Rome was the hub of the empire. The removal of the imperial capital to Byzantium (Constantinople) challenged this nascent tradition. Beginning with Constantine, the emperor regarded himself as the Church's final authority, a claim that was termed "caesaropapism." Beneath himself, he viewed the Roman Pope as the first of five leading bishops, who, in addition to Rome, represented Constantinople, Alexandria, Antioch and Jerusalem. In the emperor's eyes, they were all necessary adjuncts to his system of government.[22]

The changing shape of secular empires eventually freed the Pope from the smothering effects of caesaropapism. During the 5th and 6th centuries, Roman citizens suffered greatly as the emperor's forces fought barbarian invaders for the Italian peninsula. From this trial came a new realization. The Greek soldiers of Byzantium were foreigners as much as the barbarians. They cared nothing for the Roman citizenry. The Pope alone identified with the people's condition. Gregory the Great, the leading Pope during this period, used Church resources to feed those dispossessed by war. He ransomed captives and made treaties with barbarian kings. Officially, he served as the Byzantine emperor's viceroy. But in the eyes of his people, the Pope emerged as the only true leader of Roman civilization.

Heavy taxes and theological differences with

Constantinople ultimately severed Byzantium's imperial ties with Rome. In the 8th century, the Pope established a new viceregal relationship with the Frankish empire. He did so with the help of a document known as the Donation of Constantine. According to this official paper, the Emperor Constantine had supposedly deeded secular authority over Rome and its environs to the Pope when the move of the imperial capital to Constantinople occurred. Eventually, the document's fraudulent character was revealed. However, in the 8th century it was used effectively to free Rome from Byzantine suzerainty. Ironically, the Roman Church then became caught in a web of Frankish caesaropapism. Dominant secular power, whether it came from Byzantium or western Europe, had the same effect upon the Church. Charlemagne, the most powerful of the Frankish kings, openly dominated the affairs of the Roman Church. He named bishops and abbots and used them in administering his extensive empire. Again, relief came in the form of disaster. Viking raids in the 9th century destroyed the Frankish empire.

Meanwhile, emerging Islam increasingly threatened the Churches of Alexandria, Jerusalem and Antioch--all of which eventually fell before the Muslim advance. Indeed, the medieval millennium would end with the Muslim conquest of Constantinople itself. Because of this, Roman Catholicism would eventually emerge as the dominant Christian expression. Geography aided the cause of Rome, which was far from the centers of Muslim power. Rome was also located safely beyond the Alps, a good distance from the destructive hands of Viking marauders. Enjoying a geographic position of relative security, the Roman Church maneuvered the stormy events of the medieval period to its own advantage.[23]

The Greek Church was not as fortunate. Its troubles began with the monophysite controversy, which plagued the Byzantine empire in the 5th century. The general Church council at Chalcedon in 451 had ruled that Christ had two natures, one fully human and the other fully divine. Rome and Constantinople supported Chalcedon, but Alexandria had rebelled. For Egyptian or Coptic Christians, Christ's nature was dominated by its divine aspects. Their belief was called monophysite, as it stressed a single nature of Christ. Egyptian and Greek ethnic jealousies fueled this theological conflict within the empire. A compromise position, known as monothelitism, came too late. This held that while Christ had two natures, he had only one will, and that was divine. The Alexandrian Church

160

rejected this gesture. Shortly thereafter, Egypt fell to Islam. Coptic Christians initially welcomed the Muslims as liberators from unwanted Greek influence.

The Greek Church next suffered through the iconoclastic controversy. In the 8th and 9th centuries, Byzantine emperors demanded that their subjects destroy all religious images, whether in the form of pictures or statues. This position, called iconoclasm, was inspired by Islamic notions of religious images as idolatrous. Most Greek Christians disagreed. They claimed that religious images were in harmony with the incarnation itself, as God Himself had assumed human form. The elements of the Eucharist were also held up as symbols of Christ's body and blood. If these were not forbidden, then why were icons? Were not visual representations also religious symbols? Finally, a compromise was reached. Pictures would be tolerated. Only statues would be banned. The important result of this internal struggle was a weakened Greek Church, less capable of meeting its next historic challenge.[24]

Islam triggered the next crisis. The Byzantine empire had already lost much territory to Muslim armies, which constantly threatened to take more. Desperate, the emperor called upon the Roman Pope near the end of the 11th century for assistance against a common enemy. The outcome of this request would prove disastrous for Greek Christianity. The Pope responded by inaugurating the Christian crusades against Islam. Western European crusaders, eager for battle, too often mistook Eastern Christians for the enemy. Even when there was no excuse of mistaken identity, Greek Christian strongholds were attacked. Constantinople itself was sacked by crusaders in 1204. In comparison to the barbaric behavior of Western Christians, Muslims now appeared as highly civilized. The will to resist Islam was at an all time low for Greek Christendom. The last crusade ended in 1244. Two centuries later, Constantinople itself fell to Islam. The Patriarch survived the conquest but was forced to surrender the use of all but one of his churches to the victors. With the subsequent expansion of the Islamic Ottoman empire into Europe, the Patriarch's influence would again grow, this time over the ranks of conquered Christian peasants. But his Church would remain a captive Church.[25]

In some ways, the modern world was born in the crusades. Crusaders returned with exotic spices and other products, whetting a commercial interest that greatly encouraged the growth of trade. Ancient knowledge, long preserved by Islamic scholars, followed, causing new intellectual ferment. These influences eventually helped generate a reawakening known as the Renaissance, which appeared in different countries anywhere from the 14th to the 17th centuries. The progress of modern science and technology began in this revitalized environment. A more immediate effect of the crusades was to feed medieval credulity and superstition. Returning crusaders brought relics from the Holy Land--pieces of the true cross and Moses's burning bush, strands of the Virgin's hair as well as her finger-nail parings, and, of course, the bones of revered saints. These relics were believed to have magical power and radiate holiness much as a supernatural atomic pile.

At least one such relic has endured to our own day. It is the Shroud of Turin, claimed to be the burial cloth of Christ himself. Surfacing in southern France in the 14th century, it is believed to have been brought there by a returning crusader. The shroud is a piece of linen, measuring fourteen by four feet, with the negative imprint of a bearded man upon it. In modern times, a group of scientists has been allowed to examine it in Turin, Italy, where it is housed. Not permitted to carbon date the material, as that process would result in its partial destruction, the team nevertheless has concluded that good reasons exist to believe it is authentic. The image's accuracy in physical details, together with the fact that it was neither painted nor burned onto the cloth, caused even some prior sceptics on the team to alter their views.[26]

The relic consciousness of medieval Europe was indicative of a certain type of Christianity that emphasizes mystery and miracles more than changed lives. Roman religious services were conducted in Latin, a language increasingly unintelligible to the people. The medieval Church adopted the dogma of transubstantiation, the belief that when a priest blesses the elements of the Eucharist they actually become the body and blood of Christ while retaining their original appearance. The age also witnessed the origin of indulgences, papal dispensations reducing the agony of purgatory for their recipients. The logic of indulgences was that Christ and the saints had earned surplus merits which were left to the Pope to dispense. Indulgences were first granted to crusaders as a spur to leave home and family to fight infidels. Later, they were sold to raise money for Church construction projects. Eventually, a reaction against them would spark the Protestant revolt.[27]

Historians are often tempted to cast the Middle Ages as a time of dogmatic uniformity of belief. Such was not the case. The medieval Church encountered many challenges to its authority. One came from Peter Waldo, a wealthy merchant who gave all his possessions to the poor in 1173. His followers, known as Waldenses, attacked the Church as lacking in moral purity and spiritual devotion. Similar to the Donatists of Augustine's day, they questioned the validity of sacraments administered by immoral priests. They urged that all Christians read the Bible for its emphasis on detachment from material possessions. They spurned the official Church as oriented toward worldly values. Rome responded early in the 13th century by discouraging the faithful to read the scriptures for themselves. The Church felt itself under attack, and its monopoly of scriptural interpretation was an essential means of defense. The Waldenses were persecuted, with the idea of returning them to authorized belief rather than achieving their physical extermination. Interestingly, St. Francis of Assisi, a 13th-century contemporary of the Waldenses, shared the sect's orientation toward poverty and Christian living. However, he differed with them on one crucial issue: He remained deferential to the authority of Church and Pope.

Movements more radical than the Waldenses plagued the Roman Church. The Cathars, or Albigenses as they were also called, represented a medieval revival of the Gnostic heresy. They infiltrated and controlled the Church in southern France from the 12th through the 14th centuries. In the 13th century, the Church instituted the Inquisition, which operated on the principle that the execution of a heretic benefits his soul. Accordingly, the Cathars were exterminated by sword and fire. New ideas, stemming from Europe's reawakening, were challenging traditional Christian belief. One Meister Eckhart, a German mystic who died in 1327, described the Christian God in terms that sound akin to the Vedantist Shankara. Untouched during his lifetime, Eckhart's writings were posthumously burned. As his thought dissolved the concept of a personal deity, the Church could not long tolerate Meister Eckhart.

Ironically, the Church sought to use the

intellectual ferment causing its troubles in its own defense. Scholasticism was the result. Blossoming in the 13th century, scholasticism was a style of medieval scholarship that used reason to defend Church dogma. Scholastics accepted without question that Church dogmas were true. From that assumption, they wove intricate webs of intellectual proof supporting official Christian teaching. St. Thomas Aquinas was the most famous of these Church apologists. Unhappily for medieval Christianity, scholasticism was only a way station for increasingly curious European intellectuals. The 14th century saw the beginnings of the Renaissance that glorified the powers of the human intellect. Worldly values increasingly challenged those that had been preached by Christ. The papacy itself was caught in the snare of worldliness, as in the 15th century immorality and nepotism flourished in the Vatican. The medieval world view was apparently bankrupt. Thoughtful persons could see that if Christianity would survive this new age, something more was needed than blind obedience to corrupt Church authority. The scene was set for the emergence of the Protestant variant from the tradition of Roman Catholicism.[28]

## The Protestant Reformation

In 1517, a German monk named Martin Luther began his protest against the Roman Catholic Church. At the outset, he had no plan of grand reform. His complaints were limited, but the intransigence of the Church and Luther's own fiery rhetoric raised a confrontation that would shatter medieval Christian culture. Ironically, this disruption encouraged influences that Luther detested, namely secularism, materialism and hedonism. Of course, Luther had not intended that this would be the fruit of his efforts. His hope, and that of those who joined him, was that Christian culture would be reformed and restored to the faith that had inspired Paul and Augustine. He saw the Christianity of his own day as sorely wanting in depth and characterized by practices that at best affected only the outward behavior of men and women without changing their hearts. He knew that Christianity was more than that.

Luther was not the first person to hold this vision. John Wycliffe, an English divine of the late 14th century, propagated many beliefs later associated with Luther's revolt. In the 1370's, Wycliffe rejected the Church's doctrine of transubstantiation in favor of what he called consubstantiation. This latter belief held that when a priest blessed the bread and wine, these elements retained their original character while assuming the actual presence of Christ. More importantly, Wycliffe preceded Luther in teaching both that God's grace comes to man independent of Church authority and that scripture, not the Church, is the final Christian source of spiritual direction. Wycliffe preached that true Christians live in poverty, quite apart from the luxurious style of the Pope, whom the former identified as the Anti-Christ. John Hus, a younger contemporary of Wycliffe, agreed. Inspired by the Englishman, Hus raised his opposition from Prague. A natural death saved Wycliffe from the stake. Hus was not as fortunate. Following Hus, Luther had every reason to expect that his life too would end in flames.[29]

The invention of the modern printing press in the middle of the 15th century helped Luther succeed where Wycliffe and Hus had failed. This communications tool suddenly made the scriptures available to the multitudes. Independent interpretation of the holy writ was thereby encouraged, while making the Church's role as guardian of the Bible more difficult. During his long career, Luther published an average of one polemical tract every two weeks. His movement fed on this print-media revolution. The Church could not suppress this quick and easy flow of information. Ironically, the military expansion of Islam into Europe in the 16th century also helped Luther. At crucial junctures, Catholic attention was diverted from Luther to the advancing Ottoman Turks, who at one point came to the outskirts of Vienna. As a result, the weight of traditional, established authority was not brought against Luther, who was allowed to survive under the protection of some relatively unimportant German princes. In this way, unforeseen fortuitous timing contributed to Luther's success. Wycliffe and Hus had enjoyed no such advantage.[30]

Desiderius Erasmus, the most renowned scholar of Luther's day, helped prepare the way for the German reformer by attacking certain abuses of the Roman Church. He mocked Catholic monasteries as centers of indolence and ridiculed the silly devotion to theological minutiae that characterized Catholic scholasticism. He argued that Christ himself had preached to the multitude independent of any priestly censorship. Why then, he asked, should Christian laymen be discouraged from reading the scriptures for themselves? Luther would adopt these arguments.

165

Erasmus lacked the heart of a radical.  Unlike Luther, he never broke with the Church.  Erasmus was a humanist.  He trusted in the reasonableness of churchmen to respond appropriately to constructive criticism.  His only aim was to reform the Roman Church.  By contrast, Luther eventually sought to destroy it.  Luther's temperament saw life in the sharp contrasts of good and evil, salvation and damnation, correct belief and lies.  He did not see mankind as reasonable but rather as utterly depraved.  From Erasmus's perspective, Luther degenerated into a fanatic.  In Luther's eyes, Erasmus remained too detached and shallow in his Christian understanding. Beginning as allies, they ended as enemies.[5]

Nevertheless, the two men agreed on the primacy of scripture.  By contrast, Catholic authorities proclaimed the supremacy of the Church over scripture. During the Gnostic controversy of the second century, the Church had accepted some scriptures and had rejected others in composing the Christian Bible.  In this sense, the Church had created the Bible and therefore was superior to it.  One modern Catholic apologist has written:  "What authority have we, apart from that of the Church, to say that the Epistles of Paul are inspired, and the Epistle of Barnabas is not?" Modern Protestants, continuing the shared tradition of Erasmus and Luther, stand by this statement of the World Council of Churches:

> The fundamental Protestant idea is
> that the Church is not above
> judgment, inerrant and "self-
> authenticating" as though she were
> God Himself; she is the servant of
> God's Word, and must perpetually be
> judged by her degree of conformity
> to that Word....  The Word had its
> being before the Church and is the
> foundation of it.

Protestants note that many Catholic beliefs are not supported by scripture.  The Roman Church's doctrine concerning Papal Infallibility as well as many involving the Virgin Mary rest upon extra-biblical traditions.  Accordingly, Protestants reject Catholic claims to the Virgin's immaculate conception, her life-long virginity and her subsequent physical assumption into heaven.  The on-going debate concerning the relative importance of scripture continues to

166

divide Christianity.[32]

While together on role of scripture, Erasmus and
Luther parted company on the latter's stand on
predestination. Luther's faith was in the tradition of
Paul and Augustine, who believed that God predestined
those who would be saved. The doctrine of
predestination holds that all persons are sinners and
deserve damnation. Therefore, salvation is an
undeserved gift, bestowed by God's mercy. Luther
stressed that salvation cannot be earned by man. He
accused the Catholic Church of teaching a doctrine of
works. Through its sacramental system, the Church
implied that human beings choose when to receive God's
grace. The Church also emphasized the spiritual
benefits that derived from abstaining from butter and
cheese during Lent and from taking long pilgrimages to
Rome and other holy places. The medieval Church's sale
of indulgences was along the same pattern. Luther saw
the Church's practical emphasis on free will as
breeding human arrogance and pride. In his view,
Christian salvation could come only after ego had been
crushed. Only then could God's grace touch the human
soul. Luther's idea of predestination served to humble
the human heart. With Luther, all power rested with
God. His was a doctrine of grace.

"God works by contraries," Luther wrote, "so that
a man feels himself to be lost in the very moment when
he is on the point of being saved." In Luther's view,
any belief system that serves to make the worshipper
feel secure and safe in fact keeps God a stranger. The
Roman Catholic sacramental system, its tradition of
easy confession of sins, and the offering of
indulgences to lessen one's punishment in purgatory,
all served to breed a sense of security. For these
reasons, the Catholic Church was dangerous in Luther's
eyes.

Luther and the Frenchman John Calvin (the
second-most famous of the Protestant reformers) both
preached that humankind is utterly sinful and depraved:
As human nature is thoroughly corrupt, all human
actions, even those apparently designed to improve the
world, are stained. Human pride and self concern are
ever present. The gap between man and God is too great
to be overcome by human works. God alone can rescue
fallen man, and even those whom He touches by his[33]
saving grace do not deserve their elect status.
Luther's doctrine was too harsh for Erasmus, who
attacked the predestination concept in a pamphlet

167

entitled On Free Will, which was published in 1524. A generation later, Calvin joined the contest, arguing that God not only predestines those who will be saved but also those who will be damned. Over time, Erasmus's more gentle view defeated the predestination idea. Interestingly, few modern Protestants believe in predestination, a concept which clearly characterized the early generations of the Protestant Reformation. Predestination seems unfair and arbitrary to those raised in democratic cultures. And so, it has been passively rejected in modern times, despite the fact that the idea is still recorded as official belief in some important Protestant Churches. Unfortunately, as the idea has died, the effect that it once produced has also faded. Man is not easily humbled. His craving for security and certainty madly erect mental and material bulwarks to persuade him that he is in charge of his own destiny. The belief in predestination served a radically alternate view.

Some mistakenly think that a belief in predestination leads to lazy, passive behavior. Usually, the opposite is true. Believers in predestination sense that God has chosen them for a purpose. An active life engaged in good works feeds the hope of the believer that he is among the elect. Yet he is never sure of his true status. That knowledge belongs to God alone. Accordingly, the believer in a doctrine of grace is characterized by many good works. While Luther emphasized that good works cannot earn salvation, he did caution that good works are the necessary result of divine election. "We are not saved by works," Luther wrote, "but if there be no works, there must be something amiss with faith." Some latter-day Protestants, smugly assured of their own salvation, feel little necessity for good works. Such was not the case with the early Protestants.[34]

In breaking with Erasmus, whose Christianity was too comfortable, Luther joined company with others: the Swiss Urlich Zwingli and Calvin. They shared Luther's belief in predestination. Nevertheless, they did differ on some matters. For example, Luther and Zwingli argued over consubstantiation. Luther accepted Wycliffe's slight alteration of the medieval doctrine of transubstantiation. Zwingli went further; he saw the Eucharist's body and blood of Christ in purely symbolic terms. Luther and Calvin disagreed on the proper relationship between Church and state. Luther deferred to the state, even in the administration of his Church. He described princes as the agents of God in governing the world. Calvin saw this new version of caesaropapism as a grievous error. [35]In his view, the state should be ruled by the Church.[35]

The reformers agreed that Christianity should be applied more in daily life. They joined Erasmus in scorning monasticism, which removed Christians from the world. The elect, they claimed, have divine callings, roles intended for them by God. Such roles need not involve preaching the gospel. Indeed, they might involve something as worldly as commerce. In being called, the elect would practice a personal asceticism while serving the community. Thrift, prudence, sobriety and diligence were desirable character traits for this purpose. Worldly success might result, but the person called to serve in the world was not to enjoy the fruit of his labor. Rather, he was to serve as a steward of his accumulated wealth for the community's benefit. In this way, the monastic ideal of asceticism would be practiced in daily life. Max Weber, a 20th-century sociologist, has argued convincingly that this "Protestant ethic," because of the value it placed upon capital accumulation, fueled the rise of modern capitalism.[36]

The Protestant reformers did not intend their message to degenerate eventually into a gospel of wealth, business monopoly and special privilege. For them, the "Protestant ethic" was a corollary to a world view emphasizing the omnipotence of God and the brokenness of man. They protested a Christianity mechanically dispensing salvation through events external to deeply held faith. The Protestants proclaimed that God's grace is not the property of a human institution. They reasserted the nakedness of the person before God. For them, Christianity could not be comfortable. It was filled with anxiety concerning whether one was among the elect. It included the realization that being a pillar of the visible Church was no assurance of one's status on the day of judgment. Good works could not earn a Protestant reformer salvation. On the other hand, an absence of them was sure indication that eternal fire awaited.

## The Challenge of Secularism

In elevating holy scripture over the living institution of the Church, the Protestant reformers put final authority into the hands of the common man. At least this was so in theory. Ultimately, Luther grew wary of this democratic tendency because of a mass revolt of German peasants, many of whom quoted scripture to justify their rebellion. The spectacle of average people, untrained in Christian discipline, deciding theological questions for themselves, frightened the German reformer. Accordingly, he praised monarchy as the divine form of human government and sanctified state control of his Church. The Protestant emphasis on the depravity of man supported Luther's disdain for popular democratic yearnings. Nonetheless, as long as Protestantism valued the individual believer's direct contact with scripture, a democratic tendency was subtly encouraged.

In early Protestantism, Calvinist church government exhibited some democratic characteristics. Nevertheless, given the relatively small number of those recognized as "elect," Calvinist church organization was closer to oligarchy than democracy. Jacob Arminius, a Calvinist theologian of the late 16th century, tipped the balance more toward the democratic principle. He argued that God had predestined that all those who accept Christ will be saved. This twisted the predestination idea from a God-selecting process into one ultimately determined by human choice. In his own time, Arminius was rejected. But over the generations, his revision gradually succeeded in eroding the original Protestant understanding. This shift did not occur in a vacuum. Monarchy was increasingly under attack as an unjust form of government, and Arminianism was more in tune with rising democratic sentiment. Authority in both political and religious affairs was being won by the common man. Accordingly, fewer Protestants worried whether or not they had been chosen by God. It was enough that they had accepted Jesus Christ.[37]

A democratic secular concern for conditions in this life increasingly eroded traditional Christianity's otherworldly emphasis. Deism, popular with 18th-century intellectuals, called for the improvement of this world through the discovery and scientific application of God's natural laws. In the next century, some theologians, concerned with the human pain and isolation wrought by industrialization, would call for a "social gospel." Their goal would be the erection of equitable and just social and political systems in this world. Few Christians followed this specific call. However, most did accept the increasingly worldly trend of modern Christianity. More precisely, they accepted secular values which

170

reduced their involvement in the Church to little more than Sunday morning church attendance. Less and less Christian attention was spent on the coming day of judgment. Sin and human depravity were becoming passe and were replaced by a faith in material progress. For most 19th-century Christians in Western Europe and the United States, their religion was becoming comfortable and harmonious with the secular norms of their societies.

Soren Kierkegaard, a 19th-century Dane, criticized his contemporaries for their apparent lack of concern for the pain of the world around them. Kierkegaard urged that Christians focus upon the obligations of being saved in Christ. A Christian, he emphasized, cannot be an observer. He must be a participant. He cannot be a part-time Christian on Sunday mornings. He must live Christianity during every minute of life. Kierkegaard confessed that the consequences of truly practicing the faith would be suffering, humiliation and even death. Indeed, the life of the master himself showed that it must be so. Kierkegaard stressed that from an intellectual standpoint, Christianity is absurd. It makes sense, he concluded, only when it is lived existentially. Only by following this difficult and lonely path may one come to know the meaning of Christian redemption. This message did not appeal to most 19th-century Christians, who regarded Christian suffering as something that belonged to the unhappy medieval past.[58]

The comfortable Christianity which Kierkegaard attacked eventually drifted into two world wars marked by callous mass murder and wholesale destruction. Few German Christians dared to confront the cruel dictatorship of Adolf Hitler. Dietrich Bonhoeffer, a young theologian, was one exception. Like Kierkegaard, Bonhoeffer attacked the "cheap grace" of comfortable Christianity and in its place offered what he called "the cost of discipleship." Bonhoeffer wrote: "We have watered down the gospel into emotional uplift which makes no costly demands and which fails to distinguish between natural and Christian existence." He stressed that Christians can only share Christ's glory if they first bear his shame and suffering. He urged true Christians not to live their own relative lives, but rather let Christ live his absolute and divine life in them. He conceded that the majority would not follow this difficult path. Accordingly, in his view, Christianity is a religion for those few persons who existentially confront the world's evils and are

171

crucified as a result.  Bonhoeffer became involved in the German Resistance and was executed by the Nazis in the closing days of World War II.[39]

Another 20th-century German who squarely faced the meaning of Christianity was Albert Schweitzer.  To many, he approximated the Christian ideal better than anyone since St. Francis of Assisi.  Ironically, he rejected most of the traditional Christian creed. Schweitzer began his search intellectually, as an historian examining the life of Jesus.  In his The Quest of the Historical Jesus, which was published in 1906, he stressed the eschatological foundations of Jesus's radical love ethic.  Jesus had urged mankind to give up the natural way of living, filled with selfish concern, because a Kingdom of God was about to replace the worldly order.  Originally, this expectation had persuaded Jesus's followers of the practicality of his message.  In Schweitzer's view, few modern Christians continued to expect the establishment of this divine Kingdom.  The long delay had eroded the original belief.  For Schweitzer, the traditional Christian creed was outmoded.  For him, this was not essential, as he saw Christian behavior, not any credal scaffolding, as the substance of true religion.  In his own life, the psychological support for the Christian love ethic was what he termed "reverence for life." Similar to mystics of all religions, Schweitzer sensed the interconnectedness and divinity of all of life.  He urged each person to reflect upon this commonality in hopes that genuine Christian love would be born in the process.  For many decades, he manifested this love in equatorial Africa, serving in Christ-life suffering and service as a medical missionary.

Schweitzer's religion harmonized with modern scientific thought.  The same could not be said for traditional Christianity.  For example, Charles Darwin's theories on evolution had stressed the biological interrelatedness of all of life, much as Schweitzer had seen a spiritual bond.  Schweitzer had not drawn any rigid distinction between man and other forms of life.  By contrast, traditional Christianity held that man was a unique creation, the sole receptacle of an eternal soul.  While Darwin, who had stated his position in The Descent of Man (1871), viewed any questions concerning soul as beyond the province of his work, his Christian admirers wrestled with a fundamental issue:  When, during the evolutionary continuum, did humankind acquire that spark of the divine referred to as an immortal soul?

Schweitzer had no such problem. Apparently unconcerned about an afterlife, he focused upon the sacredness of all of life in the here-and-now.[40]

Darwin's ideas sorely tested traditional Christianity. Indeed, much of modern life subverts the ancient faith. Western culture continues to erect evermore massive idols to material power which have won the real allegiance of the nominal Christian majority. The secular norms of contemporary Western civilization have challenged Christianity as never before in its long history. Christian eschatology had revealed that the end of time would be immediately preceded by a time of tribulations which would tempt the faithful. The latter has occurred. To many traditional Christians, the nuclear arms race suggests that the Kingdom of God may be finally at hand. Fundamentalist Christianity has been fed by these conditions.[41]

Christianity has become increasingly fragmented since the days of Luther and Calvin. Because of this disunity, secularism has flourished. Facing a common challenge, a variety of Christian churches have joined hands in the Ecumenical Movement. Beginning with Protestant sectarian cooperation, the movement has entered into a dialogue with the Greek Orthodox and Roman Catholic Churches as well. Hope exists that someday all of Christianity may reunite under one banner. Should this occur, Christianity's task of reasserting its dominance within Western civilization will still be problematical. Eastern religions speak more clearly to many thoughtful Westerners than does Christianity in any form. Hindu proselytizers reveal that Darwinian theories pose no problems for their faith, as all living beings--insect, animal and human--have souls in their view. Indeed, the Hindu perspective sees one's spiritual progress as a matter of slow evolution over millions of lifetimes. In this sense, Hinduism offers a spiritual supplement to the Darwinian world view that cannot be matched by Christianity. Albert Einstein's modern physics also meshes far easier with oriental religious thought than with traditional Christianity. The notion that every physical entity has only a relative existence, an idea at the heart of Einstein's theories, is easily harmonized with China's yin-yang concept and the non-dualist Indian philosophies of Nagarjuna and Shankara. Christianity offers nothing comparable.[42]

Despite these disparate challenges, Christianity still exhibits extraordinary vitality. Few other

173

religions require an ethic so much in conflict with natural human instincts, yet some continue to choose the suffering way of the cross. Other faiths provide regimens for reducing the noise of selfish ego and promise that God or enlightenment can be found in the process. Some religions offer concepts that appeal to the rational mind. Christianity takes another approach. It tells a simple story of a man who finds victory in surrender and loves even those who hate him. These poetic contrasts appeal to the deepest human emotions as no rational program can. The demands that this religion makes are absurd and create despair among those who take them seriously. Ultimately, a leap of faith is required that transforms lives in Christian service. The process of this remains a mystery, beyond the power of words to explain.

NOTES

1. Albert Schweitzer, The Kingdom of God and Primitive Christianity (New York, 1968), p. 93; C. Milo Connick, The New Testament, An Introduction to Its History, Literature and Thought (North Scituate, Mass., 1978), pp. 89-90, 93, 97; Matthew 11:15; Ibid., 22:37-40.

2. Raymond E. Brown, The Birth of the Messiah, A Commentary on the Infancy Narratives in Matthew and Luke (New York, 1977), pp. 283-284; Alexander Jones, ed., The Jerusalem Bible (New York, 1966), 1153n; Luke 1:7; Genesis 17; Mark 1:7; Michael Grant, Jesus, an Historian's Review of the Gospels (New York, 1977), pp. 18, 46-47.

3. Xavier Leon-Dufour, Resurrection and the Message of Easter (New York, 1971) pp. 212-213; Gunther Bornkamm, Jesus of Nazareth (New York, 1956:1960), p. 181; Salo Wittmayer Baron, A Social and Religious History of the Jews (17 vols., New York, 1952-1980), I, 98-99.

4. Matthew, 21:7; I Corinthians 5:7; Exodus 12:21-23; John 19:32-33; George Brantl, Catholicism (New York, 1962), p. 98.

5. Schweitzer, Kingdom of God, pp. 115, 121-122, 127-128, 387-399; I Corinthians 15:3.

6. William A. Clebsch, Christianity in European

<u>History</u> (New York, 1979), p. 17; Paul Tillich, <u>A History of Christian Thought</u> (New York, 1968), pp. 166, 174-175, 247.

7. Connick, <u>The New Testament</u>, p. 245; Peter Brown, <u>Augustine of Hippo, A Biography</u> (Berkeley, 1969), p. 224; Acts 2:1-13, 17; Joel 2:28.

8. Oscar Cullmann, <u>Christ and Time, The Primitive Christian Conception of Time and History</u> (Philadelphia, 1949), pp. 84-85, 87, 142, 155, 158, 163, 178; Mark 13:10; Matthew 24:14.

9. Edward Schillebeeckx, <u>Jesus, An Experiment in Christology</u> (New York, 1979), p. 77; Allan Nevins, <u>The Gateway to History</u> (Garden City, New York, 1928:1962), pp. 139-140; John 8:32; Xavier Leon-Dufour, <u>The Gospels and the Jesus of History</u> (New York, 1970), p. 30.

10. Richard N. Longenecker, <u>The Christology of Early Jewish Christianity</u> (Naperville, Ill., n.d.), pp. 63-67; Bo Reicke, <u>The New Testament Era, The World of the Bible from 500 B.C. to A.D. 100</u> (Philadelphia, 1964), pp. 200-201, 212; F.E. Peters, <u>The Harvest of Hellenism</u> (New York, 1970), pp. 491, 668-669; Hugh J. Schonfield, <u>The Passover Plot, New Light on the History of Jesus</u> (New York, 1965), p. 207.

11. Peters, <u>Hellenism</u>, pp. 488-500.

12. Arthur C. McGiffert, <u>A History of Christian Thought</u> (2 vols., New York, 1932-1933), I, 24-25; Schweitzer, <u>Kingdom of God</u>, pp. 172-173; Romans 6:4-7, 11; II Corinthians 3:3; Irwin Edman, <u>The Mind of Paul</u> (New York, 1935), pp. 79, 84.

13. Robert M. Grant, <u>Augustus to Constantine, The Thrust of the Christian Movement into the Roman World</u> (New York, 1970), p. 20; Max Weber, <u>The Sociology of Religion</u> (Boston, 1922), p. 71.

14. Grant, <u>Augustus to Constantine</u>, pp. 120-121; Elaine Pagels, "The Threat of the Gnostics," <u>The New York Review of Books</u>, XXVI (Nov. 8, 1979), 43; Hans Jonas, <u>The Gnostic Religion, the Message of the Alien God and the Beginnings of Christianity</u> (Boston, 1958), p. 42.

15. Rudolf Bultmann, <u>Primitive Christianity in its Contemporary Setting</u> (New York, 1956), pp. 163-164; Robert M. Grant, <u>Gnosticism and Early Christianity</u> (New

York, 1965), pp. 13, 55, 95, 96; Jacques Lacarriere, _The Gnostics_ (New York, 1977), pp. 24-25; Jonas, _Gnostic Religion_, pp. 271-273; Elaine Pagels, "The Defeat of the Gnostics," _The New York Review of Books_, XXVI (Dec. 6, 1979), 43, 48-52; Pheme Perkins, _The Early Church and the Crisis of Gnosticism_ (New York, 1980), pp. 185-186.

16.     Lacarriere, _The Gnostics_, pp. 100-102; Nicholas Zernov, _Eastern Christendom, A Study of the Origin and Development of the Eastern Orthodox Church_ (New York, 1961), pp. 31-32; Tillich, _Christian Thought_ pp. xiv, 39; McGiffert, _Christian Thought_, I, 157-161; George Foot Moore, _History of Religions_ (2 vols., New York, 1949), II, 127-133.

17.     Grant, _Augustus to Constantine_, p. 138; Karl F. Morrison, _Tradition and Authority in the Western Church_, 300-1140 (Princeton, 1969), p. 16; Paul Johnson, _A History of Christianity_ (New York, 1976), p. 49; Kenneth S. Latourette, _A History of Christianity_ (New York, 1953), pp. 128-129; Peters, _Hellenism_ pp. 628-630.

18.     Morrison, _Tradition and Authority_, p. 9; Harold Mattingly, _Christianity in the Roman Empire_ (New York, 1954), pp. 48-49; Grant, _Augustus to Constantine_ pp. x, 93; Reicke, _New Testament Era_, pp. 284-285; Pagels, "Defeat of the Gnostics," 46; Peters, _Hellenism_, pp. 508-509, 522, 576-580; Latourette, _Christianity_, pp. 81-82, 252-253; Marina Warner, _Alone of all Her Sex_ (New York, 1976), p. 69; Johnson _Christianity_, p. 71; Max Weber, _Ancient Judaism_ (New York, 1952), p. 423.

19.     J.M. Wallace-Hadrill, _The Barbarian West, 400-1000_ (London, 1952), p. 14; Tillich, _Christian Thought_, pp. 70, 86; J.W.C. Wand, _A History of the Early Church to A.D. 500_ (London, 1937), pp. 150, 164; McGiffert, _Christian Thought_, I, 248, 249, 252-254, 266-267; _Ibid_, II, 33-34; Latourette, _Christianity_, pp. 105-107, 153-157; Peters, _Hellenism_, pp. 689, 692, 694-695.

20.     Margaret Deanesly, _A History of the Medieval Church, 590-1500_ (London, 1925), p. 93; Clebsch, _Christianity_, p. 143; Vern L. Bullough, _Sexual Variance in Society and History_ (New York, 1976), pp. 189, 320; Weber, _Sociology of Religion_, p. 238.

21.     Tillich, _Christian Thought_, pp. 123-125,

176

130-132; Wand, Early Church, pp. 80-82, 228, 230; Brown, Augustine, pp. 51, 215, 343, 346, 348; F. Vander Meer, Augustine the Bishop, Church and Society at the Dawn of the Middle Ages (New York, 1961), pp. 62-63, 124, 350, 383-385; McGiffert, Christian Thought, II, 20, 102, 134, 142, 152-153, 159; Eugene Portalie, A Guide to the Thought of Augustine (Chicago, 1960), pp. 188-189, 214, 284, 297; Bullough, Sexual Variance, p. 191; Latourette, Christianity, pp. 138-139, 179-181; Johnson, Christianity, pp. 118-119, 229-230; Brantl, Catholicism, pp. 43-44; Weber, Sociology of Religion, pp. 187-190; Warner, Alone of All Her Sex, pp. 54, 317-318.

22. Morrison, Tradition and Authority, p. 24; Zernov, Eastern Christendom, pp. 75-76; James A. Corbett, The Papacy, A Brief History (New York, 1956), pp. 11-15; Latourette, Christianity, p. 118; Johnson, Christianity, pp. 61-62.

23. Harold Mattingly, Christianity in the Roman Empire (New York, 1954), p. 75; Walter Ullman, The Growth of Papal Government in the Middle Ages (London, 1970), pp. 36, 45-49, 52-54, 81; Roland H. Bainton, The Medieval Church (Princeton, 1962), pp. 14, 25; Wallace-Hadrill, Barbarian West, pp. 40-43, 45; Deanesly, Medieval Church, pp. 25-26, 81; Corbett, Papacy, pp. 22, 24-27; Malachi Martin, The Decline and Fall of the Roman Church (New York, 1981), pp. 119-127; Latourette, Christianity, p. 365.

24. Zernov, Eastern Christendom, pp. 64, 69, 81-82, 91; Tillich, Christian Thought, p. 86; Deanesly, Medieval Church, pp. 5-6, 66, 73-74; McGiffert, Christian Thought, I, 276-286; Morrison, Tradition and Authority, pp. 147, 152, 170, 179; Bainton, Medieval Church, p. 23, 24; Latourette, Christianity pp. 172, 297.

25. Bainton, Medieval Church, p. 49; Friedrich Heer, The Medieval World, Europe, 1100-1350 (New York, 1961), p. 126; Deanesly, Medieval Church, p. 250; Gerald R. Cragg, The Church and the Age of Reason, 1648-1789 (Bristol, 1960), p. 108; Time, April 3, 1978, p. 44; Latourette, Christianity, pp. 409-414.

26. Ian Wilson, The Shroud of Turin, The Burial Cloth of Jesus Christ? (New York, 1979), pp. 85-86, 96, 253, 258; Newsweek, September 18, 1978, pp. 94-95; Warner, Alone of All Her Sex, pp. 290-294.

27.  Heer, Medieval World, pp. 199-200; McGiffert, Christian Thought, II, 321, 326; Clebsch, Christianity, p. 173; Harold J. Grimm, The Reformation Era, 1500-1650 (New York, 1954), pp. 49-51; Deanesly, Medieval Church, pp. 112-113; Latourette, Christianity, p. 531.

28.  McGiffert, Christian Thought, II, 353-357, 359-375; Heer, Medieval World, 204-214, 237-238, 241, 374-375; Corbett, Papacy, pp. 38-41; Deanesly, Medieval Church, pp. 114, 257; Bainton, Medieval Church, pp. 51-52; Clebsch, Christianity, p. 139; Martin, Roman Church, pp. 187, 207; J. Leslie Dunstan, ed., Protestantism (New York, 1962), p. 21; Latourette, Christianity, pp. 497-499, 516, 676-677.

29.  Deanesly, Medieval Church, pp. 222-227; Grimm, Reformation Era, pp. 31, 43; Bainton, Medieval Church, pp. 70-71.

30.  G.R. Elton, Reformation Europe, 1517-1559 (New York, 1963), pp. 18, 143, 152, 175; Zernov, Eastern Christendom, p. 133; Johnson, Christianity, pp. 274-275.

31.  Johan Huizinga, Erasmus and the Age of Reformation (New York, 1924:1957), pp. 102, 107, 109, 131-132, 176-177, 189, 191-192; Tillich, Christian Thought, pp. 237-238; Grimm, Reformation Era, pp. 106, 108-109, 166; McGiffert, Christian Thought, II, 384-385; Deanesly, Medieval Church, pp. 251-252; Dunstan, ed., Protestantism, pp. 29-30.

32.  Ronald Knox, The Belief of Catholics (New York, 1950), p. 106; Dunstan, ed., Protestantism, pp. 216-233; Brantl, Catholicism, p. 159.

33.  McGiffert, Christian Thought, II, 316-317; Roland H. Bainton, Here I Stand, A Life of Martin Luther (Nashville, 1950), p. 82; Gustaf Aulen, The Faith of the Christian Church (Philadelphia, 1960), pp. 278, 334-335; John Dillenberger and Claude Welch, Protestant Christianity Interpreted Through Its Development (New York, 1954), p. 29; Tillich, Christian Thought, p. 245; Elton, Reformation Europe, p. 276.

34.  Elton, Reformation Europe, pp. 31, 33, 218; McGiffert, Christian Thought, II, 392-393; Grimm, Reformation Era, pp. 352-353, 355; Huizinga, Erasmus, pp. 162-163; Dillenberger and Welch, Protestant Christianity, pp. 31, 101-103; William Niesel, The Theology of Calvin (Philadelphia, 1956), pp. 175-178;

Connick, New Testament, pp. 372-373; Max Weber, The Protestant Ethic and the Spirit of Capitalism (New York, 1958), p. 117; Weber, Sociology of Religion, p. 202.

35. Aulen, Christian Church, p. 347; Elton, Reformation Europe, pp. 71-72; Grimm, Reformation Era, pp. 88-89, 92, 99, 100, 175, 353; Bainton, Here I Stand, pp. 238-239, 246; Corbett, Papacy, p. 54; Niesel, Calvin, pp. 230-236; Basil Hall, John Calvin, Humanist and Theologian (London, 1956), p. 24; Clebsch, Christianity, p.179.

36. Bainton, Here I Stand, pp. 201, 233; Max Weber, "Anticritical Last Word on the Spirit of Capitalism," American Journal of Sociology, LXXXII (1978), 1105-1131; Weber, Protestant Ethic, pp. 3, 80-81, 158, 162, 163, 170, 172; Matthew, 25:15-30.

37. Niesel, Calvin, p. 199; Dillenberger and Welch, Protestant Christianity, pp. 90, 91; Latourette, Christianity, pp. 765, 1019-1020.

38. Cragg, Age of Reason, pp. 102, 103, 160-162, 237; Dillenberger and Welch, Protestant Christianity, pp. 247-254; Reidar Thomte, Kierkegaard's Philosophy of Religion (New York, 1948), p. 8; John A. Gates, The Life and Thought of Kierkegaard for Everyman (Philadelphia, n.d.), p. 105.

39. Dietrich Bonhoeffer, The Cost of Discipleship (New York, 1937:1949), pp. 98, 211; Andre Dumas, Dietrich Bonhoeffer, Theologian of Reality (New York, 1965), p. 204.

40. Albert Schweitzer, Out of My Life and Thought, An Autobiography (New York, 1949), pp. 53-59, 89, 114-115, 147, 157-158, 201, 219, 230, 235, 238-239; James R. Moore, The Post-Darwinian Controversy, A Study of the Protestant Struggle to Come to Terms with Darwin in Great Britain and America, 1870-1900 (Cambridge, England, 1979), p. 298; Latourette, Christianity, p. 1381.

41. John Wesley White, Re-entry, Striking Parallels Between Today's News Events and Christ's Second Coming (Minneapolis, 1971), pp. 29-58; Stanley D. Walters, "Hal Lindsey: Recalculating the Second Coming," Christian Century, 96 (Sept. 12, 1979), 839-840.

42.    Latourette, Christianity, p. 1457; Norman Goodall, Ecumenical Progress: A Decade of Change in the Ecumenical Movement, 1961-1971 (London, 1972), pp. 138-142; Fritjof Capra, The Tao of Physics, An Exploration of the Parallels Between Modern Physics and Eastern Mysticism (Berkeley, 1975), pp. 88, 161, 202-203.

# Chapter Five: Islam

## The Seal of the Prophets

Islam is the youngest of the world's great religions. It began with Muhammad the Prophet, who lived on the Arabian peninsula in the 7th century of the Christian era. He called humankind to submit to God. Indeed, the meaning of the word Islam, the name of his religion, is submission. "Those who submit" would be called Muslims--another literal translation. His religion proclaimed the oneness of God against the polytheism of his own time and place. It partially accepted and built upon the Judeo-Christian tradition, without accepting either Jewish scripture or the Christian interpretation of Jesus's ministry. It did not proclaim that Muhammad was God, but it did designate that after him there could be no further revelation of God's message to man. Because of this, Muhammad would be called the Seal of the Prophets.

Non-Muslim historians have given environmental reasons for Muhammad's emergence as a prophet of God. Specifically, the commercial condition of his home town of Mecca has received much attention. During Muhammad's lifetime, its caravan trade was booming, due to a greater than normal use of the Meccan route to Syria. Imperial wars between the Persians and Byzantines had made unreliable the traditionally favored East-West trade route through the Persian Gulf. Mecca was the beneficiary of this shift. However, this development was not an unmixed blessing. Money making and individual selfishness increasingly challenged Mecca's ancient tribal ideal of community well-being. Widows and orphans, heretofore a responsibility of the tribal communities, more and more were left to fend for themselves. Orphaned in childhood, Muhammad was better off than most. An uncle adopted him and raised him to manhood. Nevertheless, Muhammad's personal brush with destitution made him keenly sensitive to the social injustices that abounded in Mecca's increasingly survival-of-the-fittest society.

Mecca had long been a religious center, serving the tribes of Arabia, who, once a year, would journey to the Ka'ba, a cube-shaped temple located in the city. Each of Arabia's nomadic tribes had an idol housed in the Ka'ba, which was also adorned by a large jewel-like black stone, set in a corner of the structure. During an annual truce from all blood feuds, the tribes would

visit their gods. Profit-hungry Mecca exploited their
annual pilgrimage, while in other ways undermining the
communitarian feeling of this dying religious culture.
The latter situation ultimately drove Muhammad to
proclaim God's wrath and coming Day of Judgment.[2]

Muhammad's early religious education was not
confined to the ways of Mecca. As a youth, he
accompanied caravans to Syria and heard Jewish and
Christian stories that spoke to his innermost
yearnings. Later, in his mid-twenties, he married
Khadijah, a wealthy, middle-aged widow with her own
caravan business. Accordingly, he continued his trips
to Syria. Disoriented by the hedonism and social
disintegration that increasingly characterized Mecca,
Muhammad pondered life's purpose. He sought the
solitude of the many caves in the mountains near his
home. One day, near his fortieth year, he felt a
strange presence commanding him to "recite." After
discussing the experience with Khadijah, he determined
that a divine revelation, as Jewish and Christian
prophets had known before, had been visited upon him.
For the remainder of his life, Muhammad would receive
similar revelations, which would be transmitted to his
followers and memorized. Eventually, these revelations
would be compiled in the Qur'an (or Koran), which
literally means "recitation."[3]

Muhammad's message directly challenged the
polytheism of his native culture. He proclaimed that
Allah is the only God. Interestingly, Allah had been
one of the deities of Arabian tribal religion. But
Muhammad's conception was new. Arabs were used to
representing their various gods in idols of stone or
wood. Indeed, the Ka'ba had served as a storehouse of
these ancient religious art forms. Muhammad viewed
this practice as blasphemy. Allah the Magnificent
could not be limited by any human portrayal of Him, and
the same principle applied to any part of His creation.
Accordingly, with the eventual success of Muhammad, a
pall was cast upon all representative art within Arab
civilization. Architecture, embellished by intricate
geometric designs, would later fill the artistic void
required by the anti-polytheistic thrust of Muhammad's
religion.

Muhammad claimed that his revelations were not
merely approximations of God's will, but God's actual
message, accurately recorded, word for word. To this
day, most Muslims accept the Qur'an as the uncreated,
preexistent Word of God, equivalent to the status

accorded to Christ in Christianity. Many readers of its wearisome English translations find this claim ludicrous, but those able to read it in the original Arabic say that its impact is profound. Indeed, Muslims are cautioned of the necessity to read the Qur'an only in Arabic. As a language, Arabic is to any European tongue as music is to prose. It communicates more than intellectual concepts and uses cadence and tone to make a direct impact upon one's emotions. In its use of that language, the Qur'an succeeds as no other piece of Arabic literature. Muslims claim that Muhammad himself was illiterate, proof enough that the Qur'an is indeed the Word of God. Earlier prophets, Moses and Jesus among them, spoke and were misunderstood. Their messages, according to Muslims, were garbled and transcribed in imperfect form. The Qur'an is of a different nature. It is, in effect, the final and complete statement of God's Truth. As the Qur'an is the undefiled Word of God, all prophecy ends with Muhammad, making him the Seal of the Prophets.[4]

Muhammad's message attacked the selfish individualism predominant among Mecca's elite. It called for certain new minimum guarantees for women and an amelioration of the condition of slaves. It urged the giving of alms to the poor--a requirement that would later be set at an annual payment of 2.5 percent of a believer's wealth. This message of social justice made Muhammad's movement extremely controversial within Mecca. His few wealthy converts successfully relied on existing tribal connections for protection. Persecution focused more on his humbler followers who suffered brandings with hot irons, forced exposure to the desert sun and other ingenious cruelties. Eventually, at Muhammad's urging, these unfortunates fled to Christian Abyssinia, where they were given refuge. In this manner, Muhammad's movement languished for a full decade after his initial revelation. Then, suddenly, his wife and uncle, who had sustained and protected him, were dead. His life could not continue as before.

At this juncture, an invitation came to Muhammad from Yathrib to restructure that community. Located 270 miles north of Mecca, Yathrib also had been transformed by the caravan trade. Nomadic tribes had been lured to take up agriculture there in order to serve the new commerce. Jewish and pagan tribes composed Yathrib's community. The Jews had seemingly avoided the destructive blood feuds that plagued the pagan tribes. Accordingly, the leaders of Yathrib's pagan tribes invited the beleaguered prophet of Mecca to heal their communal rifts under one Muslim banner. Muhammad accepted. He ordered his followers to depart from Mecca in twos and threes so as not to raise undue suspicion. Finally, Muhammad himself left, an act known in Islam as the Hijra or "emigration." Muslims date their calendar not from Muhammad's first revelation but rather from the Hijra, the flight from Mecca to Yathrib, which henceforth would be known as Medinat un-nabi, or the City of the Prophet. Eventually, it would simply be called Medina, or "the City."[5]

The importance of the Hijra, which occurred in 622 A.D., is that it transformed Muhammad from a rejected visionary into a religious and political leader. Muhammad had long proclaimed himself to be the leader of a new community, but until the Hijra his followers would often rely on old tribal connections for protection. In Medina, the Emigrants, as these Meccan followers of the Prophet were known, were totally dependent upon Muhammad. Given the nature of their surreptitious escape from Mecca, most of their property had been left behind. Consequently, Muhammad allowed his followers to raid tribes outside of Medina, with the goal of acquiring new property. The riazza (or raid) was a traditional feature of tribal Arabia. As those tribes outside of Medina were polytheistic and idolatrous in their religious practices, these raids had religious sanction as well. Gradually, this habit of making war on non-Muslims would be termed jihad or holy war.

Muhammad's Medinese followers, known in Muslim history as the Helpers, joined the raiding, which brought them a benefit in addition to booty. By turning their aggressive feelings against outsiders, they developed a new spirit of solidarity within Medina itself. Mecca's caravan trade was a prime objective of the Muslim raiders. Each success won new converts. Other tribes were persuaded to join the faith in order to share in the spoils. One-fifth of each raid went to Muhammad, who used his new wealth to help the poor. A community of self-interest, social justice and religious impulse was arising in Arabia. A divine paradise filled with beautiful maidens was promised to those who fell in battle, whereas a share of the captured property went to those who survived. Eventually, the multifaceted appeal of Islam would prove irresistible and sweep everything before it.[6]

In the midst of this mounting success, Muhammad's

relations with Medina's Jewish tribes worsened. Initially, he had gone to great efforts in hopes of converting them to Islam. Accordingly, he had patterned many of his evolving religious practices after those of the Jews. While Islam would have no Sabbath, or day of cessation from all work, the Jewish day of Sabbath preparation (Friday) had been selected as the Muslim time for communal worship. Muhammad had adopted a modified Jewish dietary code, prohibiting pork, and had directed his followers to pray toward Jerusalem and fast during the Jewish Day of Atonement. Medina's Jews scorned these actions as a mere parody of their ancient faith. Altercations between Jews and Muslims followed, resulting in the banishment of all but one of Medina's Jewish tribes. Finally, the last Jewish tribe unsuccessfully conspired with outside forces to crush the Muslim community. With the treason revealed, punishment was swift. Muhammad ordered the execution of the tribe's adult males and the enslavement of their women and children.

Muhammad's conflicts with Medina's Jews brought some changes in Muslim practices. Specifically, Mecca was substituted for Jerusalem as the homing point for prayer, and the Yom Kippur fast was replaced by one during the daylight hours of the lunar month of Ramadan, commemorating Muhammad's first revelation. The Qur'an would proclaim that Christians are preferable to Jews, because of the Jews' presumed extraordinary arrogance. The Prophet's followers would also remember that a Jewess once tried to poison Muhammad, an attempt which partially succeeded and supposedly shortened his life. Nevertheless, in its basic outline, Islam would remain closer to Judaism than to Christianity. Muhammad, like Moses, would remain merely a human messenger of God and not be elevated to a divine status as was the case with Jesus of Nazareth. As with Judaism, Islam would trace its roots back to Abraham (Ibrahim in Arabic), the first Muslim or submitter to God. According to the Qur'an, Ibrahim had followed his son Ishmael out onto the desert, where in Mecca they had reconstructed the Ka'ba. The original, which had been destroyed in the Great Flood, had been the creation of Adam. Ishmael's descendants later strayed from Islam, until Muhammad, in the tradition of the Hebrew prophets, called them back to their true faith.

Because of the similarities between Islam and Judaism, as the former expanded and conquered distant Jewish settlements, Jews would normally be treated as a protected group. Together with Christians, they were called "People of the Book." They would be required to pay a special tax, sometimes wear identifying dress, and would be barred from military service. Their religious practices would be restricted to some degree, and, generally speaking, their condition would be substandard. Nonetheless, in comparison with Christendom's treatment of religious minorities, Islam's overall record toward its "People of the Book" has been relatively good. On the other hand, Islam gave no quarter to polytheists and idolators in their midst, at least at the beginning of the Muslim movement. When Islam conquered Sind (currently Pakistan) at the dawn of our eighth century, Muslims put polytheists to the sword in great slaughter. However, as Islam extended its conquest into India, Hindus, in spite of their polytheism and idolatry, also were accorded protection as "People of the Book." The burdens of governing subject peoples, together with a desire for revenue, would account for this subsequent modification of Muslim behavior.

Before Islam could thoroughly develop its concept of "People of the Book," it had to expand beyond Medina. To achieve this latter goal, Muhammad took numerous wives in order to build alliances with powerful tribes. He would always live humbly. His ends would always be religious. But, as we also saw with his use of raiding, he would use the worldliest of means to achieve his spiritual goals. His methods were successful. Within eight years after his flight from Mecca, Muhammad returned in triumph. Former enemies now became Muslim generals, helping the expansion of the faith that they had once sought to destroy. The idols were taken from the Ka'ba, which now became solely the temple of Allah. And the Prophet revealed that at least once in every Muslim's life a pilgrimage should be made to the Ka'ba, a commandment that insured Mecca's eternal prosperity.

Within two years after his triumphant return to Mecca, Muhammad was dead. By that time, Islam had expanded to control the Arabian peninsula. Further expansion followed at a rapid pace. Arab aggressiveness, for ages wasted in tribal blood feuds, turned outward in jihad against a non-Muslim world. Within a century after the Hijra, Muslim armies had conquered an empire spanning from Spain to the gates of India. Never before had a religion enjoyed such immediate worldly success. This condition would indelibly color the Muslim faith. Unlike Christianity,

186

which during its first three centuries suffered under state persecution, Islam successfully integrated religion and politics during its formative period. Consequently, religious developments in Islam have invariably been worked out in a political arena, a fact amply demonstrated in the section that follows.[8]

## The Islamic Schism

When Muhammad died, the young Islamic community was temporarily disoriented, for no one could effectively replace the last prophet. Nevertheless, a new leader for the burgeoning enterprise was a necessity. Muhammad's long-time companions chose Abu Bakr, who took the simple title of caliph, meaning "successor." Ali, younger cousin and son-in-law of the Prophet, nursed feelings that he should have succeeded Muhammad, for he could claim the closest blood tie from among the companions. But, two years later, Abu Bakr chose Umar, another companion of the Prophet, as the next caliph. Fifteen years beyond that, Uthman was selected. Ali would spend over a generation waiting for his opportunity, which finally came when Uthman was assassinated in 656.

Uthman had showered favors upon his clan, the Umayyads, who were part of the Meccan leadership that had opposed the Prophet right up until the time he took that city. Some puritanical fanatics claimed that this undeserving nepotism forfeited Uthman's right to rule, and they assassinated him. Ali then became caliph but not without a challenge from Mu'awiya, the surviving leader of the Umayyad clan. The two met on the field of battle. When victory was all but within Ali's grasp, Mu'awiya cleverly appealed to peaceful arbitration, which Ali weakly accepted. This outraged some of Ali's supporters, who thereupon became convinced that Ali too was unfit to lead the Muslim community. Shortly thereafter, an assassin took Ali's life. Ali's eldest son Hasan was then popularly acclaimed caliph, but he had no taste for the burdens of office. Accordingly, he abdicated in favor of Mu'awiya, who subsequently poisoned the hapless Hasan to be rid of a potential rival.[9]

At this point, the tragedy of Ali's line began to take greater focus in events that would create the major sectarian split within the Muslim community. Upon Hasan's death, his younger brother Husain reactivated his family's title to the caliphate. His claim was indirectly encouraged by the behavior of

187

Mu'awiya's son and successor Yazid, whose fondness for wine put him at direct odds with the Prophet's preaching against alcohol consumption. Also, the fact that the devout Husain was the beloved grandson of Muhammad himself strongly suggested that he should challenge Yazid. Accordingly, the inhabitants of Kufa (in present-day Iraq) called upon Husain to lead them in a popular revolt. Husain responded and set out from Medina with his family. On the way to Kufa, at a place called Karbala, he was ambushed by Yazid's forces. His caravan surrounded, Husain anxiously waited for aid. Kufa was reasonably close and knew about Husain's plight, but no one came. Death for Husain and his family could have been swift and merciful, but it was not. The agony was extended over days. Finally, with all but one of his sons dying before his eyes, Husain too was slaughtered. His head was severed as a trophy for Yazid, and his body was trampled below the hooves of Yazid's horses. As it so happened, Husain's only surviving son, the person who would carry on Ali's line, had a Persian princess for his mother. This fact, together with stories of how Ali had often worked for equality between Arab Muslims and Persian converts, later helped to endear the house of Ali to those of Persian blood.[18]

The events noted above wrought a religious schism within the Muslim community. Those who supported Ali became known as Shi'ites, whose movement comprises 10 to 15 percent of all Muslims and has its center in Iran. Those who acquiesced in the rule of whomever succeeded in holding the caliphate were called Sunnis. They constitute the overwhelming majority of Muslims. While having their origins in the historical details of the early caliphate, these two groups are significant primarily in their different approaches to the Islamic faith. Sunnis see their religion as founded on the traditions begun by the Seal of the Prophets. Shi'ites, while also venerating this tradition, pay additional emphasis to the true meaning of Islam as demonstrated in Husain's humiliating death. They also claim access to a secret knowledge of the Qur'an's inner meaning that was carried by Ali and his descendants.

Shi'ites have generally practiced a more fervent version of Islam than their Sunni rivals. For example, Shi'ites annually celebrate Husain's sacrifice during a festival known as 'Ashura. At that time, they recall their own suffering in this world, symbolized by Husain's humiliation, certain in their faith that ultimate victory awaits at the end of time. During 'Ashura, Shi'ite men march through the streets, beating themselves with chains. The meaning is stark: The good suffer in this world. One Shi'ite proverb states: "Trouble falls more quickly on a pious believer than rain to the earth." 'Ashura commemorates the Shi'ite belief that Husain died for the sins of the Islamic community and that he will intercede for believers on the day of judgment. There are certainly parallels with Christianity. Yet there are also differences, for Shi'ites yearn for vengeance, something not acceptable in Christian teaching. The style of Shi'a is one of suppressed anger, which at times explodes into unrestrained rage. This has been evident in the modern-day Shi'ite Iranian revolution led by the Ayatollah Khomeini.[11]

Shi'ites await the end of time when they will triumph over their enemies and justice will be restored. The instrument of their deliverance will be the Hidden Imam, the last known direct descendant of the Prophet through Ali's line. This Hidden Imam has been living in occultation since his mysterious disappearance from the world. Shi'ites themselves differ on when Ali's line ended. However, most believe that it occurred with the 12th Imam, or Muhammad's 12th direct descendant, who disappeared in 873 A.D. "Imam" means leader in Arabic. For Shi'ites, this means their spiritual leader, ultimately the Hidden Imam. In a more practical sense, it can mean the leading Shi'ite cleric of his time. During the Iranian revolution of the late 1970's, Ayatollah Khomeini was given this title, for he was seen as the spokesman for the Hidden Imam, with whom he had spiritual communication. Each of the 12 Shi'ite Imams supposedly enjoyed a special religious knowledge, which originated with the Prophet himself. Hence, one in communication with the Hidden Imam has extraordinary insight into God's will for mankind. Additionally, the 12 Imams were without sin. In other words, they could not make a mistake. In effect, this Shi'ite belief relegates the Qur'an to a less dominant position than is true in the Sunni religion. For Shi'ites, the pronouncements of the worldly representatives of the Hidden Imam are of paramount importance. This compromises somewhat Muhammad's own position as the Seal of the Prophets. Nevertheless, Shi'ites are quick to rejoin that an Imam cannot receive revelations from God, as Muhammad himself did. On the other hand, as an Imam can make no mistake, this distinction is somewhat theoretical.

Some of these Shi'ite beliefs have influenced the Sunni faith. For example, Sunnis agree that at least Muhammad and all earlier prophets were without sin and incapable of error. Nonetheless, they have rejected the Shi'ite claim that the 12 Imams shared in this super-human quality. Additionally, while Sunnis reject the specific Shi'ite concept of the Hidden Imam, they do largely accept the idea that at the end of time a Mahdi (one who is guided by God) will come and make all things right. Interestingly, Shi'ites interchangeably use the terms Hidden Imam and Mahdi. Sunnis concede that he will come from the blood descendants of Muhammad, although not necessarily from Ali's line. Throughout Islamic history, a variety of men have claimed this eschatological role. Interestingly, Muslims also generally believe that Jesus will assist the Mahdi at the end of time.[12]

Unlike the Shi'ites who have truly focused on charismatic Imams, Sunnis have relied more upon faceless tradition. This is not to say that Sunnis know no spiritual leadership. Both Sunnis and Shi'ites employ many religious scholars, collectively known as the ulema, whose job is to delineate the authentic Islamic traditions that guide believers. But official Sunnism knows no religious figure who can abrogate portions of the tradition by any claims to special, divine authority. For Sunnis, the scholar-jurists of the ulema, bound by the weight of tradition, constitute their principal spiritual guides.

Similar to the Talmudic scholars of Orthodox Judaism, the ulema guards Islam's religious law, the Shari'ah. In the first several centuries after Muhammad's death, the ulema evaluated Qur'anic injunctions and ruled on the relative merit of hadith, or historical details relating to the Prophet's life, in building the traditional body of Islamic religious law. Ultimately, they became collectively satisfied that no further improvements upon their creative scholarship were necessary, and the evolution of the Shari'ah largely stopped. Building on the natural conservatism of the Arabian nomad, this religious law created a cultural climate unfriendly to change.

Islamic religious tradition is almost as important for Shi'ites as Sunnis. Indeed, it is in Iran, a Shi'ite stronghold, where the loudest Islamic outcry against the Westernizing forces of modernization and change has recently been heard. We have seen that the Shi'ite religion, by looking to an infallible Imam, provides an avenue to abrogate aspects of Islamic tradition. Nonetheless, it cannot be overemphasized that Shi'ite overturning of Islamic tradition will never become a frequent occurrence. Any Shi'ite charismatic clerical leader is chosen from among the most learned of the Shi'ite ulema. Invariably, such a man is steeped in Islamic tradition. Accordingly, even in the Shi'ite faith, the weight of tradition is heavy.[13]

While the Imam's role provides some theological flexibility for Shi'ites, the concept of ijma serves in a similar manner for Sunnis. Ijma means the infallible consensus of the Sunni community of faith. The way this Sunni concept works is as follows: If something is believed widely enough within the Sunni ulema, it becomes grafted onto the religious tradition. A good example of this concerns the aforementioned belief that Muhammad was infallible. After it became widely accepted within Sunni circles, it became sanctified by the rule of ijma. A Sunni hadith supports the ijma concept. Muhammad is to have said: "My community will never agree on error." Accordingly, Sunnis call themselves "People of the Tradition and the Collectivity." "Cleave to the Collectivity," an old Sunni saying goes, "for Satan is with the one who stands alone." As Sunnis see their community as directed by God, they confidently rely on ijma.

Shi'ites look upon ijma with contempt. Were not Ali and his holy descendants spurned by those who had the acquiescence of the Sunni community? In the Shi'ite view, injustice has been the fruit of the Sunni ijma, which, after all, is a product of sinful men. For Shi'ites, religious authority derives not from the community but rather from the family of the Prophet, as represented in the male offspring of Ali and Fatima, Muhammad's daughter. This difference accounts for the Islamic schism between Shi'ites and Sunnis. Born in the early quarrels over who deserved to succeed the Prophet, this division of Muslims continues into our own day.[14]

## Islamic Beliefs

Islam, "to surrender," was the name Muhammad gave his religion. This word choice was deliberate, for in Islam the act of submission is valued more than mere belief. The Qur'an expressed this emphasis: "The wandering Arabs say: We believe, Say (unto them, O Muhammad): Ye believe not, but rather say 'We submit,'

191

obey Allah and His messenger. He will not withhold from you...(the reward of) your deeds." Nonetheless, Islamic beliefs cannot be ignored, for they reveal the contours of the Muslim way of life. Key among these beliefs is the idea that God controls everything that happens. If good fortune befalls one, it is God's will. If tragedy marks one's life, that too is God's will. Man's proper role is not to question but rather to submit.

In harmony with this emphasis on human submission, Islam is characterized by a strong tendency toward predestinarian thought. Judaism and Christianity have at times considered the concept of predestination, although both in our own day show a clear preference for the role of human free will. In Islam's early history there was a similar tension between predestination and free will. The Qur'an itself contains statements lending support alternately to divine omnipotence and the power of human choice. Suggesting a divine determinism, the Qur'an claims that God alone can change the human heart. Yet it also states that if one recognizes Allah as the only God, does not steal, does not commit adultery, does not slander neighbors and kill girl babies (an all too common practice in Muhammad's day), one will go to Paradise. This suggests a theology favoring free will. Muhammad did not resolve this contradiction, any more than did the authors of Jewish and Christian scripture. Islam's preference for divine determinism would become clear only after the Prophet's death.

Islam's ultimate emphasis of predestination was predictable given the ancient belief patterns of pre-Islamic Arabia. The nomads of the Arabian peninsula had been conditioned by their hostile environment. The experience of millennia had taught that human choice could not prevent miseries unique to the desert. In Arab eyes, luck, or better yet fate, played the larger part in the struggle for survival. This world view minimized anxiety of the unknown and was psychologically comforting. Given a choice between the Qur'an's statements harmonizing with this position and those stressing human free will, it was perhaps inevitable that the former would eventually predominate.[15] The Umayyad caliphs had recognized this and accordingly had argued that their victory over Ali's family proved that God was on their side. Of course, Shi'ites were forced to reject this early crude appeal to a predestination theology. They were joined by a formidable group of rationalist Muslims inspired by Greek philosophy. These thinkers, known as Mu'tazilites, stressed that evil men may temporarily thwart God's will. When evil seems to triumph, as in the case of the Umayyads, the Mu'tazilites held that God reverses the situation in the afterlife. This was a comforting thought for suffering Shi'ites. In addition, the Mu'tazilites argued that God could not enable evil to triumph for His nature is good.

These Mu'tazilite notions bothered Abul-Hasan al-Ash'ari. Though trained by the Mu'tazilites, he ultimately rejected their position because it placed human limits on the power of God. This, he saw, as gross human arrogance. In the 10th century, long after the overthrow of the hated Umayyads, al-Ash'ari proclaimed that God determines everything, even those deeds defined in our limited human view as "evil." He would develop a theology of fatalism which would prove irresistible to the tradition-directed Arab temperament.[16]

Al-Ash'ari regarded God as the immediate and direct author of every occurrence. He dismisssed the notion of God as First Cause and indeed all ideas of causation. He rejected natural law, substituting it with his own concept of divine habits. For example, he argued that while ice is normally cold and flame hot, these attributes are constantly recreated by God out of habit. Yet at times, God is known to suspend His habits, producing that which is called a miracle. Al-Ash'ari's theology would be called atomistic, because it claimed that every moment of time, every act, every thought—indeed, every separate thing or event, in and of itself—is directly created by God. This line of thought would later evolve to the conclusion that nothing has any real existence other than God. Al-Ash'ari's theology of divine omnipotence, predestination and determinism is more rigorous than anything comparable from Judaism or Christianity. Even the later elaborate claims of John Calvin pale when placed beside those of al-Ash'ari. Preceding Calvin by six centuries, al-Ash'ari taught that God creates belief in the Muslim and disbelief in the infidel and that any perception of human decision is in fact illusory. His philosophy, harmonizing with the ancient Arab cultural tendency toward fatalism, became established theological truth throughout most of the Muslim world.[17]

Some pockets of Muslim resistance held out for a modicum of free will. Official Shi'ite theology would continue to pay a certain homage to the belief that man has free will. This was done to avoid the unacceptable idea that God Himself had determined Ali's assassination and the horrible suffering of Husain by Yazid's minions. On the other hand, the average Shi'ite believer shares the same tendency to fatalistic thinking that characterizes other Muslims. This creates some ambivalence among Shi'ites concerning the age-old debate between those who argue for divine omnipotence and those who stress human free will. Certainly, Shi'ite theology fails to serve as an effective counterweight within Islam to that provided by al-Ash'ari. In general, al-Ash'ari's thought has dominated Islam for almost a millennium. Under the sway of his theology, the Muslim is made to feel dependent upon God for everything. "What reaches you could not possibly have missed you," one well-known Muslim proverb relates; "and what misses you could not possibly have reached you." On a more mundane level, when asked if he thinks it is going to rain, an Arab will typically respond: "insh'allah," or "as God wills."[18]

Homage to this sweeping vision of divine majesty and power is not made without some cost. Specifically, advancement in the sciences continues to be discouraged by this Islamic world view. In al-Ash'ari's own time, during the heyday of the Mu'tazilites, Islamic countries were far more advanced than Europe in the natural sciences. But as the dominant mood came to accept and submit to that which is and to that which shall be, Arab interest in science all but died. The study of the stars continued, for patterns discovered there could be used as a supplement to fatalistic beliefs. Astrology would flourish in Islam. The only other scholarly endeavor encouraged by al-Ash'ari's theology was far removed from the natural sciences. This was the study of the Shari'ah, Muslim religious law. High value was placed upon learning this unchanging divine law by means of rote memorization. The energetic age of Islamic innovation and experimentation ended soon after al-Ash'ari. That which emerged simply called upon Muslims to conform to the Shari'ah and accept God's will.[19]

To live by the Shari'ah in its infinite detail is not easily achieved. Accordingly, a catechism of sorts, composed of five precepts, was formulated to guide the average Muslim of sincere faith. These basic Islamic obligations, known as the Five Pillars of Islam, stated that believers should do the following:

194

1) Declare one's faith by proclaiming: "There is no God but Allah,
   and Muhammad is His Prophet."
2) Engage in worship five times a
   day, to be prefaced on each occasion by ritual purification
   with water or sand. Prayer is to
   be conducted by means of repeated
   prostrations, made in the direction of Mecca. Once a week, at
   Friday noon, the believer should
   engage in communal prayer in a
   a mosque, a house of prayer.
3) Pay alms to the poor.
4) Fast during the daylight hours
   of the holy month of Ramadan.
5) Participate in the hajj, the pilgrimage to Mecca, at least once
   in a lifetime.

    Several points must be highlighted when
considering Islam's guidelines on proclamation and
prayer. One of these concerns the role of Muhammad
himself. Often in the West, Islam is mistakenly called
Mohammedanism, a title which connotes an unwarranted,
exalted role for the Prophet, comparable to that of the
Christ in Christianity. In their declaration of faith,
Muslims specify that their worship is of Allah alone.
Muhammad was merely His messenger. Another aspect of
Islamic prayer life that must be acknowledged is that
no other world religion comparably pressures its
believers to acknowledge the supremacy of God on such a
regular basis. Additionally significant is the fact
that for six days of the week, this obligation is
normally met without assistance or direction by anyone
other than the worshipper himself. In Islam, man and
God normally meet without an intermediary. Then on
Friday, man is reminded that he is part of a community
of faith, a fact made poignant in the mosque by row
upon row of foreheads touching the floor in unison,
bowed in submission before God

    At times in the Islamic past, the pillar regarding
charity or alms-giving, has been administered by means
of a state tax, although normally this requirement has
been fulfilled by means of individual conscience. Even
the poor are enjoined to give to each other. Similar
to the Friday communal prayer, the Islamic requirement
of alms-giving reminds the believer that he is part of
a community. This serves to check the human

195

psychological weakness to think only of self. Islam's
obligation of fasting reminds the believer of his
inherent physical weakness as well. When the lunar
month of Ramadan falls in the summer season, a
sustained abstinence from all fluids can work a real
hardship. After sundown, the Muslim is allowed to
break the fast but moderation at such times is
preferred. Those who can afford it sleep during the
daylight hours of Ramadan and carry on a full schedule
of activities at night. In actuality, night feasting
and merriment often characterize Ramadan in much the
same way as Christmas occurs in the West. Muslims
justify this as a celebration of God's revelation of
the Qur'an, which began during the month of Ramadan.
Shi'ites revere Ramadan for yet another reason, for it
was the month of Ali's assassination.

Many exceptions are allowed to excuse Muslims from
the obligation of the hajj, the pilgrimage to Mecca.
To be sure, only a minority of Muslims are able to
afford the hajj, yet it stands as the goal of a
lifetime and the hope of every true Muslim. When a
million and a half pilgrims congregate in Mecca's
general environs during five days of the lunar month of
Dhu'l-Hijja, the meaning of the Muslim community is
burned into the attending believer's consciousness.
The pilgrim dons a simple white garment, creating an
impression of equality among the multitude of
believers. Class, nationality and race are temporarily
forgotten in the unity of the Muslim community under
God.

We have seen that Jesus of Nazareth instructed his
followers to love both God and neighbor. These ends
are likewise implicit in the Muslim's faith. At every
turn, the Muslim is called to submit before God, while
recognizing his identity with and his obligation to the
wider community. From the Muslim perspective, Islam
more perfectly meets these two emphases than does any
rival faith. Islam demands only that which is
possible. On the other hand, Muslims see the more
open-ended requirements of Christianity as too easily
encouraging hypocrisy. Real submission remains the
mark of Islam. It is encouraged by the theology of
al-Ash'ari. It is made specific in the complex
Shari'ah and simplified in the Five Pillars of Islam.
The result is praiseworthy, to the extent that Islamic
belief is actually transformed into a way of living
under God.[20]

# Sufism

Worldly success breeds hedonistic values. The last two centuries of Western civilization demonstrate this fact, as did the first several of Islam's existence. With an empire stretching from Spain to India, early Islamic society forsook the simple ways of the Prophet and indulged in displays of regal luxury. To protest this drift from authentic Islam, a few early Muslims donned clothing of a course woolen material (suf). In time, they became known as Sufis. They did more than object to the wearing of silk. They also attacked the legalistic pedantry of the ulema, the "scribes and Pharisees" of Islam. The masters of the Shari'ah, with their heads full of hadith and Qur'anic passages, had transformed Islam into an elaborate code of rules requiring outward conformity. Against this, the Sufis rebelled. One Sufi proclaimed: "Seek the real Satan in the scholastic sophist, or the hairsplitting doctor--for his is the opposite of Truth." Searching for a truer expression of Islam, the Sufis practiced asceticism learned from Christian monks in Syria. To this, they added the rich heritage of Middle-Eastern Gnosticism, which Christianity had earlier rejected. With these materials, the early Sufis fashioned a mystical religious experience surpassing anything in the Western world. Later, Sufism would intermingle with the mystical traditions of India. Sikhism, a blend of Sufism and bhakti Hinduism, would thereupon emerge as a separate faith.[21]

The Sufis emphasize what might be called experiential religion, in other words, the notion that religion must be lived rather than studied. They compare scholastic religious learning to a kiss sent by a loved one but delivered by an impersonal stranger. Using another analogy, they regard themselves as lions, who eat that which they themselves have killed, rather than foxes, who feed on the remnants of another's catch. "He who tastes not," the Sufis say, "knows not." Sufis seek to live fully in the present moment, a goal of all mystics. Harmonizing with the theology of al-Ash'ari, they see each moment as a fresh creation of God, worthy of one's complete attention. Each day, they advise, should be approached without agendas from the past or expectations concerning the future, for each moment is perfect in and of itself. Consequently, the Sufi is completely adjustable to whatever that moment might bring. He is to be ibn al-waqt (the son of the present moment). "Wisdom descends from heaven," a Sufi has written, "but does not settle into the heart of any man who pays heed to the next day."[22]

Sufism insists that one who aspires to be ibn al-waqt yoke himself to a Sufi master, called a shaykh (elder). The shaykh makes the disciple aware of his failings by asking hard questions. He humiliates the disciple by requiring him to beg in the streets and clean latrines. In the process, the student acquires an existential understanding of what it means to be a Muslim (one who submits). Sufi shaykhs use an untold variety of methods on their disciples. Indeed, one author has described Sufism as "a series of different and even contradictory experiments." But if the means employed are endless, there is an unchanging goal--direct, personal knowledge of God. The way of achieving this is self-annihilation. Each of us has a baser self, which the Sufi calls nafs. It is the source of our pride and envy, that which is generally called "selfishness." When that is destroyed, the Sufis say, all that remains is God. To know God intimately, the Sufis advise, "wipe off the dust of selfhood from thy soul." When that is done, one will experience existence beyond individuality, a condition known to mystics from every religious tradition. Al-Ash'ari's theology had described God as the sole Actor of the cosmos. The Sufis agree and urge that we surrender the fiction of separate existence. "Die before you die," they advocate.[23]

To work toward this goal, the Sufi disciple must become fully conscious of his thoughts as well as his actions. He meditates upon the Islamic concept of shirk (association). The Qur'an describes shirk as the association of other gods with God--in short, polytheism, the bete noire of early Islam. Shirk is the ultimate sin, the only one that God will not forgive. The Sufis teach that shirk is within every selfish thought. For example, if one worships God out of fear of punishment or hope of reward, he is associating himself with God and is thereby guilty of shirk. Rabi'ah-Adawia, the most famous female Sufi saint, went through the streets with a jug of water and a fiery torch. She said that her purpose was to quench the flames of hell with the water and burn up Paradise with the torch so that God would be loved for Himself alone. To use another example, Sufis warn that an exaggerated asceticism can be shirk, motivated by "idolatry of the empty stomach." In this way, Sufism realizes the wisdom of what Siddartha Gautama had called the "middle way."[24]

The Sufi disciple reflects seriously upon his own faults. When he sees a flaw in another, he is to meditate upon the same trait in himself. Through such methods, he gradually comes to appreciate the sin of his own separate existence. Concurrently, he is to practice tawakkul (complete trust in God). Jesus urged his disciples to be as lilies of the field, neither toiling nor spinning, but relying upon God alone. The Sufi is to do likewise. However, Sufis are warned of exaggerated tawakkul, which is testing God to provide for one's daily needs. One hadith claims that Muhammad advised a bedouin first to provide for his camel's requirements and then trust in God. Tawakkul should never justify inactivity. Rather, it should enable one to accept those occurrences beyond one's control.

Sufis tend to seek poverty to break all ego attachment to comfortable existence. Consequently, they are called dervishes and fakirs, two words connoting an impoverished condition. Choosing poverty for themselves, Sufis are not very alert to the material sufferings of the lower classes. Their religious orientation is not one of promoting social justice. Nonetheless, they are ever willing to aid others along the Sufi way. They teach that misfortune should be seen as "mercy in disguise," bitter medicine designed by God to cure the sickness of selfish existence. Shi'ites have condemned Sufis as escapists for holding such attitudes. In the Sufi perspective, the angry Shi'ite yearning for social justice is seen as feeding the baser instincts which Sufism seeks to annihilate.

Ironically, both the Shi'ite and Sufi traditions begin with Ali who received his presumed special gnosis from the Prophet himself. Sufis say that after Ali, mystical Sufi insights descended from master to disciple over the generations. Like the Shi'ite religion, Sufism is authoritarian in structure and charismatic in flavor. In place of the elaborate Shi'ite clerical hierarchy of mullahs, mujtahids, ayatollahs and Imams, Sufis look solely to their individual shaykhs. Nonetheless, Sufism provides the Muslim desiring religious leadership an alternative to Shi'ism. This has served to make the two expressions rivals of sorts. Accordingly, most Sufi communities see themselves as within the Sunni tradition, albeit a few insignificant Sufi orders do exist in Shi'ism.[25]

The Sufi vision provided Islam with a new kind of hero. The Sufi saint is not an Husain-like martyr nor

199

an Abu Bakr wielding the sword to expand the faith.
Sufis categorized these heroes as waging the lesser
jihad (struggle). The Sufi saint is the master of the
greater jihad, the struggle for self-annihilation. One
such Sufi hero was Husain Ibn Mansur al-Hallaj, who
lived in 10th-century Baghdad. Threatened by his
Jesus-like criticism of law-bound religion, the
authorities dismembered his hands and feet and then
crucified him. As with Jesus, he was charged with
having made the blasphemous claim of being one with
God, which of course al-Hallaj had done in the best
Sufi tradition. Al-Hallaj's poetry reveals this:

> Betwixt me and Thee there lingers
> an 'it is I' that torments me.
> Ah, of Thy grace, take this 'I'
> from between us! I am He whom
> I love, and He whom I love is I;
> We are two spirits dwelling in one
> body. If thou seest me, thou seest
> Him, And if thou seest Him, thou
> seest us both.

Also like Jesus, al-Hallaj did not try to avoid his
sentence of death. He also forgave his tormentors from
the cross. His followers also expected him someday to
return miraculously from the dead. As this example
shows, the model of Jesus of Nazareth guides the Sufi
mystics. Yet, they are in no sense Christians, for
they hold their own interpretation of the life and
death of the prophet Jesus. Sufis have said to
Christians: "You may have the cross, but we have the
meaning of the cross." For Sufis, Jesus was indeed
God, but no more so than themselves. His example
stands as a guidepost to the Sufi meaning of eternal
life. Accordingly, Sufis have entitled Jesus the "Seal
of the Saints."[26]

Sufism, drawing upon both Christian and Islamic
ideas, might have evolved into a separate religion had
it not been for Abu Hamid Muhammad al-Ghazali, who
lived in 12th-century Baghdad. He was widely regarded
as the premier Muslim theologian and greatest authority
on Islamic law of his day. He was the ultimate example
of the scholastic approach to religion which the Sufis
disdained. But al-Ghazali's development did not end
there. He experienced a spiritual crisis with the
self-realization that hope of human glory and fame had
motivated his religious studies. Serious in his search
for God, he could not continue as before. He abruptly
left his prestigious position at Baghdad's Nizamiya

University and went to live in the humble manner of the
Sufi mystics. When he returned years later, he brought
Sufism into the fold of Muslim orthodoxy. In his
writings, al-Ghazali demonstrated the essential harmony
between the theology of al-Ash'ari and Sufi teachings.
Because of al-Ghazali's great influence, a community
consensus (ijma) formed on the acceptability of Sufism,
which was then certified as part and parcel of Islam.[27]

Because of al-Ghazali, Sufism was given the title
of the "Conscience of Islam." Sufism would not always
live up to this lofty description. Given the
experimentation tolerated in Sufism, it was perhaps
inevitable that on occasion it would exhibit the worst
in human nature. Consequently, some Sufis violated
Islamic law with impunity, engaged in bizarre behavior
of the most degenerate sort, and escaped into drugs and
alcohol. They justified this by claiming that by
actively seeking society's contempt they could better
achieve the Sufi goal of self-annihilation. Such
malignant growths eventually destroyed themselves,
allowing healthier branches of Sufism to predominate.
Certainly in modern times, Sufism has not only served
as the conscience of Islam but as its proselytizing arm
as well. Millions in India and Africa have been won to
the faith by Sufi teachers. These converts, building
upon the Sufi theme of religious experimentation, have
grafted their native religious heritages onto the body
of Islam. This fact has helped make Sufism a
fountainhead of popular religious beliefs. For
example, pilgrimages to the numerous tombs of deceased
Sufi saints are commonplace in Islam. Together with
Shi'ite visitations to the burial shrines of past
Imams, these pilgrimages have often taken on the aura
of a minor hajj and, in fact, for most Muslims have
served as a substitute for the fifth pillar of Islam.
In the popular mind, these visits have positive
benefit, as those nearing the proximity of such tombs
supposedly can be cured of infertility and other
infirmities.[28]

Such practices and beliefs have grated against the
more traditional elements within Islam. Fundamentalist
Arabs were especially disturbed by the Sufi innovations
that seemed always to come from non-Arab sources. This
dissatisfaction focused in the Wahhabi reaction of the
late 18th century. Arising in the eastern Arabian
peninsula, a Wahhabi warrior community marched
northward into Iraq and westward to Mecca destroying
all Sufi tombs in its path. The Wahhabi objective was
to return Islam to the original purity that it had

known in the days of the Prophet. Ironically, this effort to go back to the fundamentals of Islam was itself heretical, for ijma (community consensus) had long before accepted Sufi experimentation and innovation into the very body of Islam. Wahhabi military might was crushed early in the 19th century, but the Wahhabi fundamentalist ideal lives on today as the state religion of Saudi Arabia.

Generally speaking, present-day Islam relies heavily upon Sufism, especially in those areas where the religion is under systematic attack from secularizing forces. Since World War I, illegal Sufi orders have kept the faith alive in both the Soviet Union and Turkey where the state has attempted to strangle Islam in hopes of thereby encouraging social modernization. The force of religion has proven stronger than the calculated policies of governments. Sufism, with its emphases on tight, authoritarian organization and on patiently enduring the vicissitudes of life, is especially well-designed to meet this challenge. Having served as both the conscience of Islam and its most effective proselytizing voice, Sufism, in our own day additionally has revealed itself as the brave preserver of the faith.[29]

## The Egalitarian Ummah

In November, 1979, radical cadre of the Ayatollah Khomeini's Iranian, Islamic revolution seized the United States' embassy in Teheran. The embassy personnel were to be held hostage for over a year and undergo many humiliations for their country's supposed transgressions against Iran. However, some Americans taken that fateful November would escape most of this ordeal. In the early weeks of the crisis, Khomeini allowed most of the Blacks and women among the hostages to go home. He justified this act on the grounds that Islam, unlike American society, respects both Blacks and women. A decade and a half before, the Black Muslim leader Malcolm X had gone to Mecca on the hajj. He had left America believing that a strict separation of the races alone could provide for racial justice. His experience on the hajj radically altered his perspective. He joyously discovered that Islam as a way of life was indeed free of all racial bias and returned home believing that Islam's egalitarian ummah (community) was humankind's surest hope for racial peace.[30]

Muhammad's own life story presents relatively

202

strong credentials for Islam in the area of racial equality. In the Qur'anic narrative, which the Prophet transmitted, Hagar, the mother of the Arab peoples, was black. One of Muhammad's wives was black. Muhammad gave one of his daughters in marriage to a Black, and Bilal, chosen by Muhammad to be Islam's first muezzin (caller for prayers), was a Black. Christians can claim that Jesus preached the brotherhood of all men, but the specific examples of Muhammad commingling with Blacks on equal terms provides a more persuasive witness to many.

Unhappily, the broader course of Muslim history is blemished on the subject of African slavery. At the outset, Muhammad's message served to ameliorate the condition of Arabia's slaves, most of whom were black Africans. He required masters to allow slaves to purchase their own freedom and exhorted good Muslims to free their slaves as a form of alms. As Islam expanded and some Whites were enslaved, slavery increasingly was restricted to domestic roles and military service. However, when there was dirty work to be done, it invariably fell to Blacks. A key example of this involved an extensive importation of black slaves into southern Iraq in Islam's third century. Their task involved a back-breaking land reclamation project. That this episode involved a degree of endemic racial prejudice is suggested by some surviving evidence. The involvement of Arab slave traders in the later movement of Africans to the New World also cannot be denied. This activity was justified at the time by a colossal misuse of the jihad concept. Slavery largely disappeared from Islamic countries in the later 19th-century, due to the pressure of Western abolitionists. Islam's long relationship with human bondage did not officially end until 1962, when again under pressure from the West, Saudi Arabia liberated its 4,000 slaves.[31]

Despite these unhappy details, Christendom's record concerning race relations is far worse. The story of Europe's exploitation of the African race in the Western hemisphere is unmatched by anything in Islamic history, a fact which has won relatively good marks for Islam from Blacks. More controversial is Islam's proclaimed respect for women. In the eyes of one observer, Muslim women occupy "an equal but different half of the Islamic universe." The Muslim perspective is as follows: A woman's devotion to her family is essential to the maintenance of a healthy society. God created male and female alike, but, in the

203

words of the Qur'an, "men are in charge of women."
Each sex has been given different gifts to offer up to
God in different ways. That a man should assume the
role divinely intended for a woman or vice versa is an
abomination. The work of each has equal value, and, in
this sense, both are equal in the eyes of God.
Unhappily, Islamic women in Arab countries suffer the
highest illiteracy rate in the world. They are kept in
a dependency relationship to males, who oppress them
not always for the greater glory of God. How can this
be justified in the name of religion?

The answer is found in Arab history. Before
Islam, Arab women were totally without rights. In
fact, the new religion improved their status. It
provided a woman with one half the inheritance of a
male. (The rationale for this inequality is that sons
have to maintain their own families whereas daughters,
supported by their husbands, do not have this expense.)
The Qur'an prohibited the killing of unwanted girl
babies, a practice which had commonly occurred in
pre-Islamic Arabia. It made adultery, viewed before
that time as the right of every Arab male, punishable
by death but required that there be at least four
witnesses to the act. It held that consent must be
given by a woman before her marriage, a right that
would be kept largely theoretical in the
father-dominated families of Islamic civilization.
Finally, the Qur'an restricted the number of wives that
a man could have to four, with the added requirement
that he treat each of them with equal favor.[32] Some
commentators have claimed that by insisting upon the
equal treatment of each of several wives, the Qur'anic
word indirectly required monogyny. Other observers
have correctly noted that if monogyny was truly the
Qur'an's intent, it would not have legislated for
polygyny. Before Islam, Arab males could take an
unlimited number of wives. Therefore, by limiting the
legal number to four and insuring for their equal
treatment, Islam improved the status of women. But, as
Muhammad was the Seal of the Prophets, no further
change was possible. In this century, some Islamic
countries, under the sway of Western thinking, have
moved against polygyny and reformed other Qur'anic
rules concerning marriage. Turkey and Tunisia have
been most notable in this regard. However, such
reforms are opposed to the clear meaning of the
Prophet's revelation. Indeed, such tampering has in
some places contributed to Islamic reactions against
Western-inspired meddling in divinely decreed
male-female relationships. Khomeini's revolution is

204

perhaps the most obvious example of this.[33]

Islam favors a healthy sexuality within marriage. However, it also promotes a chaste society. It rejects the open displays of promiscuous sexual relations that characterized Arab civilization up until Muhammad. To bring about this reform, Islam instituted a strict segregation of the sexes known as purdah (covering). Within the intimacy of the family unit, male and female are encouraged to commingle. In public, traditional Muslim women are veiled and covered with a garment designed to cancel sensual thoughts in male passers-by. Some Muslims have gone further still to insure female chastity. In some regions, female circumcision or clitorectomy is practiced to lessen the female sexual drive. In other areas, women are barred from the mosques so as to discourage any sexual fantasies of male worshippers. In still other places where women are admitted to mosques, they are required to pray behind the males so as not to distract them.[34]

Given an honorable role only within marriage, Islamic women live in constant fear of divorce. One hadith relates that the Prophet said: "Among all permissible things, divorce is the most hated act of God." Yet, Muhammad repudiated several of his own wives. By the Shari'ah, men can easily divorce their wives by a simple act of repeated proclamations. This can occur for virtually any reason. By contrast, a woman cannot divorce her husband for any reason, save possibly impotency. The Muslim woman's primary insurance against repudiation is the mahr, a payment that the bridegroom bequeaths to her at the time of marriage. The mahr provides a form of alimony if she is later divorced. However, among poorer Muslims, the mahr is virtually non-existent and so is the woman's protection against divorce. These facts create great anxiety for Muslim women and serve to keep them subservient to their husbands.

When considering women as "an equal but different half of the Islamic universe," a major problem is created by the fact that women are discouraged at several junctures from full participation in their own religion. For example, the hajj can be undertaken only by a woman who is chaperoned by her husband or close male family members. Perhaps partially as a result, the hajj is fulfilled by far fewer women than men. Interestingly, women on the hajj are discouraged from wearing the veil, an exception which at that time serves to symbolize the familial unity of the ummah.

Yet, few female faces are seen in the pilgrimage crowds of Mecca. Women more frequently visit the tombs of Sufi and Shi'ite venerables, providing a sort of substitute hajj for them. Islam's portrayal of Paradise as a realm filled with ever-virgin houris (beautiful, seductive maidens) also reminds Muslim women of their religion's preference for the male sex. Restricted at every turn within formal Islam, Muslim women commonly gravitate to more popular religious expressions involving magic and local superstitions.[35]

Traditional Muslim males are not apologetic concerning their treatment of women. They scorn the West's social disorder, which they see resulting in part from permissive sexual relations and a blurring of sex roles. They look to their own societies and see obedient children and supportive wives. Theirs is an idealized view, as is the West's own self-image as a culture of individual freedom and equality of opportunity. Clearly, the Western preference is for individual fulfillment over social order. Islam's purpose is radically different. It seeks a society living by timeless and divinely revealed standards of conduct. Its focus is not the individual but rather the well-being of the ummah, the community of Muslim believers.

In a world stained by the arrogance of racism, Islam truly approximates an egalitarian racial community. This fact has helped contribute to Islam's claims as the world's fastest growing religion. Places such as central Africa, the area of Islam's most dramatic growth, are not unduly concerned with women's liberation, which is popular only in industrialized countries. Islam's stand on race is another matter for peoples struggling to throw off the vestiges of Western colonialism. From the perspective of the Third World, Islam enjoys an egalitarian ummah, which helps explain why it is viewed by many there as the most attractive of the world's great religions.[36]

Islam and the West

Muslim belief holds that the Mahdi, the guided one of God, will come at the dawn of a new Islamic century and right all wrongs as the world ends. As Islam's lunar calendar compresses centuries into somewhat less than 100 solar years, the 14th century of Islam dawned in 1881. In that year, a Sudanese Muslim leader named Muhammad Ahmad declared himself to be the Mahdi, who, it was said, would come when Islam was severely threatened by its enemies. The 19th century had witnessed the onslaught of Western civilization against the Muslim world, both in terms of direct military encroachments and through "modernization," which fostered secular values which rivaled Islam. These signs supported the Sudanese Mahdi's claims. Eventually, his movement was crushed by a combined British and Egyptian military force. But his stout resistance gave the Western world a warning that true believing Muslims would not easily succumb to its message of "progress."[37]

Nevertheless, Western political takeovers in the Islamic world continued. By the end of the century, England controlled Muslim populations in India and Egypt, while France dominated Algeria and Tunisia. Early in the new century, Morocco also became part of France's empire. Several years later, Europe's World War I delivered the final blow to the long ailing Muslim Ottoman Empire. Its former territories were surrendered to the victorious European imperialist powers. France acquired Lebanon and Syria, while Britain gained Palestine and Iraq. Blaming the stagnant Islamic world view for this decline, Turkey's Kemal Ataturk forged a new nationalism around Western, secular ideals. Consequently, Islam as a religion was methodically persecuted by the Turkish state itself. The emergence of the Soviet Union likewise boded ill for Islam in central Asia, as mosques were closed and heavy restrictions were placed on the practice of religion. Throughout the Muslim world, traditional Shari'ah rules surrendered to the seemingly inevitable forces of modernization. Islamic criminal codes, including the cutting off of hands for stealing, were replaced with Westernized concepts of justice. Polygyny came under attack and women acquired greater rights in divorce issues. Slavery was banned, while traditional Islamic strictures against alcohol and the charging of interest were relaxed or lifted altogether. The powers of the ulema drastically declined, as governments following a Western model undertook to control matters that heretofore had been left to religion.[38]

Traditionally, Islam has divided the world into mutually exclusive spheres--Dar al-Islam (The House of Submission to Allah) and Dar al-Harb (The House of War). In the 19th and early 20th centuries, Dar al-Harb was being erected upon Islamic territory itself. Islam was losing the fight for its very existence. After World War II, the direct imperial

207

advance of European countries ceased as both Britain and France lost their will for such ventures. Slowly in some instances and hastily in others, these two nations retreated from the region, but, as they left, Westernized native elites gained control. Traditional Islam continued to decline, now suffering at the hands of Arabs with a modernizing vision.[39]

One post-war European, colonial endeavor served as a bitter reminder of an imperialism that otherwise seemed in retreat. This was Zionism, a movement having its origins in age-old Jewish hopes for a return to Palestine. Spurred by the Nazi Holocaust, European Jews flocked to their promised land. At the close of World War II, Saudi Arabia's King Ibn Saud had expressed to Franklin Roosevelt that a Jewish homeland should instead be carved from the dying carcass of Nazi Germany, but the logic of Zionism drove the persecuted Jews back to the land described in their biblical texts. By 1948, a Jewish state in Palestine was a declared fact. War ensued as neighboring Arab states challenged this new European influx. In the course of the struggle, some 780,000 Arabs fled their homes. Israel later claimed that this occurred on the orders of Arab military strategists, while others insisted that the flight occurred out of fear of Jewish terrorist tactics. In any case, these Arab refugees were not allowed by Israel to return to their homes at the end of the fighting, and a permanent class of displaced people was thereby created. Later, together with those Arabs remaining under Israeli control, they would become known as Palestinians. Their plight constantly serves to remind the Islamic world of the ongoing threat of Dar al-Harb in its midst.[40]

The 1967 Arab-Israeli war especially dramatized the danger. In six days of fighting, Israel more than doubled its territory. Muslim holy places in Jerusalem came under Israeli control. A great soul-searching swept the Middle East. How had this disaster occurred? Was it that Islamic civilization was stagnant and technologically inferior to that of the West, as represented by Israel? Or, was God punishing the Arabs for their laxity in religious matters? The fact that Egypt and Syria, two of the Arab powers defeated in that war, had pushed for secularization and socialist modernization within the Arab world for a generation seemed to suggest the possibility of divine retribution. This rationale for defeat proved irresistible, and a new wave of Islamic fervor swept throughout the entire region.[41]

208

The new Islamic fundamentalism has several faces. Nonetheless, it is unified in its view that elements in the West are actively plotting to destroy Islam. In the 1970's, King Faisal of Saudi Arabia expressed belief that Zionism and Soviet communism were in fact partners in this international conspiracy. Many leaders of the Bolshevik Revolution had been of Jewish ancestry. Also, after the Six Day War, the Soviet Union increasingly allowed its Jewish citizenry to emigrate to Israel, swelling the latter's European population. Faisal saw these disparate facts as pieces of a larger whole. Radical Islamic fundamentalists, such as the Muslim Brotherhood of Egypt, held another view. For them, it was the Christian West that was in league with Israel to humiliate the Muslim world. This theme was echoed by Islamic Shi'ite fundamentalists in Iran, led by the Ayatollah Khomeini. In 1971, a declaration by Khomeini was circulated among the hajj pilgrims in Mecca that complained that "the poisonous culture of imperialism is penetrating to the depths of towns and villages throughout the Muslim world, displacing the culture of the Qur'an." Secularism, which had emerged triumphant in Christendom, was suddenly and dramatically challenged by a vision of Islamic government. In the words of one Muslim, money is the real god of the West, and sex is its prophet. Islamic elements have proclaimed that they will no longer tolerate this typically Western version of shirk (polytheism). The modern battle lines are drawn between Dar al-Islam and Dar al-Harb.[42]

The symbols of the new Islamic resolve are everywhere and have been used even by secular elements within the Middle East. The Palestine Liberation Organization (P.L.O.) provides several examples. Even though its officially proclaimed goal is the erection of a secular, non-sectarian Palestinian state, it uses the symbols of the Islamic revival. For example, "Yasir Arafat," the widely known pseudonym used by the P.L.O.'s leader, is the name of a renowned Muslim warrior from the days of Muhammad. Additionally, al-Fatah, the central unit of the P.L.O., means in Arabic a Muslim conquest of non-Muslims. Similarly, the symbolism chosen by Egypt's President Anwar Sadat for his surprise attack on Israel in 1973 was from Islam's heroic past. The code name chosen for the combined Egyptian-Syrian attack was "Operation Badr." Every Muslim knows that Badr was an early victory of Muhammad against his Meccan enemies. Before Badr, Muhammad's movement was largely insignificant. After the battle, his strength steadily mounted. Similarly, the name given to Egypt's own movement against Israeli lines in 1973 was "Operation Saladin," after the great Muslim warrior who defeated the Western crusaders centuries before. Sadat used the symbols of the Islamic resurgence when it served his purposes. Later in the 1970's, he would outrage Muslim fundamentalists by essentially removing Egypt from the struggle against Israel. In 1981, Sadat would be assassinated for his perceived treason in behalf of Dar al-Harb[43]

Meanwhile, the Ayatollah Khomeini was also using Shi'ite symbolism to communicate to the Iranian masses. Khomeini regularly compared the hated Shah to Yazid, the Umayyad caliph who had ordered the slaughter of the beloved Husain. Consequently, Khomeini's cause was translated as an archetypal conflict between divine justice and mortal tyranny. The Iranian Shah had sought to modernize his country in the shortest time with the help of sharply rising oil revenues. Accordingly, he had imported Western technicians to Iran on a massive scale. Ironically, this fed Khomeini's claims that traditional Islamic culture was being exchanged for a mess of Western pottage. The result was the Iranian revolution of 1979. Khomeini rose to power amid speculation that he was the earthly representative of the Shi'ites' Hidden Imam.[44]

Given the recent turmoil in the Middle East, conjectures concerning Islam's future are highly tenuous. Nevertheless, some problems can be identified even now. In recent years, certain contradictions between professed Islamic beliefs and the natural preferences of Muslims have been apparent. Specifically, most Muslims want the cars, radios and television sets that are the products of the very Western values that Islamic fundamentalism vociferously rejects. As long as the region remains rich in oil, the material benefits of Western civilization will be able to be purchased in desired quantities. For the time being, this oil wealth is popularly seen as the benefit of trusting completely in God. When this treasure is finally gone, traditional Islam's reliance on Providence will be put to a severe test.

For almost a millennium, al-Ash'ari's theology has encouraged a certain style of closed-mindedness within Islam. Unfortunately, this world view serves to strangle efforts at native technological development. Islam need not look to the West for a style of mind that can harmonize faith in God with a stimulation of

210

human curiosity and inquiry which is necessary for achievements in science. Its own early history provides a model, that being the rationalistic Mu'tazilites that al-Ash'ari opposed. Mu'tazilite theology undergirded Islamic scientific leadership in the world of the 10th century. Since the late 19th century, certain Muslim thinkers have flirted with returning to the Mu'tazilite position. Should this ever occur in a complete and profound way, Islamic civilization could indeed again become technologically self-sufficient. Should this not occur, Muslims could ultimately be confronted with an unfortunate choice between their desires for a materially better life and their religious faith.[45]


NOTES

1. Bernard Lewis, The Arabs in History (London 1950), pp. 33-34; W. Montgomery Watt, Islam and the Integration of Society (Evanston, Illinois, 1961), pp. 6-8.

2. D.S. Margoliouth, Mohammed and the Rise of Islam (New York, 1905), p. 8; W. Montgomery Watt, Muhammad, Prophet and Statesman (London, 1961), p. 47.

3. Helmut Gatje, The Qur'an and Its Exegesis, Selected Texts with Classical and Modern Muslim Interpretations (Berkeley, 1976), p. 78; A.J. Arberry, Aspects of Islamic Civilization as Depicted in its Original Texts (Ann Arbor, Mich., 1967), p. 32; Margoliouth, Mohammed, p. 85; Watt, Muhammad, pp. 18-19.

4. H.A.R. Gibb, Mohammedanism, An Historical Survey (London, 1953), p. 36; Annemarie Schimmel, Mystical Dimensions of Islam (Chapel Hill, 1975), pp. 26-27; Gatje, Qur'an and Exegesis, p. 136; A.S. Tritton, Islam, Belief and Practices (London, 1951), p. 13; G.H. Jansen, Militant Islam (New York, 1979), pp. 36-37; Jonathan Raban, Arabia, A Journey Through the Labyrinth (New York, 1979), pp. 22-23; Raphael Patai, The Arab Mind (New York, 1976), p. 48; Marshall G.S. Hodgson, The Venture of Islam, Conscience and History in a World Civilization (3 vols., Chicago, 1974), I, 159-162; F.E. Peters, Allah's Commonwealth: A History of Islam in the Near East, 600-1100 A.D. (New York,

1973), p. 53; John Alden Williams, ed., Islam (New
York, 1962), p. 16.

5. T.W. Arnold, The Preaching of Islam, A History
of the Propagation of the Muslim Faith (London, 1913),
pp. 15, 25-26; Fazlur Rahman, Islam (Chicago, 1979),
pp. 36-37; Gatje, Qur'an and Exegesis, p. 10; Watt,
Islam and Integration, p. 14; Ignaz Goldziher,
Introduction to Islamic Theology and Law (Princeton,
1981:1910), p. 8

6. W. Montgomery Watt, Islamic Political Thought,
The Basic Concepts (Edinburgh, 1968), p. 15; Goldziher,
Theology and Law, pp. 8-9; Watt, Muhammad, p. 91; Watt,
Islam and Integration, p. 161; Cyriac K. Pullapilly,
ed., Islam in the Contemporary World (Notre Dame, Ind.,
1980), p. xvii; Hodgson, Venture of Islam, I, 175.

7. Gatje, Qur'an and Exegesis, pp. 11, 133;
Margoliouth, Mohammed, p. 41; Ameer Ali, The Spirit of
Islam, With a Life of the Prophet (New York, 1922), pp.
74-82; Qur'an, 5:82; Rahman, Islam, pp. 26-27; Mohammed
Marmaduke Pickthall, trans., The Meaning of the
Glorious Koran (New York, 1953), p. xxii; Gil Carl
Alroy, Behind the Middle East Conflict, The Real
Impasse Between Arab and Jew (New York, 1975), p. 182;
Jean Mathe, The Civilization of Islam (New York, 1980),
p. 6; Watt, Islamic Political Thought, p. 51; Watt,
Islam and Integration, p. 150; Robert Lacey, The
Kingdom (New York, 1981), pp. 59, 315; Michael
Edwardes, A History of India, From the Earliest Times
to the Present Day (New York, 1961), p. 101; Tritton,
Belief and Practices, p. 117; Solomon Grayzel, A
History of the Jews, From the Babylonian Exile to the
Present (New York, 1968), p. 234; Williams, Islam, p.
26; George Foot Moore, History of Religions (2 vols.,
New York, 1949), II, 402-403; Peters, Allah's
Commonwealth, pp. 63, 66, 85-86,97, 103; Hodgson,
Venture of Islam, I, 177-180; Alfred Guillaume, Islam
(New York, 1954), pp. 47-48; Kenneth S. Latourette, A
History of Christianity (New York, 1953), p. 320.

8. Watt, Islamic Political Thought, p. 17; Watt,
Islam and Integration, p. 27; Jansen, Militant Islam,
p. 29; Alroy, Behind Middle East Conflict, pp. 104-151;
Patai, Arab Mind, p. 286; Bernard Lewis, "The Return of
Islam," Commentary (January, 1976), pp. 39-49.

9. S. Husain M. Jafri, Origins and Early
Development of Shi'a Islam (New York, 1979), pp. 34,
40-45, 95, 119, 122-123, 140-141; Margoliouth,

Mohammed, pp. 340-344; Rahman, Islam, pp. 86, 259; Lewis, Arabs in History, pp. 60, 62-63, 71; W. Montgomery Watt, The Formative Period of Islamic Thought (Edinburgh, 1973), p. 15; Watt, Islam and Integration, pp. 89-124; Goldziher, Theology and Law, pp. 170-171; Hodgson, Venture of Islam, I, 213.

10. Ali, Spirit of Islam, pp. 300-302, 308; Jafri, Shi'a Islam, pp. 167, 174, 190; Tritton, Belief and Practices, p. 72; Arnold, Preaching of Islam, p. 209.

11. Goldziher, Theology and Law, pp. 179-181; Asaf A.A. Fyzee, A Shi'ite Creed, A Translation of Risalatu'l-I'tiqadat of Muhammad v. 'Ali Ibn Babwayhi al-Qummi known as Shaykh Saduq (London, 1942), p. 55; Nikki R. Keddie, ed., Scholars, Saints, and Sufis, Muslim Religious Institutions in the Middle East Since 1500 (Berkeley, 1972), p. 11; John Alden Williams, ed., Themes of Islamic Civilization (Berkeley, 1971), p. 73; Tritton, Belief and Practices, pp. 74-75; Michael M.J. Fischer, Iran, From Religious Dispute to Revolution (Cambridge, Mass., 1980), pp. 1, 171, 213; Hodgson, Venture of Islam, I, 377-379.

12. Jafri, Shi'a Islam, p. 309; Rahman, Islam, pp. 133, 175, 179, 245; Gibb, Mohammedanism, pp. 124-126; Tritton, Belief and Practices, pp. 51, 74; Gatje, Qur'an and Exegesis, p. 244; Goldziher, Theology and Law, pp. 175-177; William H. Forbis, Fall of the Peacock Throne, The Story of Iran (New York, 1981), pp. 139-164; Fischer, Iran, From Religious Dispute to Revolution, p. 6; Fyzee, Shi'ite Creed, pp. 99-100; Philip K. Hitti, Islam, A Way of Life (Chicago, 1970), p. 46; Lacey, The Kingdom, pp. 478-487; Hodgson, Venture of Islam, II, 454; San Francisco Sunday Examiner and Chronicle, Nov. 18, 1979, p. B-2; Peters, Allah's Commonwealth, p. 599.

13. Keddie, ed., Scholars, Saints, and Sufis, pp. 3, 33; Watt, Islamic Political Thought, p. 123; Fred Brenner, "Khomeini's Dream of an Islamic Republic," Liberty, LXXIV (1979), 11; Peters, Allah's Commonwealth, pp. 583-584.

14. Hitti, Islam, p. 46; Rahman, Islam, p. 173; Williams, ed., Themes of Islamic Civilization, pp. 28, 35; Goldziher, Theology and Law, pp. 162-163, 191; Hodgson, Venture of Islam, II, 451.

15. Pickthall, trans., Glorious Koran, p. 369;

P.M. Holt, Ann K.S. Lambton, Bernard Lewis, eds., <u>The Cambridge History of Islam</u> (2 vols., Cambridge, Eng., 1970), IIB, xiv-xv; Watt, <u>Formative Period</u>, pp. 88-89, 92-93, 301; Hitti, <u>Islam</u>, p. 48; Lacey, <u>The Kingdom</u>, pp. 37, 270; Peters, <u>Allah's</u> Commonwealth, p. 59.

16. Watt, <u>Formative Period</u>, p. 95; Gibb, Mohammedanism, pp. 112-114; Goldziher, <u>Theology and Law</u>, pp. 84, 91; Williams, ed., <u>Themes of Islamic Civilization</u>, pp. 179-180; Rahman, <u>Islam</u>, pp. 88-90; Peters, <u>Allah's</u> Commonwealth, pp. 181, 184-186, 591.

17. Lewis, <u>Arabs in History</u>, p. 143; Goldziher, <u>Theology and Law</u>, pp. 101-102, 113-115; Richard J. McCarthy, ed., <u>The Theology of Al-Ash'ari</u> (Beirut, 1953), pp. 6-7, 33-34, 36-37, 55, 56, 63-67, 98-100; Moore, <u>History of Religions</u>, II, 418, 426, 427; Hodgson, <u>Venture of Islam</u>, I, 443; Peters, <u>Allah's</u> Commonwealth, p. 587.

18. Fyzee, <u>Shi'ite Creed</u>, pp. 31-36; Hamid Algar, ed., <u>On the Sociology of Islam, Lectures by Ali Shari'ati</u> (Berkeley, 1979), p. 78; Keddie, ed., <u>Scholars, Saints and Sufis</u>, p. 350; Goldziher, <u>Theology and Law</u>, p. 81; Watt, <u>Islam</u> and Integration, p. 281; Lacey, <u>The Kingdom</u>, p. 519; Fischer, <u>Iran, From Religious Dispute to Revolution</u>, p. 67.

19. Lewis, <u>Arabs in History</u>, p. 137; Mathe, <u>Civilization of Islam</u>, p. 120; Williams, ed., <u>Themes of Islamic Civilization</u>, p. 171; Keddie, ed., <u>Scholars, Saints and Sufis</u>, p. 71; Lacey, <u>The Kingdom</u>, p. 176; Ali, <u>Spirit of Islam</u>, p. 454; Patai, <u>Arab</u> Mind, pp. 262-263; Rahman, <u>Islam</u>, p. 263; Peters, <u>Allah's</u> Commonwealth, p. 372.

20. Mathe, <u>Civilization of Islam</u>, pp. 156-157; Jansen, <u>Militant Islam</u>, pp. 32-34, 81; Hitti, <u>Islam</u>, p. 36; Lacey, <u>The Kingdom</u>, pp. 43, 517; Fischer, <u>Iran, From Religious Dispute to Revolution</u>, pp. 172-173; Schimmel, <u>Mystical Dimensions</u>, p. xxi; Peters, <u>Allah's</u> Commonwealth, p. 60; Huston Smith, <u>The Religions of Man</u> (New York, 1958), pp. 213-214.

21. Idries Shah, <u>The Sufis</u> (New York, 1964), p. 361; Rahman, <u>Islam</u> pp. 6, 136-137, 142-143, 201; P. David Devanandan, <u>The Concept of Maya, An Essay in Historical Survey of the Hindu Theory of the World, With Special Reference to the Vedanta</u> (London, 1950), pp. 172-174; Peters, <u>Allah's</u> Commonwealth, pp. 416-418.

22. Shah, _Sufis_, pp. 20-21, 62; Schimmel, _Mystical Dimensions_, pp. 130, 362; Geoffrey Parrinder, _Mysticism in the World's Religions_ (New York, 1976), p. 126; Reshad Feild, _The Last Barrier_ (New York, 1976), pp. 39, 91, 100; Goldziher, _Theology_ and _Law_, p. 133; Hodgson, _Venture of Islam_, I, 398.

23. Schimmel, _Mystical_ Dimensions, pp. 25-26, 104, 135; Shah, _Sufis_, pp. 93, 171-172, 282-283, 289, 391; Rahman, _Islam_, p. 154; Keddie, ed., _Scholars, Saints and Sufis_, pp. 327-328; Kenneth Cragg, _The Wisdom of the Sufis_ (New York, 1976), pp. 25, 31, 81; Feild, _The Last Barrier_, pp. 86, 101; Parrinder, _Mysticism in the World's Religions_, p. 134.

24. Constantine K. Zurayk, "Tensions in Islamic Civilization," _Contemporary Arab Studies_ (Washington, D.C., 1978), p. 5; Goldziher, _Theology and Law_, p. 42; Hitti, _Islam_, pp. 31-32; Parrinder, _Mysticism in the World's Religions_, p. 132; Schimmel, _Mystical Dimensions_, pp. 38-39, 116-117; Hodgson, _Venture of Islam_, I, 402.

25. Schimmel, _Mystical Dimensions_, pp. 83, 117-120, 198,200; Shah, _Sufis_, p. 66; Goldziher, _Theology_ and _Law_, pp. 133-134, 139-140; Tritton, _Belief and Practices_, pp. 100, 179; Ali, _Spirit of Islam_, p. 460; Pullapilly, ed., _Contemporary World_, p. 178; Algar, ed., _Sociology of Islam_, p. 68; Schimmel, _Mystical Dimensions_, pp. 83, 200; Rahman, _Islam_, p. 156; Williams, ed., _Themes of Islamic Civilization_, p. 327.

26. Goldziher, _Theology_ and _Law_, p. 155; Williams, ed., _Themes of Islamic Civilization_, p. 281; Schimmel, _Mystical Dimensions_, pp. 69, 73; Algar, ed., _Sociology of Islam_, p. 68; Shah, _Sufis_, pp. 263, 425; Hodgson, _Venture of Islam_, I, 409; Williams, ed., _Islam_, pp. 147-149.

27. W. Montgomery Watt, trans., _The Faith and Practice of al-Ghazali_ (London, 1953), pp. 54-59; Shah, _Sufis_, pp. 169-170; Rahman, _Islam_, pp. 110, 140.

28. Schimmel, _Mystical Dimensions_, pp. 59, 84, 96, 149, 206, 208, 214, 335-336; Tritton, _Belief and Practices_, p. 98; Goldziher, _Theology and Law_, pp. 149-150, 152-153; Rahman, _Islam_, pp. 153-155; Gibb, _Mohammedanism_, pp. 138, 144; Keddie, ed., _Scholars, Saints and Sufis_, p. 79; Williams, ed., _Themes of Islamic Civilization_, p. 330; Hitti, _Islam_, p. 66;

Williams, ed., Islam, p. 152.

29. Pullapilly, ed., Contemporary World, pp. 35, 233; Lewis, Arabs in History, pp. 160-161; Gibb, Mohammedanism, pp. 166-169; Rahman, Islam, pp. 7, 196-197, 199; Goldziher, Theology and Law, pp. 244-245.

30. Malcolm X, The Autobiography of Malcolm X (New York, 1965), pp. 318-342; Fischer, Iran, From Religious Dispute to Revolution, p. 235.

31. Ali, Spirit of Islam, p. 27; Bernard Lewis, Race and Color in Islam (New York, 1970), pp. 22, 38; Rahman, Islam, pp. 38-39; Tritton, Belief and Practices, pp. 137-138; Gibb, Mohammedanism, p. 184; Lacey, The Kingdom, pp. 177, 345; Peters, Allah's Commonwealth, p. 408n; Smith, Religions of Man, p. 220.

32. Keddie, ed., Scholars, Saints and Sufis, p. 385; Qur'an, IV:34; Pullapilly, ed., Contemporary World, p. 394; Tritton, Belief and Practices, p. 66; Lois Beck and Nikki Keddie, eds., Women in the Muslim World (Cambridge, Mass., 1978), p. 26; Muhammad Abdul-Rauf, The Islamic View of Women and the Family (New York, 1977), pp. 132-133.

33. Rahman, Islam, pp. 231-232; Hitti, Belief and Practices, p. 29; Abdul-Rauf, Islamic View of Women, p. 147; Daniel Pipes, "'This World is Political!!' The Islamic Revival of the Seventies," Orbis, XXIV (Spring, 1980), 10; Fred Brenner, "Khomeini's Dream of an Islamic Republic," Liberty, LXXIV (1979), 11-12.

34. Qur'an, XXIV:31; Patai, Arab Mind, pp. 33, 130-131; Mathe, Civilization of Islam, p. 35; Pullapilly, ed., Contemporary World, pp. 375, 392; Goldziher, Theology and Law, p. 52; Keddie, ed., Scholars, Saints and Sufis, pp. 385-386.

35. Abdul-Rauf, Islamic View of Women, pp. 119-120; Mathe, Civilization of Islam, pp. 31, 46; Keddie, ed., Scholars, Saints and Sufis, pp. 388, 390; Jansen, Militant Islam, p. 34; Ali Shari'ati, Hajj (Houston, 1977), p. 18; Patai, Arab Mind, p. 154; Guillaume, Islam, pp. 71, 174-177; Hodgson, Venture of Islam, I, 181-182, 340-342.

36. James A. Bill and Carl Leiden, Politics in the Middle East (Boston, 1979), p. 64; Abdul-Rauf, Islamic View of Women, pp. 21, 141; Patai, Arab Mind, p. 10.

37. Keddie, ed., Scholars, Saints and Sufis, pp. 6, 368, 372, 384; Williams, ed., Themes of Islamic Civilization, pp. 233, 238-239; Lacey, The Kingdom, pp. 478-487.

38. Arberry, Aspects of Islamic Civilization, p. 17; Jansen, Militant Islam, pp. 112-120; Pullapilly, ed., Contemporary World, pp. 35, 233; Keddie, ed., Scholars, Saints and Sufis, p. 208; Pipes, "'This World is Political!!,'" p. 13.

39. Dana Adams Schmidt, Armageddon in the Middle East (New York, 1974), p. 35; Patai, Arab Mind, p. 14.

40. Lacey, The Kingdom, pp. 269, 271-171, 391; Kenneth Ray Bain, The March to Zion, United States Policy and the Founding of Israel (College Station, Texas, 1979), pp. 25-26; Wilbur Crane Eveland, Ropes of Sand, America's Failure in the Middle East (New York, 1980), pp. 350, 353n; John W. Amos, Arab-Israeli Military/Political Relations, Arab Perceptions and the Politics of Escalation (New York, 1979), p. 269; Schmidt, Armageddon, pp.4-5; William R. Polk, The Arab World (Cambridge, Mass., 1980), p. 182.

41. Bill and Leiden, Politics in the Middle East, p. 51; Fuad Ajami, The Arab Predicament (New York, 1981), pp. 32, 63.

42. Lacey, The Kingdom, pp. 241, 385-386; Amos, Arab-Israeli Relations, pp. 21, 161; Keddie, ed., Scholars, Saints and Sufis, p. 253; Frances Fitzgerald, "Giving the Shah Everything He Wants," Harper's, CCIX (Nov., 1976), 77; V.S. Naipaul, Among the Believers, An Islamic Journey (New York, 1981), p. 92; Shari'ati, Hajj, pp. 131, 142, 151.

43. Pipes, "'This World is Political!!,'" p. 38; Polk, Arab World, pp. 256-257; Amos, Arab-Israeli Relations, pp. 148-149, 197-198, 214; Margoliouth, Mohammed, p. 269; Schmidt, Armageddon, p. 203; Christopher S. Wren, "The Moslem World Rekindles Its Militancy," New York Times, June 18, 1978, p. E-3.

44. Keddie, ed., Scholars, Saints and Sufis, pp. 228, 233; Fitzgerald, "Giving the Shah," p. 78; Pipes, "This World is Political!!,'" pp. 12, 33-34, 36; Naipaul, Among the Believers, pp. 9, 406, 423; Forbis, Fall of the Peacock Throne, pp. 139-164; Fischer, Iran, From Religious Dispute to Revolution, p. 191; Ayatollah

Ruhollah Khomeini, Islamic Government (New York, 1979), pp. 5-7, 10-11, 13-17, 23-24, 26.

45. Naipaul, Among the Believers, p. 33; Pipes, "'This World is Political!!,'" pp. 19-21; Gibb, Mohammedanism, pp. 112-113; Watt, Formative Period, pp. 179, 242-245; Goldziher, Theology and Law, pp. 87-88, 91; Manfred Halpern, The Politics of Social Change in the Middle East and North Africa (Princeton, 1963), p. 120; Nadav Safran, Egypt in Search of Political Community (Cambridge, 1961), pp. 62-84; Pullapilly, ed., Contemporary World, pp. 293-303; Newsweek, January 22, 1979, p. 47.

# Epilogue

Occasionally, an author writing about the world's great religions has a hidden agenda. In such cases, while a variety of faiths may be reviewed, the work is essentially motivated by the belief that one religion alone is true and correct. Consequently, readers are presented with richness and life in only that part of the volume concerned with the favored religion. Certainly, in the conclusion to the book, such an author guides the reader to that perception. The fundamental premise of this survey is of a different sort. Simply stated, it is that each and every path portrayed herein leads to God. This author has not sought to evaluate any of the world's great religions by any external standard. Rather, he has tried to make each of them understandable to the reader in terms delineated by its own tradition. Hopefully, as a result, the reader has acquired a greater appreciation of these varied paths.

While the narrative was designed to be objective and impartial, it has not been neutral concerning whether or not humanity's reaching out to God is a valid enterprise. Great respect has been given to those from each of the world's great religious traditions who, in their own unique and varied ways, have searched for God. Elements within each faith claim to have found Him or an impersonal, divine equivalent. This account has attempted to convey the internal logic, excitement, wonder and meaning involved in each of these discoveries. It has sought to be ecumenical in its appreciation of the unique contribution made by each tradition represented in these pages.

Each of the world's great religions possesses a special insight. From Judaism, we recall that humankind must actively wrestle with the divine and translate it into daily life. From Hinduism, we remember the parable of the blind men and the elephant. The beauty of this story is that it doubly portrays the majesty of God and our human inability to grasp Him. A logical conclusion of this inherent fallibility is religious tolerance. Buddhism offers us a method for greater self-control and realization of the divine in everyday existence, while Christianity urges us to care for our neighbors. Finally, Islam requires our real submission before God. Groping in the dim light of a common search, members from each of the faith traditions represented in this volume can learn from

the others.  Indeed, each can serve as an inspiration
for the others.  Collectively considered, they serve to
enrich and deepen human faith.  This belief has been
the unspoken premise of the foregoing chapters.

INDEX

223

Palestine Liberation
Organization (PLO), 209
Palestinians, 40, 208
Papacy, 159-160, 164
parable of the arrow
(Buddhist), 101
parable of the blind man
(Buddhist), 107
parable of the blind men
and the elephant
(Hindu), 74, 80
parable of the chariot
(Buddhist), 108-109
parable of the elephant
seeking its escape
(Buddhist), 103
parable of the farmer's
runaway horse
(Chinese), 125
parable of the raft
(Buddhist), 110, 112,
128
Paradise (heaven), 198,
206
Passover, 144
Patriarch of Constan-
tinople, 159, 161
Paul, St., 148-150, 152,
159, 164
Pelagianism, 156-158
Pentateuch, 10
Pentecost, 145-146
People of the Book, 186
personal Godhead, 80, 83,
85, 163
Peter, St., 148
Pharisees, 20, 21, 25
Philistines, 7
Pinsker, Leon 37, 38
polygyny, 204, 207
polytheism, 49, 73, 75,
80, 120, 181, 182, 184,
186
prasada, 87
predestination, 2, 5, 87,
157-158, 167-168, 170,
192-194
"Protestant ethic," 169
Protestant Reformation,
163-170
purdah, 205

Pure Land, 118, 119, 127
purgatory, 158, 167

quietism, 124
Qur'an, 30, 182, 183,
188, 191 -192, 198,
203, 204

rabbi, 21
Rabi'ah-Adawia, 198
racism, 26, 38, 202-203,
206
Ramadan, 185, 196
Ramakrishna, 74
rebbe, 35
Reconstructionism, 36
reincarnation, 47, 52, 54,
55, 60, 61, 65, 109,
115-116
Reform Judaism, 35, 36
relics, 162
Renaissance, 162, 164
resurrection, 13, 15, 16,
19, 142-143, 145, 152
Rig-Veda, 47, 49, 51,
57
Rinzai, 132
Rita, 50
Roman Catholic Church,
156-167, 173
Rudra, 49

Sabbath, 13, 19, 22, 28
sacraments, 157-158, 163,
167
sacred cows, 75
Sadat, Anwar, 209-210
Sadducees, 20, 21
sadhus, 71-72
Samaritans, 10
samsara, 54-61, 65, 87,
109
sanatana dharma, 54
"Sanskritization," 67, 68
Sarah, 2
Satan, 15
sati, 58, 59
satori, 128-129, 131, 132

vegetarianism, 68, 115
virgin birth, 142
Vishnu, 50, 76-78, 85,
  113
Vivekanada, Swami, 73
Vritra, 48, 49


Wahhabis, 201-202
Waldenses, 163
Washington, George, 147
Weber, Max, 169
Weems, Mason, 147
women, 36, 57, 58, 102,
  183, 202-206
wu-wei, 123-124
Wycliffe, John, 164


Yama and Yami, 52
yantra, 54
Yathrib (see Medina)
Yazid, 188, 210
YHWH, 14
yin-yang concept, 125-126, 173
yogi, 59
yogini, 59


zazen, 130
Zealots, 18, 22
Zen (Ch'an), 112, 117, 125,
  127-133
Zevi, Shabbatai, 34
Zionism, 37-40, 208-209
Zohar, 31
Zoroastrianism, 15, 16, 78
Zwingli, Urlich, 168